D1566893

LONG MARCH AHEAD

THE PUBLIC INFLUENCES

OF AFRICAN AMERICAN CHURCHES,

VOLUME II

LONG MARCH AHEAD

AFRICAN AMERICAN CHURCHES

AND PUBLIC POLICY IN

POST–CIVIL RIGHTS

AMERICA

EDITED BY R. DREW SMITH

DUKE UNIVERSITY PRESS

Durham and London

2004

© 2004 *Duke University Press*
All rights reserved
Printed in the United States of America on
acid-free paper ∞ Designed by Amy Ruth Buchanan
Typeset in Minion by Tseng Information Systems, Inc.
Library of Congress Cataloging-in-Publication Data
appear on the last printed page of this book.

A PROJECT OF THE LEADERSHIP CENTER
AT MOREHOUSE COLLEGE, FUNDED BY
THE PEW CHARITABLE TRUSTS.

Facing the rising sun of our new day begun,

Let us march on till victory is won.

JAMES WELDON JOHNSON

"Lift Every Voice and Sing"

CONTENTS

PREFACE

This volume is the second of two to be published by Duke University Press featuring research developed as part of the Public Influences of African-American Churches Project (PIAAC). The aim of this research initiative, which is based at the Leadership Center at Morehouse College, is to examine the relation of African American churches to American political life in the late twentieth century, the period since the civil rights movement. This focus recognizes the fact that American politics in general, and African American politics in particular, has changed dramatically since the 1960s. It also acknowledges, not just new configurations of the political landscape, but a troubling lack of research on recent black church involvements within that political landscape — this despite a substantial body of scholarship on earlier black church activism.

Working with thirty scholars over a three-year period, the PIAAC Project has had as its primary goal remedying this lack. Essays in the first volume, *New Day Begun: African American Churches and Civic Culture in Post–Civil Rights America*, ed. R. Drew Smith (Durham: Duke University Press, 2003), focused on relations between ecclesiastical and civic culture and, specifically, on ways in which black churches draw on civil religious ideas, black nationalist concerns, and community and economic development objectives. They also explore ways in which the political dispositions of black churches are shaped by theological, gender, and other cultural considerations. Essays in this second volume analyze black church activism on such national public policy issues as affirmative action, health care, welfare reform, and public education. Both volumes provide analysis of data from the 1,956 black churches surveyed by the PIAAC Project. Those churches were located in nineteen major cities across the country and in twenty-six small rural counties in the South. However, the vast majority were urban. Also, almost 90 percent of respondents were pastors.

The hope is that our interdisciplinary focus will help fill in a few of the historical and analytic gaps in the scholarship on black churches and politics since the 1960s. To the extent that these two volumes achieve those ends, there are many who helped make that possible. I extend thanks to each of the project scholars with whom I had the good fortune to work during this project. I am also grateful to the numerous church leaders across the country who participated in the national survey and in interviews and discussions with researchers connected with the project. I am extremely appreciative of the Pew Charitable Trust's commitments to research on religion and American public life and certainly appreciative of their generous funding of our three-year project. Thanks go out, in particular, to Luis Lugo, who invited me to develop a national project on black churches and public life, and to Kimon Sargeant, who has been supportive of this project in numerous ways. I am indebted to Raphael Allen at Duke University Press and to the manuscript review team for their many helpful suggestions about ways to strengthen the organization of the volumes and arguments within individual chapters. I cannot offer enough thanks to my colleagues at the Leadership Center at Morehouse College — especially Walter Fluker, whose vision and trust have facilitated countless opportunities for ministerial and professional collaboration between the two of us, and Alexis Simmons, who has worked tirelessly to ensure the success of the PIAAC Project. I am thankful, as well, for the important contributions that our data team made to this project, especially Mark and Robin Nichols at Spectrum Data Link and our lead survey research assistant, Jerriline Smith. Finally, to Angelique Walker-Smith, I will be forever grateful for your counsel, commitment, and partnership throughout this process.

INTRODUCTION

R. Drew Smith

African American churches emerged from the civil rights movement with
political momentum stemming both from their successful mass-based public
policy activism and from legally enhanced electoral opportunities achieved
as a result of that activism. Although there is ample evidence that African
American churches have built effectively on the electoral momentum produced by mid-1960s civil rights legislation,[1] there is less evidence of significant public policy involvement on their part over the last forty years.
Contributors to this volume explore the extent to which African American
churches have been willing and able to push beyond their newfound electoral
strength into forms of political activism aimed at shaping and monitoring
the policy content of the government leaders they elect.

There are very few assurances, in fact, that citizen power to elect government officials will necessarily carry over into citizen influence on the political priorities, interests, and actions of government. While the procedural
constraints on voting participation are fairly uniform and technical in nature (e.g., mainly age requirements), the procedural constraints on monitoring and lobbying government may be far more subjective, inequitable, and
insurmountable (e.g., such actions require resources and favor those with
the most resources). The civil rights movement removed many barriers to
African American participation in the electoral arena, but the marginaliza-
tion of rank-and-file citizens relative to public policy matters (while not a
threat to constitutional integrity) remains a serious problem facing American
democracy.[2]

Nevertheless, democratic governments could not survive without the existence of a discursive and procedural space that affords a reasonable expectation of effective and direct citizen scrutiny, contestation, and negotiation
of government policies and actions. This is partly captured by the electoral
process, but it occurs in a more ongoing and systematic way by means of a
growing range of organized activities aimed at monitoring and lobbying the

government and educating and mobilizing citizens on public policy matters. Essays in this volume outline dimensions and dynamics of this policy advocacy sector within the contemporary U.S. context as well as contributions and limitations of policy activism by African American churches on key public policy initiatives in recent years.

Various internal and external factors have constrained public policy involvements by African American churches, but two that are especially important and discussed in one way or another in each of the essays are tensions between religious imperatives and political activism and deficits in the organizational capacity of African American churches.

Tensions between Religious and Political Imperatives

Some have argued that, during the civil rights movement, political leadership was thrust on African American clergy almost by default, given African American exclusion from the formal political process and structures of government.[3] But, with the removal of barriers to African American social and political participation, as formalized through the 1964 Civil Rights Act and the 1965 Voting Rights Act, a rapidly expanding sector of black government officials and other black public policy professionals increasingly assumed political leadership responsibilities. This has sometimes led to competition between black clergy activists and black political professionals,[4] but more often it has resulted in active and passive alliances between clergy activists and political professionals. By *active alliances* I mean, for example, church facilitation of election-related activities, direct political contacts and interactions with government officials, and lobbying-related collaborations with advocacy organizations. By *passive alliances* I mean those where voters entrust the governing process to persons they elect while seeking no further direct input into the process until the next election. Political activism by African American clergy has generally taken one or both of these forms of conventional (or procedural) activism.

African American clergy have also been associated with protest responses to government or legal frameworks in the decades since the civil rights movement, although they have appealed to protest far less than they have to conventional forms of activism.[5] In addition, racial nationalist orientations have persisted among some African American clergy and have resulted in tactics of political separatism and noncooperation despite the political open-ings produced by the civil rights movement. Relatively few African American clergy have in recent years promoted a literal political separation from main-stream America,[6] but quite a few have been sympathetic to the emphasis by black nationalists on economic autonomy and on individual moral respon-sibility. Evidence of support for the latter includes the prominent leadership provided by African American clergy to the 1991 Million Man March. Never-theless, where African American clergy have refrained from participating in American political life, it has most often been as a result of religious devotion rather than racial separatism.

Religious devotion is, however, a complex factor, one that has gener-ated both quietist and activist postures among African Americans. As Albert Raboteau points out, beginning with the earliest expressions of African American Christianity, an African American "allegiance to a 'higher au-thority' than their own" has produced "docility" as well as "rebellion" among African American Christians.[7] The quietist strand emphasizes the transcen-dent aspects of Christian faith and spirituality as a basis for social withdrawal and otherworldliness, while the activist strand emphasizes them as a basis for relativizing and challenging temporal authority and social structures. Schol-ars have tended to point to the prevalence of the former among African American churches,[8] but important attention has been given as well to rich traditions of spiritually driven African American political activism.[9]

Sometimes the choice has been, not between a willingness and an unwill-ingness to engage the political space, but rather, as the theologian Reinhold Niebuhr suggests, between moral absolutism and moral approximation in efforts to extend Christian influence and values into the political realm.[10] One of the practical implications of Niebuhr's argument is that there are inevi-table trade-offs between religious and political imperatives when pursuing public objectives through the formal American political process. There has sometimes been a spiritual and temporal urgency to the imperatives of Afri-can American churches that has made compromise unacceptable to them and distanced them, not only from public policy debates framed in objectionable ways, but often from the public policy process in general. Emilie M. Townes's essay on churches and reproductive health rights and Cathy J. Cohen's on churches and HIV/AIDS draw attention to the religious caution of African American churches on certain controversial public policy matters. Other essays in this volume also examine ways in which religious imperatives encouraged and discouraged African American church engagement of strategic public policy agendas.

Organizational Obstacles to Black Church Public Policy Activism

The public policy activism of African American church leaders has been constrained as well by the technical requirements of public policy advocacy. Lobby and advocacy groups have grown significantly in numbers and in degree of professionalization and are engaging the public policy process via increasingly sophisticated communications linkages to the constituencies and public officials they seek to influence. One indicator of the explosive growth of professional lobby and advocacy groups is that the number of individuals registered to lobby the federal government grew from approximately one thousand during the early 1970s to fourteen thousand by the mid-1990s. Many of these organizations have a highly specialized focus and staff, and the most influential tend to be heavily funded.[11]

Policy influence therefore requires a commitment of time, energy, and resources that, apparently, African American churches have not yet made, considering the rather limited scale of their formal lobbying infrastructure. Only the African Methodist Episcopal Church and the Progressive National Baptist Convention, for example, have had an institutional lobby apparatus operating under their own denominational auspices—both these denominations maintained Washington lobbyists during most of the last twenty years. Recently, however, the National Baptist Convention, USA, and the Church of God in Christ have taken steps to form denominational divisions devoted to public policy.

Moreover, African American churches have collaborated with numerous ecumenical and secular lobby organizations outside their specific denominational structures. Nevertheless, the limited Washington presence of African American denominations reflects the multiple pressures and demands on the resources and energy of churches and the priority given by churches to ecclesiastical rather than political matters (as evidenced, e.g., by the lack of attention given to political advocacy as a component of the training that clergy receive in seminary, Bible colleges, and Bible schools). I explore many of these issues more fully in my essay, which looks at gaps between African

American churches and the rest of the advocacy group sector on matters related to diversification of infrastructure and issue orientation.

Policy Substance within African American Church Activism

Despite these tactical, and sometimes theological, barriers to church-based policy advocacy, African American churches have shown potential for affecting American public policy in certain key areas. Where they have engaged in policy activism, that activism has tended to focus on racial justice and black economic development.[12] African American churches emerged in force on both issues during the 1950s and 1960s, often utilizing economic boycotts as a method for advancing black political and economic opportunity. During the 1970s, African American churches continued to promote racial justice through their involvements with the Southern Christian Leadership Conference and the National Association for the Advancement of Colored People, and they channeled a great deal of their advocacy on economic development matters through Operation Breadbasket and the Urban League. By the 1980s, however, African American advocacy of political and economic opportunity contended against a growing counteremphasis by the American public on individual rights and agency — displayed most clearly in challenges to affirmative action and welfare policies and in the championing of small government and private-sphere interests. This had the effect, as Preston Smith points out, of both "valorizing privatism" and "making public action increasingly illegitimate."[13]

In many respects, this is where the case studies in the present volume pick up on the story. The essay by Barbara Dianne Savage looks at African American church opposition to the One Florida Plan, an initiative aimed at ending affirmative action in Florida's government contracts, hiring, and institutions of higher education. Savage details an extensive range of African American church involvements in the effort to defeat the One Florida Plan and suggests that the broad coalition of African American churches, women's groups, and others that came together against the plan signals a much larger mobilizing potential for affirmative action issues nationally.

Tensions over private and public social responsibility have been at the heart of recent shifts in social welfare policy, as represented by the sweeping and suggestively named Personal Responsibility and Work Opportunity Reconciliation Act of 1996. The essays by Megan E. McLaughlin and by Michael Leo Owens examine the extent to which African American churches engaged in these debates and how they responded, in particular, to the policy shifts resulting from the "charitable choice" provision of this 1996 legislation. McLaughlin and Owens agree that African American churches had a fairly limited role in the debate leading up to the legislation, mainly because many of the traditionally activist African American church leaders regarded the legislation as a government abdication of responsibility in the fight against poverty. Nevertheless, McLaughlin and Owens point out that the 1996 welfare legislation, and George W. Bush's subsequent "faith-based initiative," have generated support among an increasingly activist element of conservative African American churches that have resonated with the implicit emphasis within these policies on character, values, and the "faith factor."

The character and values issue is also relevant, but in a somewhat different way, to Cohen's and Townes's essays on African American churches and health care issues. As mentioned above, Cohen and Townes show that churches have been consistently reluctant to engage health issues that they associate with objectionable behaviors. Both authors argue that African American churches fulfill their own moral mandates when providing, not withholding, public policy support on issues affecting marginalized and stigmatized segments of African Americans.

Public support for greater equity and justice in the education and criminal justice systems has ebbed and flowed in the years since the civil rights movement, and the essays by Desiree Pedescleaux and Christopher Winship examine where African American churches have been positioned around these issues. Pedescleaux's essay examines African American clergy participation in recent urban education reform movements, pointing out the strategic value that African American churches bring to these movements as institutions that frequently emphasize education issues and that include teachers and principals among their membership base. Winship's essay on Boston's Ten Point Coalition (a well-known contemporary initiative by African American churches to affect law enforcement policies and practices) interrogates the widely embraced idea that Ten Point churches were strategic to homicide reduction and police reform in Boston. Winship argues that factors other than church involvement may account more for homicide reductions and for police crime-fighting innovations but that partnerships between African

American churches and the police did contribute directly to improved race relations in Boston. Columba Aham Nnorum's essay on antiapartheid activism by African American churches shifts the policy focus to racial justice in a foreign context with close parallels to the domestic American context. Nnorum credits African American churches with providing crucial support in the successful passing of the Comprehensive Anti-Apartheid Act of 1986, which, among other things, formalized U.S. sanctions against South Africa. Nevertheless, Nnorum draws attention to the unreliability of African American churches on Africa issues, specifically identifying institutional parochialism as an impediment to broader and more aggressive Africa advocacy.

The volume's contributors examine, then, a variety of U.S. policy issues and responses to these issues by African American churches at municipal, state, national, and international levels. A consistent refrain is that there is a potential for — or at least an expectation of — black church public policy influence that has been, to this point, largely unfulfilled. Whether or not this is an appropriate burden to place on African American churches, it is one that they inherited as a result of their civil rights movement involvements. To the extent that African American churches embrace the challenge that this burden represents, the authors in this volume help identify factors that have contributed to and hindered effective policy activism.

Notes

1 Data on African American church involvement in a wide range of electoral activities are outlined in R. Drew Smith and Corwin Smidt, "System Confidence, Congregational Resources, and Black Church Civic Engagement," in *New Day Begun: African American Churches and Civic Culture in Post–Civil Rights America*, ed. R. Drew Smith (Durham: Duke University Press, 2003).

2 See William Greider, *Who Will Tell the People: The Betrayal of American Democracy* (New York: Simon and Schuster, 1992); and John B. Judis, *The Paradox of American Democracy: Elites, Special Interests, and the Betrayal of the Public Trust* (New York: Pantheon, 2000).

3 See, e.g., Adam Fairclough, *To Redeem the Soul of America: The Southern Christian Leadership Conference and Martin Luther King, Jr.* (Athens: University of Georgia Press, 1987), 14–18.

4 See Adolph Reed Jr., *The Jesse Jackson Phenomenon: The Crisis of Purpose in Afro-American Politics* (New Haven: Yale University Press, 1986), chap. 1.

5 According to data from the 1999–2000 Black Churches and Politics Survey, 84 percent of respondents indicated that their congregations had organized voter registration activities in the ten years prior to the survey, but only 17 percent indicated that their congregations had been involved with protest activities (see Smith and Smidt, "System Confidence," 60).

6 See C. R. D. Halisi, "Blyden's Ghost: African American Christianity and Racial Republicanism," in Smith, ed., *New Day Begun*.

7 Albert Raboteau, *Slave Religion: The "Invisible Institution" in the Antebellum South* (New York: Oxford University Press, 1978), 298.

8 See, e.g., E. Franklin Frazier, *The Negro Church in America* (Liverpool: University of Liverpool Press, 1963); Gary T. Marx, "Religion: Opiate or Inspiration of Civil Rights Militancy among Negroes?" *American Sociological Review* 32 (February 1967): 64–72; and Reed, *The Jesse Jackson Phenomenon*.

9 See, e.g., Vincent Harding, *There Is a River: The Black Struggle for Freedom in America* (New York: Vintage, 1981); and Fairclough, *To Redeem the Soul of America*.

10 Reinhold Niebuhr, *Moral Man and Immoral Society* (New York: Scribner's, 1932).

11 For example, the top ten public relations firms in the Washington, D.C., area had 1998 revenues in excess of $10 million, while the top ten revenue-generating lobbying firms brought in more than $5 million in fees during the first six months of 1999 (see Neil Lewis, "Once the Enclave of a Few Old Hands, Lobbying Is Corporate and Fast-Merging," *New York Times*, November 16, 1999, C1). There are also lobby groups (as opposed to lobby firms and public relations organizations) whose clout and resources emanate mainly from the extensiveness of their grassroots constituencies. A 1997 *Fortune* magazine survey of 329 public policy professionals in the Washington, D.C., area ranks the most influential of these lobby groups on the national political scene. Of the 120 organizations considered to be most influential, there were no explicitly black-oriented organizations. Nevertheless, the growth of African American professional, trade, and lobby organizations—which numbered approximately four hundred by the early 1990s—has been impressive. (See "The Power 25," *Fortune*, December 8, 1997, 144–50.)

12 This is consistent with the dual emphasis within African American politics in general on racial justice and economics (see Robert Smith, *We Have No Leaders: African Americans in the Post–Civil Rights Era* [Albany: State University of New York Press, 1996], 165–66; and Dona Hamilton and Charles Hamilton, "The Dual Agenda of African American Organizations since the New Deal: Social Welfare Policies and Civil Rights," *Political Science Quarterly* 107, no. 3 [fall 1992]: 435–52).

13 Preston H. Smith, " 'Self Help,' Black Conservatives, and the Reemergence of Black Privatism," in *Without Justice for All: The New Liberalism and Our Retreat from Racial Equality*, ed. Adolph Reed Jr. (Boulder: Westview, 1999), 284.

1

ASSESSING THE PUBLIC POLICY PRACTICES

OF AFRICAN AMERICAN CHURCHES

R. Drew Smith

Although pivotal in channeling black political grievances and dissatisfaction into mass protest during the 1950s and 1960s, African American churches have struggled to maintain political momentum within the contemporary American political context. Contributing to this has been the lack of consensus since the civil rights movement about an African American public policy agenda — unlike the 1950s and 1960s, when a broad consensus around a civil rights agenda existed. The lack of consensus is, in one respect, evidence of an evolving African American social and political diversity in a context where race functions somewhat less than it once did as a determinant of social prospects for African Americans — indeed, for all groups — within American society. And this diversity has become increasingly evident, translating into a more wide-ranging approach to African American public policy activism — especially with respect to its organizational auspices.

African American policy activism has since the mid-twentieth century been advanced mainly by three black institutional sectors — black advocacy organizations, black elected officials, and black churches.[1] In assessing the relation of African American churches to the contemporary public policy process, it is important to understand the shifting dynamics within and between these three sectors. The trend within all three through at least the mid-twentieth century (and, in some cases, well beyond) was toward the centralizing and collectivizing of actions through national bureaucracies. For example, African American churches formed national denominational structures beginning in the nineteenth century and into the twentieth, developing national offices and divisions designed to centralize and collectivize a range of actions. African American advocacy organizations such as the National Association for the Advancement of Colored People (NAACP) and the Urban League and, later, the Southern Christian Leadership Conference (SCLC) and Operation PUSH evolved national structures that centralized and collectivized the activities of their emergent local chapters and units. And African American elected officials have generally channeled their leadership through national political parties that have centralized and collectivized the policy agendas and political actions of those operating under their party banner. These centralizing and bureaucratizing tendencies have by no means been unique to African American institutional life and have, in fact, closely paralleled patterns operative in the institutional life of the majority culture.

Beginning in at least the 1960s, African American institutions and majority culture institutions have also been on parallel courses in their growing dissatisfaction with the national institutional bureaucracies through which so much of their activity had come to be channeled. According to a number of scholars, denominational structures and political party structures are examples of national bureaucracies whose institutional relevance and support have diminished in recent years. Craig Dykstra and James Hudnut-Beumler argue, for example, that American denominations began losing considerable moral influence and institutional clout in the 1960s owing to the erosion of ideological consensus within denominations as the society became more polarized on issues and "the tremendous rise in the number and kinds of . . . special-interest groups" and of the organizational vehicles that they created to promote their social concerns and interests. At about the same time, according to John Bibby, and for similar reasons, political parties also started to experience a significant decline in their influence and clout. Bibby contends that the extended reach and effectiveness of special interest groups and the media over the last few decades have broken the monopoly that political parties once held in shaping political reality and setting the political agenda for political candidates, officeholders, and the public.[2] The combined effect of these broad institutional trends, and of the significant racial reforms of the 1950s and 1960s that led to the dismantling of politically constrictive Jim Crow policies, has been that the context of African American church activism has in recent years been characterized by greater political variegation and decentralization than it had been prior to and during the civil rights movement.

Acknowledging these contextual differences is an essential starting point in assessing and critiquing contemporary black church policy activism, and these contextual distinctions will receive close attention in my analysis of public policy involvements of African American churches during the 1990s. Utilizing data from the 1999–2000 Black Churches and Politics (BCAP) Survey, I examine recent public policy priorities of African American churches, the methods that they have used to engage public policy, and the auspices under which this policy activism has been pursued. The data shed important light on the increased institutional range of black church policy activism and on modest increases in the ideological range of this activism.

Policy Priorities

As Charles Hamilton and Dona Hamilton point out, since at least the 1930s the public policy focus of African Americans, including leading organizations such as the NAACP and the Urban League, has centered around a "dual agenda" of "social welfare" (including socioeconomic development) and "civil rights" (encompassing racial justice politics in a broad sense). Hamilton and Hamilton note that various balances have been reached between the two agendas since the 1930s, with priority given to socioeconomic development during the 1930s and 1940s, civil rights during the 1950s and 1960s, and both civil rights and the socioeconomic development of the black underclass from the mid-1960s through the 1990s.[3]

Throughout most of the 1900s, the public policy commitments of African American churches, it is fair to say, largely mirrored the policy agenda of the broader African American community as outlined by Hamilton and Hamilton. More than one scholar has drawn attention, for example, to the importance that African American churches assigned to socioeconomic development, and to education as a form of socioeconomic development, during the period from the late nineteenth century through the mid-twentieth.[4] Considerably more documentation exists on the emphasis that African American churches placed on civil rights during the 1950s and 1960s. Doug McAdam, for example, codes *New York Times* newspaper accounts of African American political activism anywhere in the nation during the period covered by the civil rights movement, isolating in particular black church–based activism for subperiod 1955–60. He shows that the *Times* reported fifty-seven

TABLE 1 Issue Involvements by African American Churches

	% Yes[a]
Public education policies	41
Civil rights policies	31
Public welfare policies	27
Affirmative action policies	24
Criminal justice policies	23
Government economic development policies	19
Social rights and empowerment of women policies	17
U.S. Africa policies	13
U.S. Caribbean and Latin America policies	5

Source: BCAP Survey (*N* = 1,956).

[a]That is, percentage responding yes to the question, *During the last ten years has your congregation been directly involved with any of the following as part of their congregational mission?*

instances of black church–initiated activism during this subperiod (not including actions initiated by Martin Luther King Jr. or the SCLC, which he considers formal "movement organization" activities) and that at least 95 percent of this activism was focused on black civil rights or black educational and economic empowerment.[5] Similarly, 38 percent of respondents surveyed for a study of activism by African American clergy in Buffalo during the 1960s reported systematic involvements in political issues — all of which were civil rights related.[6] As the American social context became more diversified, polarized, and decentralized after the civil rights movement, one of the effects was that the public policy involvements of African American churches expanded in a few additional directions. Data from the BCAP Survey confirm some of this expansion.

The BCAP Survey asked respondents (mostly pastors) from 1,956 congregations about their congregational involvement with a list of public policy issues during the 1990s. The issue identified by congregations as receiving the greatest attention was public education, followed by (in order) civil rights, public welfare, affirmative action, criminal justice, and government economic development (for more details, see table 1). The data reveal, therefore, a rela-

TABLE 2 Issue Orientation of Civic/Political Organizations

	Local		National	
	%	N	%	N
Civil rights	19	378	10	202
Community/economic development	10	202	3	61
Ecumenical	6	131	3	59
Government/electoral	3	70	.8	17
Neighborhood associations	3	69	. . .	
Education	1	28	.4	8
Criminal justice/Anticrime	1	26	.2	5
Cultural	1	19	.7	15
Public health	.7	15	.3	6
Other	5	98	1	27
No answer	47	920	79	1,556

Source: BCAP Survey (N = 1,956).

tively strong twofold emphasis on racial justice and economic development policies. Half the top six issue categories listed in table 1 (civil rights, affirmative action, and criminal justice) could be considered racial justice issues, while the other half (including public welfare and public education)[7] could be considered socioeconomic development issues.

Moreover, the types of advocacy organizations cited by BCAP respondents reflect a similar twofold emphasis. When BCAP respondents were asked about their involvements with civic or political organizations, the NAACP was most frequently cited, 16 percent being involved at the local level and 8 percent at the national level—twice the frequency of involvement with any other organization or category of organizations. When these figures are combined with figures on involvement with other civil rights organizations such as the SCLC or the Rainbow/PUSH Coalition, 19 percent of respondents are shown to be involved locally with civil rights organizations generally and 10 percent nationally (see table 2). Community/economic development organizations were the second most frequently cited, 10 percent of respondents being involved locally and 3 percent nationally. (Another 1 percent cited involvements with local education-related organizations.) It could be said, then,

TABLE 3 Agreement with School Vouchers and Government Funding of Church-Based Social Services

	School Vouchers (%)	Church-Based Social Services (%)
Strongly agree	10	8
Agree	33	37
Don't know	1	1
Disagree	19	19
Strongly disagree	35	33

Source: BCAP Survey (*N* = 324).

that, at best, 11 percent of the congregations were involved locally with socio-economic development organizations and just over 3 percent were involved nationally (for more details, see table 2).

Although African American churches have placed a priority on racial justice and socioeconomic development issues, there were strong differences of opinion about how justice and social empowerment are best achieved — especially as these goals relate to approaches to education and welfare policies. For example, when a subsample of 324 respondents was asked about government interest in channeling education tax dollars toward vouchers for private education, 43 percent of the respondents agreed with the policy (10 percent strongly agreeing), but 54 percent disagreed (35 percent strongly disagreeing). When asked about government interest in funding churches to provide social services, 46 percent agreed with this initiative (8 percent strongly agreeing), but 52 percent disagreed (33 percent strongly disagreeing). Complete data are reported in table 3.

Two policy areas that represent emerging frontiers of black church policy activism in the post–civil rights movement era are women's rights and foreign policy. However, while it is important to acknowledge black church expansion into nontraditional policy areas, it must also be noted that African American church activism in these areas has proceeded fairly slowly. It has been well established that African American churches have been generally unsupportive of many aspects of the women's movement, especially women's leadership aspirations. A number of historically black denominations, for example, continue to resist, if not prohibit, the ordination of women. And,

TABLE 4 African American Churches on Women in Leadership

	Women as Ministers and Church Leaders		Women as Leaders in the Community	
	Male (%)	Female (%)	Male (%)	Female (%)
Strongly agree	41	74	52	73
Agree	30	15	44	22
Disagree	6	0	1	1
Strongly disagree	16	6[a]	0	0

Source: BCAP Survey (valid cases = 1,917).
[a]Likely from the handful of nonclergy respondents.

while, in a survey of black clergy conducted by C. Eric Lincoln and Lawrence Mamiya as late as the 1980s, 81 percent of female respondents approved of women as pastors (as opposed to their holding a ministerial position other than pastor), male respondents were split fifty-fifty on the issue.[8]

The BCAP Survey inquired similarly about African American church supportiveness of female leadership in the church and the broader society. While the Lincoln and Mamiya survey asked about approval of women specifically as pastors, the comparable BCAP question asked about congregational support for women taking on "ministerial and other leadership positions in the church." Seventy-one percent of male BCAP respondents and 89 percent of female respondents indicated support for women as ministers and leaders within the church (see table 4). The stronger support of female clergy in the BCAP Survey than in the Lincoln and Mamiya survey may be due in part to the wording of the question—Lincoln and Mamiya made the pastoral role explicit, while the BCAP Survey left it implicit—a fact that has relevance to the extent that respondents would support women as "ministers" but not as "pastors." But it is more likely due to incremental progress made during the period between the two surveys in the acceptance of women as ministers and as pastors within African American churches.

Either way, the significance of 71 percent male support among BCAP respondents for female leadership within churches, and 96 percent male support for female leadership in the broader community (see table 4), should not be overlooked as an indicator of growing conceptual affirmation among

African American churches of the rights and social interests of women. However, given that only 17 percent of the BCAP respondents reported congregational involvement in public policy activism related to women's rights or empowerment (see table 1 above) and that only a handful of BCAP respondents listed congregational involvements with organizations that concentrate on any aspect of women's social interests, there is obviously a great distance yet between conceptual support and policy advocacy/actual practice.

BCAP respondents reported least involvement in foreign policy matters relating to Africa and the Caribbean. Herschelle Challenor points out that factors constraining black foreign policy advocacy historically have included "the immediacy of local survival" issues for African Americans, American diplomatic disinterest in black life globally, and "official discouragement" of black "interference" in American foreign policy. Roger Wilkins notes that certain cultural dynamics historically unfavorable to African American foreign policy advocacy, including African American negativity toward Africa, have evolved in more favorable directions owing to greater firsthand and secondary exposure to Africans on the continent and in the diaspora.[9]

The creation of organizations such as Operation Crossroads Africa (which has sent hundreds of young Americans to Africa annually for short-term volunteer experiences since its founding by a black Presbyterian minister in 1957) and TransAfrica (founded in 1977 by the Congressional Black Caucus to promote public awareness and U.S. government support of Africa and the Caribbean) illustrates a growing African American seriousness about African affairs. Moreover, other organizations have shared the Africa policy stage in the United States with TransAfrica, including the American Committee on Africa, the Washington Office on Africa, and the Constituency for Africa — with some of these combining to form an organization called Africa Action in 2001. But, while 55 percent of African Americans surveyed in 1984 indicated feeling close to Africans, those affinities have yet to translate into comparable levels of engagement with Africa public policy matters.[10] African American churches have played an active part in Africa-related advocacy; still, few (only 13 percent) of churches in the BCAP sample said that they were involved with Africa policy matters and even fewer (only 5 percent) that they were involved with Caribbean policy matters (see table 1 above). These numbers are certainly small, but it is likely that the number of African American churches with Africa policy involvements was considerably smaller prior to the historic changes brought about in the United States, and in Africa, during the 1950s and 1960s.

Therefore, to the extent that African American churches are involved in public policy matters, their policy focus remains somewhat narrowly centered around civil rights and black community economic development issues. This may suggest the intractability of problems related to racial and economic fairness in the United States just as much as it suggests the relative inability of African American churches to broaden their focus in ways that reflect the contemporary diversity of political demands and interests in a now globalized context. Nevertheless, as the data on black church policy and advocacy group involvements suggest, there are signs that black churches are taking steps toward diversifying their advocacy. Not only have they become somewhat more involved in Africa and women's rights advocacy than before, but their advocacy interests have also become more wide-ranging. Table 2 above outlines the directions in which advocacy interests have moved, but behind these summary categories are the names of quite a number of advocacy organizations, community economic development organizations, ecumenical organizations, and government or electoral organizations with which African American churches have collaborated.[11] This increase in African American church involvement with advocacy groups, including the number of organizations with which activist churches are involved and the types of involvements that activist churches have with these organizations, will be examined more closely in the next section.

African American Churches and Advocacy Organizations

For the first half of the twentieth century, there were two primary black advocacy organizations with which black churches could potentially align — the NAACP and the Urban League. It is not clear what level of institutional collaboration existed during this period between black churches and these two organizations, although the strategic role of activist cadres of ministers throughout the early decades of the NAACP's history has been documented. Charles Kellogg points out, for example, that two African American clergymen were among the half dozen or so people involved in the initial organizing meetings of the NAACP in 1909.[12]

The NAACP leadership involvements of African American clergy were very apparent by the 1950s. In his study of the institutional channels of civil rights movement protest, Doug McAdams reports that a quarter of the local NAACP leaders who headed up protest activities in the South from 1955 to 1960 were African American ministers acting in their capacity as NAACP leaders.[13] During this period, the SCLC emerged as another African American advocacy organization with national stature. Its leadership core was composed primarily of African American clergy, including Martin Luther King Jr. and Ralph Abernathy. Like the NAACP and the Urban League, the SCLC received considerable support from African American churches across the South and the nation—although that support may have been limited to a small activist core. As Adam Fairclough notes: "During the Birmingham protests of 1963—which was one of the most organized and effective of all the civil rights campaigns—only about 20 of the city's 250 African American ministers actively supported SCLC."[14] That translates into only 8 percent of African American ministers being SCLC supporters in a context where a far greater number would have been expected.

By the 1970s, the numbers of black advocacy organizations with which black churches could potentially align began rapidly expanding. Quite a few organizations targeting black issues and constituencies were formed during the 1970s and early 1980s, including Operation PUSH, TransAfrica, the Washington Office on Africa, the Congress of National Black Churches, the Children's Defense Fund, the National Center for Neighborhood Enterprise, and the Rainbow Coalition. The development of such organizations was part of a much broader explosion of U.S. civic and political organizations during that period. For example, the number of individuals and organizations registered to lobby the national government went from approximately 1,000 in 1976 to 17,000 in 2000 (and these figures do not include the additional thousands registered to lobby state and local government).[15] Ronald Hrebenar and Ruth Scott examine other dimensions of the growth of national organizations during this period, estimating that there were approximately 20,000 national nonprofit organizations and 200,000 state and local organizations in 1990—with political organizations representing the largest number of new organizations developed during the 1980s.[16]

Not surprisingly, the percentage of BCAP respondents citing involvement with civic and political organizations was significantly higher than the approximately 8 percent involved with the SCLC during the 1963 Birmingham

TABLE 5 Congregational Involvement with Civic/Political Organizations

	%	N
Yes	49	973
No	50	983

Source: BCAP Survey (N = 1,956).
Note: Response to the question, *Is your congregation currently involved in the activities of any civic or political organization?*

TABLE 6 Instrumental Church Involvements in Civic/Political Organizations

	%	N
Attended meetings	45	898
Given money	41	819
Participated in programs or events	40	792
Advocated issues with public policy officials	35	695
Served on a board or committee	31	608

Source: BCAP Survey (N = 1,956).
Note: Churches may be counted in more than one category of instrumental involvement.

protests. Perhaps reflecting the much broader opportunities for such involvement today than in 1963, a full 49 percent of BCAP respondents reported congregational involvement with political or civic organizations (see table 5). BCAP respondents were also asked about the type and extent of their congregation's participation with civic and political organizations. The types of involvements most frequently cited were attending meetings (45 percent), giving money (41 percent), and participating in programs and events (40 percent) (see table 6). Thirty-five percent indicated participating through issue advocacy and 31 percent through committee or board service, both of which represent a more systematic form of activism than giving money, attending meetings, or participating in programs and events.

To assess the extent of involvement by BCAP respondents in these organizational activities, a subsample of BCAP respondents was asked about the

TABLE 7 Frequency of Instrumental Involvements in Civic/Political
Organizations

	Frequently (%)	Sometimes (%)	Rarely (%)	Never (%)
Given money	13	39	33	12
Attended meetings	2	35	19	42
Advocated issues	2	27	18	52
Served on board/committee	.6	13	21	64

Source: BCAP Survey (*N* = 324).

frequency of some of their involvements with civic and political organizations. The data reported in table 7 show that 52 percent of the subsample
frequently or sometimes gives money to civic and political organizations,
48 percent rarely or never. Approximately one-third of the subsample reported frequently or sometimes attending advocacy group meetings or engaging in an organization's direct advocacy work, two-thirds rarely or never.
Less than one-fifth of the respondents said that they participate in the board
or committee work of advocacy organizations frequently or sometimes, four-
fifths rarely or never (see table 7). When table 6 above and table 7 are taken
together, it would appear that between one-third and half of the overall
BCAP sample were involved in some aspect of the work of civic and political
organizations.

However, the inference from the subsample data is that those involvements
were probably very infrequent for most and frequent for only a very small
number. The data also suggest that the involvements that African American churches have with these organizations tend to be fairly passive. Attending meetings and making financial contributions are not actions that convey
the same level of personal commitment or political engagement as do participation in direct advocacy or leadership functions. The conclusion to be
drawn would, therefore, seem to be that only a small minority of African
American churches can be considered as extensively involved with activist
organizations.

Channels of Policy Activism

Because of the growth and influence of advocacy organizations, policy activism undertaken by congregations will almost certainly have to intersect at some point with the work of these organizations. Nevertheless, congregational policy activism can be and has been pursued through a variety of channels—with advocacy organizations representing only one and, not necessarily, the most frequently utilized channel. Policy activism may take place as part of congregations' involvement with denominational or interdenominational bodies whose primary work is ecclesiastical in nature. Also, congregations may choose not to channel their activism through intermediary structures at all but may, instead, engage policymakers via face-to-face contact or other congregationally initiated actions (such as protest activities). Then, in certain cases, the activism attributed to a congregation may actually be the individual activism of the pastor, acting on behalf of the congregation—and with or without the congregation's active consent.

BCAP respondents were asked to rank which of these channels they were most likely to work through when addressing political concerns.[17] Forty-seven percent indicated that their congregation's policy activism would most likely result from the pastor acting individually, 38 percent that it would most likely be channeled through community organizations, 37 percent that it would most likely result from the congregation acting collectively on its own behalf, 17 percent that it would most likely be channeled through denominational structures, and 13 percent that it would most likely be channeled through interdenominational structures (see table 8).

The distributions seen in table 8 can be placed in a somewhat fuller context by examining factors relating to the governance structures of African American churches. In their contemporary policy activism, as in their ecclesiastical affairs over a much longer period of time, the majority of African American churches have been characterized by decentralization and a lack of hierarchy. This derives, in part, from the fact that the overwhelming majority of African American churches are affiliated with ecclesiastical traditions (such as the Baptist) that emphasize the independence of congregations.[18] Often, within these traditions, the pastor embodies (or, in some cases, individually mirrors) the congregation's independence of authority and action. It is not surprising,

TABLE 8 Channels of Political Activism

	%	N
Individual basis	47	438
Community basis	38	355
Congregation basis	37	351
Demonimation basis	17	158
Interdenomination basis	13	124

Source: BCAP Survey (valid cases = 927).
Note: The 927 respondents who answered this question were asked to rank channels in terms of most likely to least likely to be used. The numbers in table 9 below reflect instances where these channels were ranked first and second most likely to be used.

then, that almost half the BCAP respondents report that their congregation's policy activism results most often from the individual actions of the pastor.

Also contributing to a decentralized approach to activism by African American churches is a fairly weak administrative infrastructure at the denominational level — even among denominations whose polity calls for *episcopal* oversight of member congregations. The infrastructure weakness is particularly pronounced with respect to denominational capacity in responding to public affairs. Although African American congregations within mainline denominations (including the Presbyterians, Episcopalians, United Methodists, American Baptists, Lutherans, Disciples of Christ, United Churches of Christ, and Roman Catholics) have been able to draw on their respective denominational lobbyists on Capitol Hill and on denominational offices and divisions devoted to public affairs, this kind of advocacy infrastructure has generally not existed within the historically black denominations. Two of the historically black church bodies (the African Methodist Episcopal Church and the Progressive National Baptist Convention) have, however, had Washington lobbyists off and on during the last twenty years. Also, many of the historically black denominations — and all the mainline denominations (except for the Roman Catholics, who have had their own structures) — have engaged in advocacy via initiatives of ecumenical bodies such as the National Council of Churches of Christ, USA, and the World Council of Churches. It must be remembered as well that African American church activism is often channeled through advocacy organizations that are not explicitly religious or ecclesiastical, such as the NAACP, the Urban League, or TransAfrica.

Table 9 more systematically examines the relation between types of congregations and channels of activism, analyzing three variables related to the type of congregation (membership size, congregational income, and denominational affiliation) and four variables related to the channels of political activism reported by the survey respondent (individual actions of the pastor, congregation-based activism, denomination-based activism, and community-based activism). The clearest correlation is between congregational income and channels of activism. As table 9 shows, the larger the income of the congregation, the more likely that that congregation's policy activism has been pursued in collaboration with community groups or initiatives ($r = .21$) or that it has been initiated by the congregation acting collectively on its own behalf ($r = .14$). There is an even stronger correlation between congregational income and activism pursued through denominational channels ($r = .22$). In this instance, middle-income congregations (those whose incomes range from \$50,000 to \$249,999) have pursued their policy activism through denominational channels more frequently than have congregations with greater or lesser incomes.

There is, however, a fairly weak correlation between channels of activism and variables related to congregational capacity, such as congregational membership size or denominational affiliation ($r > .06$). Although the relation between these latter two variables and variables pertaining to channels of activism has a higher probability of being random, the analysis of these variables, and of the variables discussed above where the correlations were stronger, supports the overall proposition that congregations pursue policy activism in a manner consistent with the institutional strengths of the congregation. As shown in table 9, that includes an ability and inclination by congregations with higher incomes and larger memberships to facilitate activism through channels internal to the congregations and to form advocacy partnerships with community groups and an inclination by congregations affiliated with denominations characterized by an extensive infrastructure (Catholics and mainline Protestants) to channel their policy activism through their denominations.

TABLE 9 Correlation of Congregational Capacity with Channels of Activism

	N	Individual %	r	Congregation %	r	Denomination %	r	Community %	r
Size			.035		-.053		-.038		-.009
1–99	226	51		34		14		39	
100–999	587	47		38		18		38	
1,000 or more	119	40		41		15		33	
Church income			.048		.146		.221		.219
$1–$49,999	238	42		25		15		37	
$50,000–$249,999	426	50		39		19		39	
$250,000 and over	207	48		51		15		42	
Denomination			.061		.067		.062		.034
Historically black	424	45		39		18		34	
Mainline Protestant	136	52		39		22		48	
Pentecostal/Nondenom.	113	57		37		6		38	
Catholic	60	51		38		25		41	

Conclusion

A relatively small percentage of African American congregations have been actively engaged in public policy activism in recent years, but that activism has been characterized by greater diversity with respect to issue orientation and the organizational channels through which it has moved. Issue orientation has moved beyond racial justice and community economic development concerns to include a greater emphasis on Africa-related policies and women's rights. Although only a small percentage of African American congregations are engaged on these issues, the organizational (and intellectual) infrastructure that has grown up around them since the 1970s should ensure that they maintain a relatively stable footing within African American churches.[19]

A consequence, however, of the broader issue and organizational range of black church activism may be that the policy influence of black churches appears less rather than more obvious. Although there may actually be quantitative and qualitative increases in black church policy activism, the activist core of black churches is relatively small and, potentially, spread more thinly. Impact and influence are achieved quite differently within the current American public policy context, with its diversity and complexity, than during the era of the civil rights movement, when black churches derived a noticeable degree of influence through the concentration of their institutional strengths on one or two issues. That level of influence would likely require either a similar recentering of black church energies around a relatively small range of policy concerns or a marked increase in the number of activist black congregations and in the intensity of their activism. Serious attention to either of these tactical considerations could greatly improve chances for a systematic public policy impact by African American churches.

Notes

1 The leading role of the Nation of Islam in the Million Man March is suggestive of the advocacy potential of other black religious groups; nevertheless, policy activism from within the black faith sector has come almost exclusively from churches.

2 Craig Dykstra and James Hudnut-Beumler, "The National Organizational Structures of Protestant Denominations: An Invitation to a Conversation," in *The Orga-*

nizational Revolution: Presbyterians and American Denominationalism, ed. Milton J. Coalter et al. (Louisville: Westminster/John Knox, 1992), 318–20; John F. Bibby, *Politics, Parties, and Elections in America* (Chicago: Nelson-Hall, 1987), 12–13.

3 Dona Hamilton and Charles Hamilton, "The Dual Agenda of African American Organizations since the New Deal: Social Welfare Policies and Civil Rights," *Political Science Quarterly* 107, no. 3 (fall 1992): 435–52.

4 See, e.g., W. E. B. Du Bois, *The Philadelphia Negro* (1899; New York: Schocken, 1970), and *Economic Cooperation among Negro Americans* (Atlanta: Atlanta University Press, 1907); and C. Eric Lincoln and Lawrence Mamiya, *The Black Church in the African American Experience* (Durham: Duke University Press, 1990).

5 Doug McAdam, *Political Process and the Development of Black Insurgency, 1930–1970* (Chicago: University of Chicago Press, 1982), 137.

6 Ronny Turner, "The Black Minister: Uncle Tom or Abolitionist?" *Phylon* 34, no. 1 (1973): 89.

7 Lincoln and Mamiya argue for a strong relation between education matters and economic development matters. They write: "Education is traditionally considered the primary means of achieving economic mobility, and personal and social fulfillment" (*The Black Church*, 251).

8 Ibid., 290. For a fuller discussion of African American denominational practices relative to women in the ministry, see ibid., 285–89.

9 Herschelle Challenor, "The Influence of Black Americans on U.S. Foreign Policy toward Africa," in *Ethnicity and U.S. Foreign Policy*, ed. Abdul Aziz Said (New York: Praeger, 1981), 173; Roger Wilkins, "What Africa Means to Blacks," *Foreign Policy*, no. 16 (summer 1974): 130–142.

10 Katherine Tate et al., *The 1984 National Black Election Study Sourcebook* (Ann Arbor: University of Michigan, Institute for Social Research, 1988).

11 Some of the national organizations mentioned more than once by respondents included development organizations such as the Opportunities Industrialization Center of America, the Campaign for Human Development, Habitat for Humanity, and One Church/One School and ecumenical organizations such as the Congress of National Black Churches and the National Council of Churches of Christ, USA. A wide range of national lobby and civic groups were also mentioned, including the American Committee on Africa, Bread for the World, the United Negro College Fund, the United Farm Workers, the National Education Association, the National Council of Negro Women, the Children's Defense Fund, the Coalition for Public Justice, and the Boy Scouts and Girl Scouts of America.

12 Charles F. Kellogg, *NAACP: A History of the National Association for the Advancement of Colored People* (Baltimore: Johns Hopkins University Press, 1967), 1:12.

13 See Doug McAdam, *Political Process and the Development of Black Insurgency, 1930–1970* (Chicago: University of Chicago Press, 1982), 254–55. Aldon Morris (*The Ori-*

gins of the Civil Rights Movement: Black Communities Organizing for Change [New York: Free Press, 1984], 15, 14) notes differences between the Southern and the Northern wings of the NAACP, pointing out that the Southern chapters (which were first being formed eight years after the founding of the organization in the North) generally "wanted to move faster than the national office." He remarks further that this "produced uneasiness and tensions between the Northern-based NAACP and its all-black Southern branches."

14 Adam Fairclough, *To Redeem the Soul of America: The Southern Christian Leadership Conference and Martin Luther King, Jr.* (Athens: University of Georgia Press, 1987), 35.

15 See Karen DeWitt, "Lobbying: Key to Lasting Political Influence," *Black Enterprise* 7, no. 2 (September 1976): 44; and J. Valerie Steele, ed., *Washington Representative*, 24th annual ed. (Washington, D.C.: Columbia, 2000).

16 Ronald J. Hrebenar and Ruth K. Scott, *Interest Group Politics in America* (Englewood Cliffs: Prentice-Hall, 1990), 10, 13.

17 Respondents were asked to rank seven different channels of activism, including individual actions of the pastor, congregation-based activism, denomination-based activism, and community-based activism. For purposes of this analysis, I interpret channels that received a ranking of 1 or 2 as those through which respondents' activism was most likely to operate.

18 For example, 57 percent of the churches in the BCAP sample reported affiliation with some form of Baptist, nondenominational, or *independent* church communion.

19 Not only have important advocacy organizations related to Africa and women's rights become well established in recent decades, but so too have women's studies and African studies programs within colleges, graduate schools, and seminaries.

2

AFRICAN AMERICAN CHURCHES,

AFFIRMATIVE ACTION, AND THE CAMPAIGN

AGAINST THE ONE FLORIDA PLAN

Barbara Dianne Savage

African American religious institutions, leaders, and laypeople played a crucial role in many of the campaigns in the modern civil rights movement. Civil rights era activists worked to end legally sanctioned segregation and discrimination in all aspects of American economic and political life. In the post–civil rights period, attention necessarily shifted to monitoring and implementing those new legal requirements and racial policies.

Among those policies is affirmative action, a constellation of requirements designed to remedy the continuing effects of racial discrimination. Affirmative action — whether in education, employment, or contracting — has always been resisted and remains one of the most volatile issues in contemporary American politics. Recent highly publicized anti–affirmative action campaigns further illustrate the persistence of this opposition. This essay presents a case study of the response of African American religious leadership to challenges to affirmative action. Rather than focusing on national-level politics or on the discursive or legal realms, this case study looks to the local.

Ward Connerly, the conservative African American businessman who had spearheaded the successful initiative against affirmative action in California, headed for Florida in 1999 with the goal of placing a statewide referendum on the issue on the ballot for the 2000 elections. As a consequence of that and other political factors, Florida Governor Jeb Bush proposed what he called the One Florida Plan — his administrative proposal to end existing affirmative action programs in state-funded jobs, contracts, and educational institutions.

African American churches played a significant role in the campaign against these anti–affirmative action efforts. Churches engaged in issue-based organizing and employed a variety of mobilization strategies. Churches formed coalitions across denominations with labor unions, the National Association for the Advancement of Colored People (NAACP), and women's groups. Religious leaders coordinated their efforts with black elected officials and with national groups like People for the American Way (PFAW) and the National Organization for Women (NOW).

The ability of African American churches to lend their congregations to powerful political action is well demonstrated in what follows and is seen by all involved as a key component in the anti–affirmative action campaign in Florida. However, working in coalition with several partners brings both opportunity and challenge, and this case is no different in that way as the tensions inherent in coalition building certainly are part of this story as well. And, while organizing to protest Governor Bush's proposal was masterfully executed, translating that activism into a more permanent oppositional presence remains a concern. A lesson also emerges about affirmative action itself and the ways in which it can serve as a particularly appealing issue for black church–based political organizing.

The Politics of Affirmative Action

In 1996, California voters approved Proposition 209, a statewide ballot anti–affirmative action initiative. Ward Connerly had led the publicity campaign for the measure with financial and political support from a wide range of affirmative action opponents based within and outside California. The campaign leading up to the referendum vote generated an enormous amount of national attention and controversy. Minority and women's groups and civil rights and education activists worked hard against the measure, but the majority of California voters voted in favor of it.

Organized opposition to the measure continued after its passage, but activists transferred their energies into a massive voter registration and get-out-the-vote campaign. In elections held in California in 1998, that new voting power was trained against state officials who had supported Proposition 209, most of whom were Republicans. Those newly registered voters are credited with helping California Democrats win control of the state legislature, the congressional delegation, and almost every major statewide position.[1]

In the meantime, Connerly had moved on, taking his well-funded campaign for another statewide anti–affirmative action ballot measure to Washington State. There, in November 1998, he scored another victory despite the opposition of the governor and powerful local corporate employers such as Microsoft and Boeing. Almost as soon as the votes had been tallied, Connerly announced that he planned to lead initiative efforts in other states that permitted such ballot measures. And Florida was the next state on his list. By the summer of 1999, he had started gathering the first round of signatures of registered voters, the first step necessary to place the measure on the ballot during the 2000 presidential election — and force a national debate on the issue.[2]

As a battleground state in the national elections, a state with a large minority population (unlike Washington), and a state with a Republican governor whose views on affirmative action had not been tested, Florida presented Connerly and his supporters with an unusually rich opportunity. It seemed the perfect place to stage a campaign to position affirmative action as a more prominent issue in national Republican and Democratic politics.

For Jeb Bush, Connerly's intervention was especially unwelcome as it would force him to confront this controversial issue head-on during his first term as governor. Perhaps just as important, Connerly's timing raised the specter that an energized coalition of minorities and women might vote in large numbers in the fall 2000 elections, to the detriment of Bush's brother Texas Governor George W. Bush in his bid for Florida's large slate of electoral votes.

National political considerations aside, the attention to the affirmative action issue also intertwined with other developments in Florida state politics, especially around the issue of education. In 1999, under Bush's leadership, the Florida legislature had passed his statewide voucher proposal, the Opportunity Scholarship Program.[3] Despite Bush's attempt to avoid the use of the word *voucher*, the program earned the enmity of many African American and education activists, including some prominent religious leaders and NAACP chapters.[4] That statewide network of activists was, then, already active when the anti–affirmative action campaign emerged. For many already fighting against the implementation of the voucher program, the new campaign was seen as another attack on educational opportunity for low-income and minority students. This would become the key issue that galvanized African Americans who opposed changes to affirmative action programs in Florida.

More broadly, the recent history of racial antagonism in Florida had kindled and strengthened black political organizing and activism in many of the state's large cities. Riots and allegations of police brutality in Miami in the 1980s heightened attention to the persistence of poverty and oppression in a state whose image did not fit the typical Southern racial paradigm, in part because of a diverse ethnic presence, and in part because of its tourism industry.

Indeed, Florida has an often-overlooked but long-standing history of black political activism. The historian Clarence Taylor, for example, demonstrates that a rich variety of black religious activism and political engagement forms a crucial part of Miami's political life and history.[5] African American activism also has strong bases of local support in cities scattered across Florida's wide expanse, in other key population centers like Jacksonville, Tallahassee, Tampa, and Sarasota. In each of those locations, as we will see, religious networks intertwine with the NAACP and other local black civic and political groups. So, in many ways, groups that coalesced around the fight for affirmative action turned to preexisting local black networks — city and county based, but with key congregations, denominations, and religious leaders forming core leadership and resource components.

The One Florida Plan

This then was the complicated political world that Ward Connerly entered into in 1999 when he began building support within Florida for placing an initiative on the November 2000 ballot. Despite his outsider status and Jeb Bush's opposition, Connerly's effort quickly garnered support and financial backing from many Floridians — including a core group of conservative Republican supporters. By the end of October, Connerly had gathered the 43,500 signatures necessary to earn state supreme court review of his proposed ballot measure, a required legal step. African American political leaders in Florida had not been hesitant in criticizing Connerly; perhaps State

Senator Betty Holtzendorf of Jacksonville expressed it most bluntly when she said: "He needs to take his little black butt to California and leave us the hell alone."[6]

In what he hoped was a preemptive strike, Jeb Bush on November 9, 1999, announced his One Florida Plan, which through executive order would end nearly two decades of affirmative action programs in college admissions and state contracts. The proposal eliminated race and ethnicity as factors in state university admissions and contracts. It also established a so-called Talented 20 program that guaranteed state university admission to the top 20 percent of each high school's graduating class, regardless of the students' ACT or SAT scores. And it would provide additional funding for college financial aid. As far as state-issued contracts were concerned, Bush proposed the elimination of all racial set-asides and other racial preferences in state contracting, instead holding each state agency accountable for increased diversity in contracts. Bush asserted that his initiative ended "racial preferences, racial set-asides and race-based university admissions, not affirmative action properly understood."[7]

Bush's move was designed in part to defuse any urgency surrounding the ballot initiative and to avoid divisive attention to the issue during his brother's presidential campaign. The governor had also portrayed his plan as a compromise that would be both less divisive and less harmful to minority interests than Connerly's initiative. George W. Bush felt well served by his brother's actions, saying when asked: "It's awfully handy to have a brother doing a fine job in an important political state and who's for me."[8]

Jeb Bush's hopes that his proposal would short-circuit efforts for a ballot initiative were dashed when Connerly insisted that he would proceed as planned. However, a month later, Connerly announced that he was postponing his petition drive for a ballot initiative pending the outcome of a March state supreme court decision on the wording of the referendum. The long delay led Connerly to fear that he would not have the time needed to gather the larger number of signatures necessary to place the initiative on the ballot or to mount the public campaign needed to ensure its passage. Connerly pledged that, in either event, he would renew his campaign in time for the next available election.

Opposition to the One Florida Plan

Rather than easing matters, Connerly's retreat simply shifted most of the attention toward Jeb Bush's anti–affirmative action proposal and the speed with which Bush was trying to implement it. Initially, some African American political leaders had been willing to give Bush the benefit of the doubt, among them State Senator Daryl Jones, the head of the legislature's black caucus. But, after closer consideration of the proposal, and under pressure from his colleagues, Jones withdrew his support for the One Florida Plan within a week of Bush's announcement.

One of the initial concerns about the Talented 20 plan was that many of Florida's high schools serving poor and minority students offered neither college preparatory nor AP-level courses. As a result, students could graduate in the top 20 percent of their classes or even with an A average and still be denied college admission because they had no opportunity to satisfy the usual college preparatory course requirements. So, despite the 20 percent promise, these students would never be admitted to college and, in particular, to the flagship universities in the state. For those students, the success of a plan like Bush's would depend first on improving their high schools, yet there was no provision for doing that.

Moreover, in terms of education policy, the other aspect of Bush's plan that troubled its opponents — and especially black college students who rallied against it — was the apparent dismissal of the "lower 80 percent." The plan ignored the needs and potential of the vast majority of Florida's minority and low-income high school students. Combined with abandoning affirmative action and the absence of any commitment to better school funding or any remedial assistance, the fear was that fewer, rather than more, black and poor students in Florida would actually make it to college. The Talented 20 plan became perceived as, in some ways, a true quota — excluding the vast majority, and perhaps not even helping those in the top 20 percent of their classes.[9]

Many African American civic and political activists in Florida, including the Reverend Willie Holley, the president of the Sarasota branch of the NAACP, immediately expressed grave reservations about these and other aspects of the plan. Holley called for proceeding "with caution" because he saw the plan as a "nice political maneuver" whose eventual success depended on providing funding to improve high schools serving poor and minority students. Holley had long worked in coalition with other ministers, NAACP members, and black business owners on school equity issues, both at the local level and in opposition to Bush's statewide voucher plan. The affirmative action measure came to be associated easily and instantly with the ongoing school voucher battle. The proposal was seen by Holley and others as another attempt to avoid investing public funding in elementary and secondary schools serving minority and low-income students.[10]

Holley's early opposition to the One Florida Plan is also one example of the overlapping religious and activist networks that were already in place and at work on the issue of education when the affirmative action issue emerged. The state NAACP also had a long-standing interest in education equity issues, a commitment that continued under Adora Obi Nweze, its newly elected president, herself an educator and the head of alternative education and dropout prevention program for the Miami-Dade public schools.[11]

In addition, the connection between the NAACP and Florida's churches was unusually strong. Holley was only one of many ministers across the state who also served as NAACP chapter presidents; another was Bishop Victor T. Curry, a charismatic and influential young minister who became president of the powerful Miami-Dade branch when Nweze assumed the statewide position. State convention meetings of the Florida NAACP are often held in Curry's large New Birth Baptist Church sanctuary.

Religious leadership formed an important part of the earliest opposition to Bush's plan in other ways as well. Leon Russell, a longtime Florida activist and former president of the state NAACP, was leading a coalition of civil rights groups called FREE that wanted to place on the 2000 ballot a constitutional amendment protecting affirmative action. On December 5, ministers at African Methodist Episcopal churches around the state, at the request of their bishop, distributed petitions to their congregations as part of Russell's campaign to gather the necessary signatures for that ballot initiative.[12]

Strong links between the Florida NAACP branches and the national office and between state legislators and members of Florida's congressional delegation helped generate national attention as well. The One Florida Plan drew fire almost immediately from the NAACP's Washington office, which portrayed Bush as "trying to play 'good cop' to Ward Connerly's 'bad cop.'"[13] Congresswoman Corrine Brown of Jacksonville and other members of the

Congressional Black Caucus also voiced their opposition to the plan, with Brown accusing Bush of acting like a "dictator" by ending affirmative action while racial discrimination was still "widespread and persistent."[14]

Bush's decision to impose his plan via executive order rather than through the legislative process led to repeated criticism that he was acting behind closed doors and foreclosing any opportunity for public hearings or amendment. That aspect of Bush's approach became an early rallying cry in building opposition to his action. It also allowed the conflict to be easily cast in religious terms and portrayed as a battle between good and evil. For example, when seventy thousand Florida A&M and Bethune-Cookman alumni and fans came to Orlando for their annual football game, state legislators and religious and NAACP leaders sponsored an informational meeting on Bush's plan. State Representative Chris Smith told a crowd at that meeting: "When you are doing wrong, you've got to do it in the back room. Because we're on the side of God, because we're doing the right thing, we can do it out in the open."[15]

Black members of the state legislature were especially disturbed by Bush's procedural rush outside the legislative process; they also saw the governor's failure to consult them before he introduced his plan as both disrespectful and politically suspect. Still, without clarifying the vagueness of the proposal, the Board of Regents gave preliminary approval to the education component of the plan a week after Bush announced it. To those who were opposed to Bush's proposal or were suspicious of it, it looked like the wheels toward implementation were already turning quickly.

The final vote by the Board of Regents was scheduled for January 21. On the eve of that vote, State Representative Tony Hill and State Senator Kendrick Meek met with Bush in his lieutenant governor's office, where they tried to convince the governor to delay the vote and to hold public hearings on this proposal. But Bush was unmoved and told the legislators that he had his mind firmly made up on the issue. According to Hill, as the meeting was ending the governor said: "If you think you are going to change my mind on this, you might as well send for some blankets."[16] And, on that dare, Hill and Meek decided to hold an impromptu sit-in in the lieutenant governor's office, refusing to leave until some agreement had been reached on hearings about the proposal. They ended their twenty-five-hour protest only after Bush agreed to appoint a legislative task force to hold three public hearings around the state during the coming month and to postpone the Board of Regents vote until February 17, after the hearings.

Hill and Meek's sit-in electrified African Americans in Florida and drew national attention to Bush's political difficulties. The use of an old civil rights tactic, however spontaneous, sparked a tremendous response. About a hundred demonstrators convened outside the governor's offices; the group included NAACP officials, college students from Florida A&M, and Congresswoman Carrie Meek, Senator Kendrick Meek's mother. They were joined by labor union members, who had gathered in support of Representative Hill — a state American Federation of Labor and Congress of Industrial Organizations (AFL-CIO) official. The group prayed and sang "We Shall Overcome." This was a small version of the coalition that would be joined by religious and church leaders to marshal public opposition to Bush's plan.[17]

The scheduled public hearings became the focal point for mobilizing opposition to the One Florida Plan. When the first hearing was held in Tampa on January 28, over six hundred people attended and offered public comment on the plan, making for a five-hour hearing. Bush was roundly criticized for failing to attend that meeting; under pressure, he attended the next hearing, held on February 3 in Miami. There, booed by a crowd of five thousand that had turned out despite the pouring rain, he left after two and one half hours, although the hearing lasted for seven. A week later, the last public hearing drew over eight hundred people to Tallahassee.

Black churches throughout the state helped publicize the hearings and bus people to the task force meetings. Bishop Curry, the president of the Miami-Dade NAACP chapter, used his church's popular gospel radio station to broadcast information, debates, and interviews about the issue and the hearings.[18] At the Miami hearing, where five thousand people turned out, one state representative pointedly thanked a minister for paying for buses to bring people representing twenty-one churches. Some of those in the audience who gave public comment at the hearings sometimes made biblical and other religious references in the course of their testimony. "I am here to tell you that there is a great spirit in this place," stated one man who had driven four hours to get to the hearing, "and I need to go one step further and say God's spirit is in this place. And where the spirit of the Lord is, there is liberty."[19]

Representative Tony Hill, who had led the sit-in and who is a devout Baptist, spoke near the end of the Miami hearing. He cast his own involvement—and that of the others who had come—in starkly religious terms: "Two weeks ago, Kendrick [Senator Meek] and I took the 137 Psalm where the Babylonians called the Israelites; and I was in Atlanta, Georgia, prior to coming to a committee meeting, and I heard Reverend Lawrence say sometimes we have to sing a song in a strange land; and I don't know what more we can say for this committee to take back."[20]

Apparently, Governor Bush had sought out reaction to his proposal from black ministers who had supported his election. At the Tallahassee hearing, the Reverend James B. Sampson, who was an activist pastor of a large church in Jacksonville, blasted the governor for seeking advice only from those black ministers who, in his view, were being rewarded for their support through various state grants: " 'I want him to know,' Sampson said to wild applause, 'God has still got some preachers that won't sell their souls.' "[21] Bush actually had lost the support of his most outspoken black supporter, the Reverend R. B. Holmes, pastor of the six-thousand-member Bethel Missionary Baptist Church in Tallahassee and a Democrat. Holmes said that he felt "double-crossed and embarrassed" by the governor. "Instead of One Florida," said Holmes, "it's divisive Florida."[22]

While the hearings were proceeding, there was lots of other activity as well. The NAACP had filed suit against the governor's proposal. College students became an important part of the opposition to the proposal. Students at predominately black Florida A&M became especially energized by this issue as many of them were Florida high school graduates. On February 8, over a thousand students marched on and held a four-hour rally at the state capitol, where they were addressed by Meek and Hill (the initiators of the sit-in). Under pressure, the governor agreed to meet with several of the student representatives concerning his plan.[23]

March on the Capitol

The idea of a larger march on the state capitol had already emerged as a larger-scale mobilization and lobbying strategy among One Florida opponents. The march was announced for March 7, the day of Jeb Bush's State of the State address marking the start of the legislative session. And, from a symbolic point of view, of equal importance, that date also marked the thirty-fifth anniversary of the "Bloody Sunday" march at Selma across the Pettus Bridge, one of the turning points in the civil rights movement. Designed to bring more pressure on the governor by attracting statewide and national media attention, the march as a strategy also proved especially well suited for church-based organizing efforts and for issue-based coalition building. Indeed, almost as soon as the march was announced, its potential success was linked to Florida's black religious institutions; the *St. Petersburg Times*, for example, predicted as early as January that "church buses are expected to converge on Tallahassee on March 7."[24]

The march would prove to be a highly successful event, with a crowd of marchers estimated to be anywhere from ten or twenty to fifty thousand (depending on the source) — far exceeding the organizers' expectations. It brought together what became known as the coalition of conscience, which consisted of organizers and supporters from the state AFL-CIO, the local and national NAACP offices, NOW, and college students. The union support was important, with about three thousand union members joining the march in addition to several prominent leaders of national labor unions.[25]

But the large turnout for the march would, in Representative Hill's view, have been impossible without the support of black churches and religious leaders — who did, indeed, literally bus in thousands from across the state to attend the rally. Many of the informational meetings about the One Florida Plan and many of the rallies leading up to the march were also held in black churches representing a variety of denominations. The Florida convention of the Primitive Baptist Church played a major role in this organizing effort, according to Hill, as did churches in the Florida General Baptist Convention (affiliated with the National Baptist Convention).[26]

Organizing efforts in key locations were coordinated out of local churches in the cities of Miami, Jacksonville, and Tallahassee. The Reverend James Sampson, pastor of the First New Zion Missionary Baptist Church in Jacksonville, estimated that his church alone sent twenty-five buses to the state capitol. His church also hosted several rallies and prayer vigils in preparation for the march, including a training session for black ministers on organizing for the march. According to Sampson, the members of his church made most of the posters for the marchers.[27] Bishop Curry, president of the Miami-Dade NAACP and pastor of one of the largest churches in Miami (New Birth Baptist), also continued, as he had during the hearings, to use his church's local radio station to broadcast information about the events leading up to the march and to urge listeners to make the trip to Tallahassee. Churches in the state capital were especially active; Bethel African Methodist Episcopal Church in Tallahassee hosted several large rallies leading up to the march; a well-publicized candlelight prayer vigil was held the night before the march at St. Mary's Primitive Baptist Church, which is pastored by the Reverend R. N. Gooden.[28]

The national organizations involved in the march worked through and with local religious leadership and networks in their efforts in Florida. In 1996, the national NAACP had initiated a new campaign aimed at encouraging faith communities toward greater activism, with African American churches serving as the focus of this campaign. The Reverend Julius Hope of Detroit, who holds the position of director of religious affairs for the NAACP, joined the fight against the One Florida Plan. In conjunction with the national branch and local Florida branches of the NAACP, he worked closely with existing ministerial and religious leaders in Florida.[29]

An additional development that was something of a surprise was that the liberal, Washington-based PFAW also established relations with black religious leaders through the formation of their African American Ministers Leadership Council. That group works with black ministers and churches across the country on issue-based campaigns and was founded in part as a counterforce to the prominence of religious leadership in right-wing politics. Formed in 1997, the group worked initially with the NAACP and black pastors in opposition to school voucher proposals. That collaboration, called Partners for Public Education, focused on about fifty ministers in strategic cities in about a dozen states, including Florida. Staff at the national PFAW office found that the ministerial networks in Florida were very strong and well organized in key cities like Jacksonville and statewide. When the One Florida Plan was announced, some of the ministers who had been involved with PFAW in the voucher fight contacted the organization, asking for assistance on affirmative action, which they saw as linked to broader education issues.[30]

What is surprising about this connection is that PFAW is actively engaged in a number of political issues that are not likely to be embraced by the ministers with whom they work, including efforts against prayer in public schools or in favor of gay and lesbian rights. Nonetheless, the partnering between the group, black ministers, and the NAACP rested here on the common ground of education equity, opposition to school vouchers, and, in Florida, opposition to the One Florida Plan. This does suggest the possibilities for single-issue-based organizing and functional coalition building among disparate groups, including black religious groups.

PFAW's African American Ministers Leadership Council is headed by the Reverend Timothy McDonald, pastor of the First Iconium Baptist Church in Atlanta. McDonald and a PFAW organizer helped coordinate the group's efforts in Florida. The two worked closely with state legislators Kendrick and Hill and with Reverend Sampson in Jacksonville, NAACP officials, and other Florida ministers. Together, they organized a series of public information meetings on the One Florida Plan and the march for pastors, laypeople, and church officials from a variety of denominations, with the goal of having churches bus large numbers of their members to the march.[31]

That work was made easier because existing ministerial alliances were already in place and already active on civic and political issues, especially the issue of education. The broader aim was, not only to help foster religious support for and coordination around education and affirmative action, but also to translate the campaign into a massive voter registration and get-out-the-vote effort for state and national elections. Some of the ministers had such programs already in place at their churches; Reverend Sampson's church, for example, sponsors a voter registration drive every three months. Other pastors were encouraged to organize voter registration drives, arrange transportation to the polls, and provide information on absentee voting where necessary.[32]

Not surprisingly, perhaps, those involved with the ministerial effort considered black churches to be essential to the success of the march and the voter turnout campaign. "Black folks . . . are not going to do anything positive for long unless they hear it from the preacher," said one pastor at an organizing meeting. "God has placed on our shoulders the burden of leadership," he concluded. Following on that, the Reverend Julius Hope argued: "It's time for that leadership to step forward." He concluded: "Black churches are the best thing to happen to black America; if we are going to make it to the promised land, we need black churches to get us there." In a similar way, Reverend McDonald declared: "As black churches go, so do black people." Directing his remarks to Governor Bush, he warned: "You have awakened a sleeping giant called the black church. Jeb Bush, you asked for a fight, you've got a fight."[33]

In most cases, activities leading up to the march on the capitol were held in black churches across the state. These events and the entire campaign were infused with a sense of religious mission and black religious culture. One grassroots organizer who traveled around the state helping plan for the march said that she "had been to church more times in the last year than in the previous twenty years."[34] Speaking after the church service and the candlelight prayer vigil held the night before the march, Representative Meek observed that both set the spiritual tone intended for the march itself.[35] At the service, people sang and prayed for God's intervention in the One Florida dispute. Reverend Gooden, the pastor of St. Mary's Primitive Baptist Church, where the meeting was held, told those gathered: "Some of us are tired because we've marched for issues like this before and we thought that demon was finished. Thirty years hence, and we're here again."[36]

By any measure the march was a success, both in terms of turnout and in terms of local and national media coverage. The numbers of marchers exceeded the organizers' expectations as busloads of people, predominately black, converged for what many believed was the largest rally ever held at the state capitol. Protestors came from all across the state, and some were still arriving even as the rally was drawing to an end. Speeches were interspersed with religious and protest songs from the crowd, including "Amazing Grace," "We Shall Overcome," and "Lift Ev'ry Voice and Sing." The march drew statewide and national media coverage in print and on the air. Many reports contrasted views of the large crowd on the capitol grounds with the image of Governor Jeb Bush delivering his brief State of the State address to a sparsely attended opening-day legislative session.[37]

For all their success in helping turn out thousands of people for the march, black religious leaders from Florida were largely excluded from the speakers' platform at the rally and were, therefore, rendered largely invisible in the coverage of the event. Predictably, most of the attention in both the national and the local media focused on the well-known figures of the Reverend Jesse Jackson, NAACP President Kweisi Mfume, and Martin Luther King III, all of whom spoke. There was resentment, then, of the reliance on star performers as focal points of the rally when local leadership actually turned out the crowd. But the complaint was more specific than that. Nearly three dozen people addressed the rally, but the Floridians who were among the speakers were not chosen from among the religious leadership. According to one account, there was only one Florida minister (Bishop Curry, president of the Miami NAACP) among the speakers, with another giving the benediction (Reverend Sampson of Jacksonville).

It appears this was no accident but, rather, the result of a set of political assumptions made by certain organizers of the coalition. It reflected a strategic decision to try to reframe the affirmative action debate as a majority issue rather than a racial minority or a black issue. This was achieved by emphasizing that women, white women in particular, had been the greatest beneficiaries of affirmative action programs.[38] In trying to recast the One Florida fight as being about both race and gender, one participant reported, the organizers had given prominence to Florida women, and especially white women, on the speakers' podium. The two primary rally leaders were Florida NAACP President Adora Obi Nweze, the first woman to hold that position, and Marilyn Lenard, president of the Florida AFL-CIO.

From the onset, the campaign had garnered support from NOW, both locally and nationally. But the tensions generated from emphasizing white women as beneficiaries had been present during the campaign as well. Florida NOW President Toni Van Pelt observed: "When I go out and speak to black groups the first thing I tell them is that white women have been the greatest beneficiaries of affirmative action and there's this wave of 'amens,' and the next wave I feel come over them is a wave of resentment." For her, that reaction fit into "Bush's divide and conquer strategy": "When they say black and Hispanic, they mean black and Hispanic men. When they say women, they mean white women. When does a woman stop being a woman? Black women and Hispanic women aren't even in the mix."[39]

This is one more indicator of the tensions and potential for conflict inherent in trying to build and maintain a coalition around a single issue, especially one that touches on volatile matters such as merit, racial inferiority/superiority, and complex intra- and interracial gender dynamics. Lost in the mix are African American women. It seems likely, for example, that affirmative action could be presented as a black woman's issue—appealing to women who may have been beneficiaries, especially in view of the gender disparities among black college students, or women who as parents or aunts might be especially invested in seeing the continuation of these policies. But that kind of argument does not appear to have been emphasized in this campaign, which is deeply ironic given that black churchwomen likely formed the core organizing strength for the religious networks involved.

For several reasons, then, the decision about speakers irked pastors who had worked hard to deliver the busloads of people assembled that day. Not only did ministers recognize their own exclusion from the podium and from the media coverage, but they recognized as well that the choice of speakers did not reflect the fact that the people who would be most directly harmed by the One Florida Plan were young black people, not white women. In many ways, this concern about the faces on the podium and the faces in the crowd characterized the strains inherent in issue-based coalition building. This is especially true when there are layers of local mobilization and several national organizations representing somewhat different interests. In this instance, the latter included the NAACP, the AFL-CIO, PFAW, and NOW, to name a few. One pastor came away feeling that the churches had been used by the national organizations simply to ensure a large turnout and that the local politicians involved in the march did not keep the religious leadership well informed or well represented when tactical decisions were being made. This reflects another pressure, one that is more frequent in the post–civil rights era — namely, the potential for conflict between black elected officials and black religious leadership who are engaged in the same battle but operating from contrasting insider versus outsider perspectives.

Next Steps

The larger concerns expressed in the wake of the march were how to keep the issue alive and how to transfer the church-based organizational energy and commitment into a voter registration campaign. The concern with voter registration was related to the 2000 national election, but also to local and state races, including sixty open seats in the state legislature.[40] The interim CEO of the Urban League of Palm Beach County, S. Bruce McDonald, rode a bus to the march out of a sense of commitment to the earlier struggles for civil rights, even though, at age seventy-one, the retired school principal thought it would be the last thing he would do. The Florida Urban League chapters plan to make voter registration a priority. The day of the march was filled with promise, he said, but, "now that the marching is over, it's time for the real work to begin." Relying on a sports metaphor, McDonald said: "We're known as sprint runners, but we've got to become long distance runners in this race."[41]

Once again, it seems that the success of that effort will depend on the continued commitment of individual congregations across the state of Florida. State Representative Hill is working with many of the members of the coalition that rallied for the march (including the NAACP and labor unions) in a new campaign, called Arrive with Five — encouraging each voter to bring along five other voters on election day. Traveling around the state, Hill and others involved have been holding meetings "morning, noon, and night" to expand the base of voters. Many of the ministers involved in the One Florida campaign see this as the essential next step and also as a way of continuing to build local and new leadership. And the church is seen as the center of that work simply, in the words of Reverend Sampson, "because the black church has the people."[42]

These actions aimed at elections are necessary because, despite all the negative publicity, and the public pressure, and the opposition to the plan, including that from members of his own party, Bush remained firmly committed to his proposal. The Board of Regents approved the education component of the plan and is proceeding with implementation. The NAACP's lawsuit against the plan failed, although the decision was appealed, forcing, as a result, a postponement in implementing the plan. In the meantime, a judge found Governor Bush's school voucher plan to be unconstitutional. And the state supreme court rejected the language in Connerly's proposal as too broad and misleading, denying him access to the ballot — at least in the 2000 elections.[43] In 2002, the NAACP appeal was thrown out and the education plan implemented.

Perhaps in some recognition of the continuing opposition and of the role that religious leadership held in it, when the governor appointed an advisory panel to oversee the implementation of the One Florida Plan, he chose Bishop Frank Cummings, presiding bishop of the African Methodist Episcopal Church's Eleventh Episcopal District in Jacksonville, to chair the fifteen-member panel. Cummings had supported Bush's Democratic opponent in the gubernatorial campaign.[44]

Conclusion

This case study provides evidence of the potential and power that black churches and denominations have in political mobilization campaigns. Religious institutions and leaders played an essential role in organizing against the One Florida Plan, assuming responsibility for public education on the issue and for rallying community members to attend opposition hearings, meetings, rallies, and marches. Many ministers in key Florida cities pastor churches whose members are civic-minded, and several are involved in working with networks of teachers, the NAACP and the Urban League, and other groups on issues of education equity and school funding. This example, then, teaches us about the continuing political appeal of education and education-related issues for organizing in religious black communities.

In important ways, the issue of affirmative action connects easily to this interest in education. It is viewed by many African Americans as linked to the traditionally sacred black political values of opportunity, education, and jobs. The commitment to affirmative action is a contemporary manifestation of African American political thought that reveres individual mobility as both evidence of and argument for group racial advancement. It is an appealing political issue for that reason.

Of equal importance, the issue of affirmative action avoids some of the stigmas associated with other political issues affecting black communities, issues such as crime, AIDS, welfare reform, drugs, and climbing imprisonment rates. These are public policy issues that trigger conflicts over notions of personal responsibility and morality; as a consequence, these issues also often evoke feelings of condemnation or shame among some middle-class black people. Many simply do not want to be associated with these problems or with advocating on behalf of ameliorative policies, even when structural arguments can be made about them. Clearly, underneath this reluctance are class-biased perceptions as well. Organizing politically on these matters, whether through churches or otherwise, has proved difficult for these and other reasons — with, in my view, unfortunate consequences for African Americans and poor people as a whole.

Affirmative action, in contrast, offers a different appeal and has greater potential as a unifying issue among African Americans, perhaps even across class lines. Many middle-class African Americans achieved their status because affirmative action opened to them, or to their parents, opportunities for jobs, education, and training long denied prior generations of black people. Those opportunities included skilled-labor jobs as well as white-collar administrative positions, apprenticeship programs as well as greater access to college and professional training at white institutions, and new employment possibilities in both the public and the private sector. Affirmative action debates often focus on college and professional school admissions as the most significant area of concern, but, in fact, the largest numbers of affirmative action programs and beneficiaries are elsewhere: in public-sector jobs with federal, state, and local governments and in laboring and skilled positions in the blue-collar construction and service economy. And it is that reality that opens the possibility for African American intraclass unity on this issue.

The argument that affirmative action itself marks black people as inferior — a favorite jibe from its opponents — has been rejected by most of its beneficiaries, who see the policy as a justified and necessary corrective to the stigma and practices of white racism. Evidence of the continued existence of those practices convinces many middle-class African Americans, regardless of their own achievements, security, or status, that their children's and their grandchildren's economic futures will still depend on the preservation of affirmative action programs. Working to protect affirmative action, then, rests on both self- and group interest in safeguarding black access to good education, good training, and good jobs. And, in the end, if all politics is, indeed, local, then self-interested advocates are the easiest to mobilize and to motivate, as here the political merges with the personal often in very powerful ways, as do individual, kinship, and group interests as well.

This look at the opposition to the One Florida Plan also exposes both the advantages and the tensions that come with single-issue coalition politics, especially where the coalition is composed of groups with otherwise divergent interests and missions. Here, affirmative action opponents included many of its past and future beneficiaries — groups of black students, small businesswomen, minority contractors, union members, and white women. This kind of coalition works best when organized around a specific event or rallying point, such as a march, a rally, or a hearing, or getting out the vote on election day. The choice of mobilization strategies, then, becomes very important, as each group is, in the end, left with the job of maintaining its own group's commitment to the broader issue through repeated appeals to the group's self-interest. When many interests are affected, as in this campaign, tensions involved in assigning priority to certain interests do arise and, in the longer term, pose deeper threats to the coalition's work.

One aspect of the post–civil rights era is the involvement of black elected officials in campaigns like this one that are aimed against other public officials and policymakers. As political officials themselves, these black elected officials assume varied roles, sometimes as activist outsiders, sometimes as savvy insider politicians. For those in the African American community who work alongside or follow the leadership of black elected officials, there will be inevitable tensions related to this duality and the frequent role shifting.

While black elected officials have access to certain avenues for power and access, many black ministers also stand in a strong position of power because of the resources of facilities, fund-raising, and congregations that they are uniquely positioned to inspire, direct, or control. In some ways, the two positions of power can and do work well together, but a competition for leadership can develop even over honest differences of opinion about strategies. This may be one of the ironic aspects of the struggle for African American empowerment in the post–civil rights era. In this case, it seems that those tensions have not been destructive as the affirmative action mobilizing coalition — of religious leaders, black elected officials, the NAACP, labor unions, and women's organizations — forged a strong campaign to increase black voter turnout in the 2000 elections in Florida.

Notes

1 William Schneider, "Clearing an Obstacle for George W.," *National Journal*, November 20, 1999, 3–30.

2 "Flush with Washington I-200 Victory, Connerly Is Looking at Other States," *Seattle Post-Intelligencer*, November 10, 1998; "Battleground Moves to Florida; Opponents of Affirmative Action Programs Are Taking Their Cause South in an Effort to Force a National Debate," *Seattle Post-Intelligencer*, July 8, 1999.

3 For more on the Florida Department of Education's Opportunity Scholarship Program, see http://www.opportunityschools.org (copy on file with author).

4 Bush purposely avoided the use of the term *voucher* in his proposal, later telling a congressional committee that he did not "like the v-word" and that he avoided using it in an effort to avoid becoming a part of the national debate over vouchers ("Bush Tells Congress of Voucher Program," *St. Petersburg Times*, September 24, 1999).

5   Clarence Taylor, "Miami's Black Religious Community in the Twenty-First Century" (Florida International University, 2003, typescript).

6   "Battleground Moves to Florida."

7   "Remarks by Governor Bush: Announcement of the One Florida Initiative, Tallahassee, Florida," November 9, 1999, available at http://www.state.fl.us/eog/one_florida (copy on file with author).

8   "Clearing an Obstacle for George W."

9   Similar criticisms had met similar plans that had been implemented in California after the success of the ballot initiative and in Texas after a lawsuit outlawed race-based affirmative action programs. In Texas, African American and Hispanic legislators developed a plan entitling 10 percent of each graduating class to admission to any state university, including the flagship, the University of Texas at Austin, or Texas A&M. This plan, unlike the Florida proposal, also included a variety of college preparatory initiatives, remedial programs, alumni-sponsored minority scholarships, and college retention programs. Still, according to a report from the U.S. Commission on Civil Rights, while the number of minority students admitted under the plan matches that of classes before the policy change, the actual yield for minority applicants is lower—i.e., students who are not in the top 10 percent of their high school classes who might have been admitted under affirmative action have lost that opportunity. The commission criticized Bush for issuing the One Florida Plan without adequate review and consultation and for failing to provide sufficient remedial and retention efforts. For a more detailed analysis of the Texas, California, and Florida plans, see U.S. Commission on Civil Rights, "Toward an Understanding of Percentage Plans in Higher Education: Are They Effective Substitutes for Affirmative Action?" April 13, 2000, available at http://www.usccr.gov/percent/stmnt.htm (copy on file with author).

10 Reverend Willie Holley, telephone interview with author, July 31, 2000. Similarly, Leonard M. Chappell, the president of the Charlotte County branch of the NAACP, also raised questions about the practical feasibility of Bush's plan ("Bush: End Race-Based Preferences," *Sarasota Herald-Tribune*, November 10, 1999).

11 "First Woman President, NAACP," *AP Wire*, October 10, 1999.

12 "Group Begins Battle of Pen," *St. Petersburg Times*, November 21, 1999.

13 "Attacks on Bush Initiative Mount," *Lakeland Ledger*, November 17, 1999.

14 "Governor Hit from Both Sides," *Florida Times-Union* (Jacksonville), November 18, 1999. See also "Attacks on Bush Initiative Mount."

15 "Group Begins Battle of Pen."

16 Florida State Representative Tony Hill, telephone interview with author, July 23, 1999.

17 "Sit-In Leads to Affirmative Steps; Bush Agrees to One Florida Hearings, Puts Off

Vote on University Admissions," *Florida Times-Union* (Jacksonville), January 20, 2000; "Florida Sit-In Spurs Dialogue on Bias," *Washington Post*, January 20, 2000.

18 "Florida Affirmative Action Meeting Faces Political Battle over Location," *Miami Herald*, February 3, 2000.

19 Full transcripts of the three hearings can be found on Governor Bush's website: http://www.state.fl.us/eog/one_florida (copy on file with author).

20 Psalm 137 concerns the constancy of Israel while in captivity under the Babylonians: "For there they that carried us away captive required of us a song; and they that wasted us required of us mirth, saying Sing us one of the songs of Zion. How shall we sing the Lord's song in a strange land?" (AV).

21 "Bush Determined to Keep Plan Alive," *Sarasota Herald-Tribune*, February 11, 2000.

22 "Jeb Bush Roils Florida on Affirmative Action," *New York Times*, February 4, 2000.

23 "FAMU Students March on Capitol," *Tallahassee Democrat*, February 9, 2000.

24 "Governor Stealing Unwanted Thunder," *St. Petersburg Times*, January 31, 2000.

25 "Taking Affirmative Action in the Street: Over 3000 Union Members March on Tallahassee," Florida AFL-CIO press release, March 2000.

26 Florida State Representative Tony Hill, telephone interview with author.

27 Reverend James B. Sampson, telephone interview with author, July 28, 2000.

28 "Anti–One Florida Forces Plan Prayer Vigil, March on Capitol Steps," Associated Press State and Wire Service, March 6, 2000; "United in Prayer against One Florida," *Florida Times-Union* (Jacksonville), March 7, 2000; Barbara De Vane, Academy of Florida Trial Lawyers, telephone interview with author, July 24, 2000.

29 "NAACP Forges New Agenda with Faith Community: Two-Day Religious Summit Champions Increased Activism," NAACP Press Release, February 2000.

30 Kurt Clay, People for the American Way Foundation, telephone interview with author, July 25, 2000.

31 Reverend Timothy McDonald, telephone interview with author, July 25, 2000; Reverend James B. Sampson, telephone interview with author.

32 Reverend Timothy McDonald, telephone interview with author; Reverend James B. Sampson, telephone interview with author.

33 "NAACP, Pastors Call for Activism; One Florida Plan Galvanizing Blacks," *Florida Times-Union* (Jacksonville), February 29, 2000.

34 Barbara De Vane, telephone interview with author.

35 "Anti–One Florida Forces Plan Prayer Vigil."

36 "United in Prayer against One Florida."

37 "Thousands Protest One Florida," *St. Petersburg Times*, March 8, 2000; "Thousands March on Florida Capitol—Protesters Assail Gov. Bush's Plan That Replaces Affirmative Action," *Boston Globe*, March 8, 2000; "Marchers Bring Bush a Message," *St. Petersburg Times*, March 8, 2000; "Jeb Bush's Anti–Affirmative Action Plan Ig-

nites Firestorm," *Los Angeles Times*, March 7, 2000; "How Jeb Bush Suddenly Became Bull Connor," *National Journal*, March 18, 2000, 843–44; "Ending Affirmative Action Proves Harder Than It Looks," *Christian Science Monitor*, March 10, 2000.

38   Barbara De Vane, telephone interview with author.

39   "Judge Upholds Bush's Anti Affirmative Action Plan," *Women's Enews*, July 18, 2000, http://www.womensnews.org (copy on file with author).

40   "Opponents Haven't Given Up One Florida Fight," *Lakeland Ledger*, May 21, 2000.

41   "One Florida Protests Draw Veteran Leader," *Palm Beach Post*, March 11, 2000.

42   "One Florida Protest Organizers Turn Efforts toward Voter Drive," *Palm Beach Post*, June 20, 2000; Florida State Representative Tony Hill, telephone interview with author; Barbara De Vane, telephone interview with author; Reverend James B. Sampson, telephone interview with author.

43   Governor Jeb Bush, " 'One Florida'—the Next Step Forward," February 16, 2000, available at http://www.state.fl.us/eog/one_florida/remarks_nextstep.html (copy on file with author); "Court Bars Affirmative Action from 2000 Ballot," *St. Petersburg Times*, July 14, 2000; "Suit Stalls One Florida Admission Guarantee," *Palm Beach Post*, April 1, 2000; "Students Targeted to Bolster One Florida," *Palm Beach Post*, May 16, 2000; "Bush Suffers Legal Setback as Judge Declares Vouchers Are Unconstitutional," *Miami Herald*, March 15, 2000.

44   "One Florida Panel Headed by AME Bishop," *AP State and Local Wire*, May 1, 2000.

3

THE ROLE OF AFRICAN AMERICAN CHURCHES IN

CRAFTING THE 1996 WELFARE REFORM POLICY

Megan E. McLaughlin

Maulana Karenga remarks: "In a society divided and defined by race and class, interests and the conflicts around them assume a race and class character."[1] Divergent class and race interests have in recent decades been played on and exaggerated in public social policy debates around welfare reform, among other policy issues. It is not an accident that, in order to gain public support for changes in welfare, conservatives carefully cultivated in the public's mind an image of the average recipient as "black welfare queen" riding in a Cadillac to get home to her big-screen television. In *Why Americans Hate Welfare*, Martin Gilens asserts: "Racial stereotypes play a central role in generating opposition to welfare in America. In particular, centuries-old stereotypes of African Americans as lazy remain credible for large numbers of white Americans. This stereotype grew out of, and was used to defend, slavery, and it has been perpetuated over the years by continuing economic disparities between black and white Americans."[2]

In discussing recent debates over welfare reform, Gilens quotes a statement from the *Minneapolis/Saint Paul Star Tribune* as saying, " 'Welfare' and 'urban' have often been used as political code words that really mean 'minority,' " and the University of Minnesota Law School professor Paul Powell as saying, "A lot of this discussion is racism in drag. . . . When you talk about welfare, vouchers, urban strategies, crime, poverty, you're really talking about race." Gilens also calls attention to the fact that "perceptions of blacks continue to play the dominant role in shaping public's attitudes toward welfare."[3] Gilens's conclusion is by no means unique. In fact, most advocates have articulated the view that, in order to "end welfare as we know it," it is necessary to get the public to believe that welfare is a program that primarily serves blacks. Public debates have often focused, for example, on high out-of-wedlock birthrates among African Americans and Latinos, thereby casting the issue and social targets in racial terms.

Recent public social legislation has radically redefined the government's responsibility for the poor. Simultaneously, these policies have redefined the role of civil society as it pertains to the poor. The Personal Responsibility and Work Opportunity Reconciliation Act of 1996 (PRWORA) devolved responsibility for the poor from the federal government to state and local governments and, further, to the individual and civil society. This change has significantly affected black families and communities and has major implications for civil society. For example, in 1993, blacks constituted 12 percent of the nation's population overall but 33 percent of the nation's poor population, more than 50 percent of all black children were poor, and more than 39 percent of the children receiving Aid to Families with Dependent Children (AFDC) were black.[4] In view of the significant way in which race has factored into the development of welfare policy, the involvement of black institutions (including black churches) in the deliberations over the 1996 welfare reform policy should have been a given. Unfortunately, it was not.

Social policies embody values and determine priorities and the use of resources. Policy planners will make different choices depending on their values and priorities. Therefore, a thorough analysis of any social policy should include answers to such questions as, Who plans? To whom are the planners accountable? Whose values guide the choices?[5]

This essay seeks to explore the role of African American churches in the evolution and formulation of PRWORA. The major assumptions guiding this analysis are as follows:

1. Public policies and programs will have a more positive effect on African American families and communities if representatives from the key black institutions are involved in their formulation.
2. African American churches should, as historic and influential representatives of black civil society, constitute a primary site where the interface between black civil society and public policymakers can take place.
3. The absence of African American churches from the the process by which social welfare policy is formulated signals the possibility that the best interests of black families and communities are being excluded.

4. Strategies for increasing the influence of African American churches on public social welfare policy are needed.

PRWORA: An Overview

Civil society, simply defined, is a realm that we create for ourselves through associated common action in families, clans, churches, and communities. It is "a 'third sector' [the other two are the state and the market] that mediates between our specific individuality as economic producers and consumers and our abstract collectivity as members of a sovereign people."[6] Since the 1980s, the concept of civil society has gained currency, and people on all points of the political spectrum — left, right, and center — have found it appealing. Some suggest that the current focus on civil society is related to the debate about the role of government, specifically, the antigovernment mood that has permeated American life since the 1970s. For some, it is a strategy to increase social supports for individuals and families on a community level, and, for others, it is a strategy to transfer responsibility for the poor from the government to civil society and to enforce personal responsibility.[7] For others still, it is a strategy to implement their view that poverty is the result more of a lack of values than of economic issues.[8]

A role for civil society and faith communities, in particular, was defined in Section 104 of PRWORA. The charitable choice provision encourages states to engage faith-based organizations to provide welfare services using federal dollars. It obligates the government to respect the religious identity and mission of churches and faith-based organizations that accept government money to help the poor.[9] Section 104 of Public Law 104-193, for example, allows "states to contract with religious organizations, or to accept certificates, vouchers, or other forms of disbursement under any program described . . . so long as the programs are implemented consistent with the Establishment Clause." Originally promulgated by Senator John Ashcroft in 1995, the charitable choice provision allows charitable and faith-based organizations to compete for contracts or participate in voucher programs whenever a state chooses to use private-sector providers for delivering welfare services to the poor. The provision provides for several safeguards, protecting religious organizations' freedom of expression: "A religious organization with a contract . . . shall retain its independence from federal, state and local governments, including such organization's control over the definition, development, practice, and expression of its religious beliefs."[10] In 1999, the Charitable Choice Expansion Act pushed the federal provision further, indicating that the government must equally consider faith-based organizations and other private institutions when contracting or using vouchers for social services: "Faith-based organizations then would be allowed to provide services or programs with federal funds without being required to form separate corporations or remove religious symbols from their premises."[11]

Of course, the charitable choice provision should be viewed in the context of PRWORA. PRWORA radically changed the safety net program that had been in existence since 1935. It ended altogether the entitlement status that guaranteed aid and cash assistance for poor children and families by making welfare the responsibility of the state rather than the federal government; established a five-year lifetime limit on receipt of welfare and imposed strict time limits barring adults who are not working from receiving food stamps for more than three months in a thirty-six-month period unless they are disabled, caring for a child, over the age of fifty, pregnant, or otherwise exempt from the work requirements; and mandated work requirements and included child exclusions permitting states to deny benefit increases to a woman or teenage girl who has another child if she receives AFDC or qualifies as a dependent child.[12]

There has been a great deal of emphasis placed on Temporary Assistance for Needy Families (TANF) — the program that replaces welfare. However, it is important to recognize that PRWORA was much broader than TANF. In the area of child care, for example, PRWORA eliminated the guarantee of child-care assistance for families on welfare who are working or are in school or training programs; replaced child-care entitlement programs with a single block grant; targeted 70 percent of the funds for families on welfare or at risk of being on welfare; required both parents to work in order to receive child-care assistance; and eliminated language in the 1996 Family Support Act that required states to pay market rates for child care. Not only in child-care but in other existing social welfare provisions, guarantees were removed, more flexibility was given to states, benefits were reduced, and additional restrictions were placed on eligibility.[13] PRWORA is particularly harsh on legal immigrants, a high proportion of whom are blacks or other people of color.

They are generally banned from receiving any "federal public benefit" — with some exceptions for emergency medical care. PRWORA ends supplemental security income and food stamps for all legal immigrants and gives states the option to deny Medicaid. All future legal immigrants will be ineligible for most social welfare benefits and social services in their first five years in the United States.

Numerous studies have attempted to document the impact of welfare changes. Some paint a picture suggesting that families have fared well, while others report more disturbing findings. Early portraits of welfare reform, in particular, highlight declines in welfare rolls, increases in recipients finding employment, and a slight decline in the overall child poverty rate.[14] For the most part, welfare reform has been declared a success, with success gauged largely by dramatic reductions in the number of welfare cases. Since 1994, the year in which the caseload peaked nationally, the number of welfare cases in the United States has been cut by more than half, with 2.6 million families leaving the rolls — a 52 percent decline.[15] Caseload declines, however, are by no means the whole story and should not be the major criterion with which to judge success.

On the other side, there is mounting evidence that welfare reform is adversely affecting poor families. According to a joint study by the Children's Defense Fund and the National Coalition for the Homeless,[16] early findings on the impact of welfare reform from less well-publicized data reveal an increase in extreme childhood poverty, a proliferation of inadequately paid employment, and signs of rising hardship for many families leaving welfare. The report found that many families leaving welfare are experiencing serious economic struggles getting food, shelter, and needed medical care and other hardships. Moreover, many families are not getting the basic help — such as child care, medical coverage, food, and transportation — that might enable them to sustain work and care for their children on very low wages. Welfare reform has also reduced food stamp receipt for those still eligible and contributed to the loss of health care coverage for many others. Moreover, welfare reform has resulted in high rates of unemployment for those leaving the welfare rolls.[17]

Welfare changes have had major repercussions for all low-income families, but blacks and other minorities have continued to be especially hard hit. According to a fifty-state Associated Press survey, the proportion of blacks and other people of color on assistance has grown nationwide, in some cases dramatically, primarily because whites are leaving welfare at a faster rate. The survey found that, in thirty-three states, the proportion of white welfare recipients has dropped since 1994, when caseloads peaked nationally. The survey also revealed that, of the sixteen largest states, home to 76 percent of people on welfare, fourteen have seen whites leave welfare faster than blacks or Hispanics. In Ohio, for example, among those on welfare, blacks now out-number whites for the first time: in 1995, 54 percent of the people on welfare in Ohio were white and 42 percent black, but, by 1999, 53 percent were black and 42 percent white.[18]

A study released by the Brookings Institution Center on Urban and Metro-politan Policy, *Unfinished Business*, examined welfare caseloads between 1994 and 1999 in the eighty-nine urban counties that contain the one hundred largest U.S. cities, with additional analysis of racial and ethnic trends. One of the study's key findings is that, since 1996, the overall racial composition of the welfare caseload in twenty of those eighty-nine counties has changed only slightly, black and Hispanic welfare recipients leaving the welfare rolls at roughly the same rate as white welfare recipients and at only slightly slower rates than national welfare declines. Specifically, the proportion of the case-load that was black increased 0.6 percentage points between 1996 and 1999, the proportion that was Hispanic increased by 2.7 percentage points, the pro-portion that was white decreased by 3.3 percentage points, and the propor-tion that was "other" remained stable.[19]

The disproportionate impact on blacks is not limited to the numbers leaving welfare. One study shows differences in the support provided black and white welfare clients by caseworkers. Black welfare recipients report sig-nificantly less discretionary transportation assistance and receive less case-worker support in increasing their formal education than do their white counterparts as they attempt to become economically self-sufficient.[20] An-other study, this one examining the treatment that black and white welfare recipients receive from employers (another important component of achiev-ing self-sufficiency), found that, in five of ten indicators, blacks receive more negative treatment than do whites. Black respondents reported shorter inter-view lengths, a greater number of required preemployment tests, more differ-ences between the positions described at the interview and the tasks actually performed, more evening working hours, and a more negative relationship with their supervisor.[21] A recent article on the employment status of white and black welfare recipients who are participating in a state welfare reform program, the Virginia Initiative for Employment Not Welfare, also found significant racial disparities. Its findings suggest that black and white welfare recipients with similar human capital do not have similar employment outcomes and that this phenomenon is an understudied dimension of welfare policy.[22]

PRWORA codifies as public policy the movement by many elected officials to abandon social problems and to disinvest in the poor. These officials claim that the public sector tried and failed and that "faith-communities should now assume the responsibility for ridding the society of the burdens associated with the poor and needy whose condition is a result of moral failure."[23] Charitable choice is the mechanism to provide funding for faith-based initiatives meant to implement the new welfare policies. Public officials are looking to African American churches to take the lead in caring for the myriad of social problems in the African American community—although not necessarily inviting African American church input on the policy guidelines or parameters. The Reverend Johnny Ray Youngblood, an activist black pastor involved in St. Paul's Community Baptist Church in Brooklyn, commented in an op-ed piece in the *New York Times*: "One would think that major candidates who stress faith-based solutions would want to sit down with our bishops and rabbis, priests and ministers to discuss these matters. That has not been the case. None of the candidates have accepted our invitation. As soon as they hear that we are not interested in a luncheon photo-op, but in serious conversation about wages and equity, they stop returning calls."[24] The Reverend Dr. Calvin Butts, senior pastor of the Abyssinian Baptist Church, expressed a similar view in an interview, indicating that the public sector never "engaged the black church in serious discussions about policy" and that any discussions that have ensued "came out of the churches' desire to help."[25]

Lincoln and Mamiya question whether, given their multiple responsibilities, African American churches are really in a position to make public policy formation a priority. According to Lincoln and Mamiya: "Today's Black Church is struggling for relevance in the resolution of today's black problems: racism; drug abuse; child care; health and welfare; housing; counseling; unemployment; teenage pregnancy; the false securities of conspicuous consumption; and the whole tragic malaise with which society is burdened."[26] Given scarce resources, the question therefore is, How important is involvement in the development of public social policy? In the area of civil rights, it was recognized that legislative changes were necessary in order to extend benefits to the largest number of people. The same applies in the area of social policy.

The Policymaking Process and the Role of African American Churches

It is difficult to ascertain the full extent of African American church involvement in the development of PRWORA given that African American churches do not function as monolithic entities with central hierarchies that approve, disseminate, and advocate for policy positions in the manner of the Catholic Church. African American churches are, instead, characterized by multiple centers of power and decisionmaking where influence may be exerted through individual leaders and members. The public social policy process can be, and often is, influenced by individuals working behind the scenes. Thus, individual African American church leaders may exert influence on public policy issues in ways that remain largely invisible.

I do not mean to minimize the fact that many concerned individual churches and coalitions worked hard to voice their concerns about the foreseeable impact of welfare reform, and many authors (some within this very volume) have chronicled those efforts. I do, however, seek to highlight the critical place within the formulation of PRWORA where African American churches did not have a strong voice.

A review of seventeen legislative hearings, from 1993 through 1996, covering a broad range of issues such as welfare hotels, child care, welfare reform, the Republicans' Contract with America, the Clinton administration's view on welfare reform, teenage parents, welfare to work, child welfare programs, and causes of poverty, sought to identify witnesses representing major African American religious denominations. Among the more than 285 witnesses identified, not a single one specifically representing an African American denomination, religious coalition, or congregation was found.

Interviews with twenty prominent African American ministers and individuals active in major advocacy organizations sought to determine the level of involvement of African American church leaders in the process by which welfare reform policy was formulated and to document some of the reasons for those levels of involvement.[27] The findings were definitive. African American churches had no measurable involvement in welfare reform policy formation. This lack of involvement was not, however, limited to African American churches; participation by religious institutions in general was fragmented and largely ineffective. The notable exceptions were the efforts of Catholic Charities and the Christian Coalition.

The clergy interviewed were all aware of the ongoing national debate about welfare reform. The Reverend Dr. William Epps, of the Second Baptist Church, Los Angeles, indicated that he worked with other groups, including the Southern Christian Leadership Conference, the National Association for the Advancement of Colored People, and Bread for the World, to educate his congregation and community about welfare reform and also participated in demonstrations and letter-writing campaigns to express disagreement with the proposed policies.[28] The other pastors interviewed indicated that they had not been actively involved in efforts to influence that debate. According to Reverend Butts: "Public policy debate and how you do that is one of the greatest challenges we [the black church] have."[29] Richard Roper, deacon of the Bethany Baptist Church, stated that African American church leaders were against most of the welfare reform proposals. They had, according to Roper, actively opposed and protested against key components of New Jersey's child exclusion provision when a black legislator, Assemblyman (now State Senator) Wayne Bryant of Camden, introduced the bill in 1991. However, to Roper's knowledge, there was no organized opposition to similar policies in the 1985 welfare reform legislation.[30]

Barbara Blum, of the National Center for Children in Poverty, acknowledged: "The presence of organized religious opposition to welfare reform was virtually nonexistent."[31] Michael Laracy, of the Annie E. Casey Foundation, added: "Faith-based organizations were not very effective in influencing the legislation."[32] Even religious organizations with manifestly conservative platforms currently claim to have had little or no input in the formation of welfare reform legislation. Organizations like Focus on the Family and the Family Research Council claim to have focused on specific issues within the proposed legislation but not on supporting or opposing PRWORA itself. The Christian Coalition — presumed by some to be the philosophical architect of PRWORA — indicated that it could find no material in its files relating to coalition participation in activity related to national welfare reform,[33] although representatives of the organization did appear as witnesses in legislative hearings reviewed for this essay.

Edward LaMonte and Michelle Coghlan conclude: "By and large national denominational representation spoke with a tone of weary discouragement over their failure to be more effective in welfare reform."[34] Interviews focusing on representatives of major African American religious and nonreligious organizations revealed similar perspectives regarding the level and impact of African American churches on welfare reform policy formation. Dr. William Sprigg, at the National Urban League, characterized the participation of African American churches as "minimal," even with welfare reform's "measurably negative impact on poor black communities."[35] Sullivan Robinson, of the Congress of National Black Churches, an ecumenical coalition of eight historically African American denominations representing over sixty-five thousand African American churches with a collective membership of more than twenty million people, expressed "surprise at the lack of participation by the membership."[36]

Activists within the black advocacy sector confirmed the lack of involvement, not just by African American churches, but by black civil society institutions in general. Emblematic of the latter was that the Congressional Black Caucus (CBC) held no hearings on welfare reform, choosing instead to work informally with other legislators on the issue. Andrea Martin, the policy director of the CBC, stated: "We felt it would be more effective to focus on specific items that affect our constituents rather than focus on the entire bill. We focused on saving school lunches, child immunization, and senior citizens programs. We feel strongly that a broader approach might have left these and other important items extremely vulnerable. The caucus decided that separate hearings would be counterproductive. We needed to reserve our resources to address the specific items in the bill that we opposed. We were able to significantly minimize the damage to the programs we were concerned about."[37]

In assessing the lack of involvement by these sectors in the welfare policy formation process, it is important to acknowledge that some of the reasons offered for minimal participation are complex and, for those offering them, quite real. Among the reasons offered were perceived structural barriers and the conflicting perspectives on welfare.[38]

Martin confirmed that Congress had absolute control over who would be invited to testify and over what written submissions would be entered into the permanent record. While it has been customary for the chair of the committee holding hearings to allow the ranking minority member some privileges on these matters, courtesy was not always observed. The frenzied determination of the "Republican Revolution" made it impossible, some suggest, for dissenting arguments to be presented during *key* legislative hearings. Many felt that the die was cast and that their advocacy would make no significant difference, and they therefore withheld their views. Anna Rhee, the director of religious affairs of the Children's Defense Fund, put it bluntly: "Black Churches are only approached by policymakers to be showcased. They are never asked to be legitimate partners. If their participation level in the welfare reform dialogue was less than vigorous, that was probably as much by design as it was an effect." Rhee also cautioned against the notion that African American churches are natural vehicles for advocacy: "Public perceptions aside, black churches are not comfortable engaging in advocacy."[39]

Another significant factor was the greatly misunderstood lobbying restrictions on 501c(3) tax-exempt organizations and the complexities of welfare policies. The skills and resources necessary for mounting an effective advocacy campaign simply were not available to most African American churches—already overtaxed by their commitments to providing religious and social services to their constituents. The Reverend Dr. Frances Manning, of New Hope Baptist Church, acknowledged a lack of understanding by many African American clergy: "Most of us were not aware of the specific developments in the welfare reform process; we simply didn't understand the issues."[40] This view was expressed by other clergy interviewed and by James Ferguson, policy director of the Congress of National Black Churches, who noted: "Most churches don't have the resources or the expertise to effectively engage in, and influence, complex policy discussions."[41] These perspectives are consistent with those observed by the National Council of Churches, which stated that welfare reform occurred within the context of a complex budget reconciliation process, that it was part of a budget deficit reduction package.[42]

Those who withdrew from the process because they felt that decisions had already been made were accurate in their assessment. The content of the 1996 Welfare Reform Act (as passed) was decided on over an extended period of time by a limited number of scholars, policy analysts, and researchers—many of whom were paid to work full-time on these issues. They generated significant amounts of data and analysis and distributed their findings through the media and scholarly journals. Through this process, they were effective in influencing public perceptions. They also worked directly with legislators and their staffs in crafting legislation and moving it through the legislative process. Lucy A. Williams summarized the evolution of this powerful force as follows:

> Often it seems that this attack on welfare (euphemistically called "reform") is a new political phenomenon. Because it is so closely associated with the Newt Gingrich Congress, it is easy to see it as the brainchild of the New Right and the "new Republicans" who dominated the 104th Congress. However, the targeting of welfare dates to the "Old" Right of the 1960's, the movement headed by Barry Goldwater and identified with the John Birch Society. In the 30 years since the 1960's, right wing think tanks and intellectuals have polished and refined the critique, and developed the policies that were captured in the current bill.[43]

Conservative foundations have, in fact, been particularly strategically important to the formulation of the most recent welfare policy reforms. In 1999, David Callahan projected that conservative think tanks would expend more than $1 billion during the 1990s. In 1996 alone, the top twenty conservative think tanks spent $158 million promoting their agenda. Comments from the president of the National Committee for Responsive Philanthropy, quoted by Callahan, shed light on the capacity of conservative foundations to shape policy: "When it comes to 'winning' political battles, ultimate success results less from who's doing the right thing and more from whose view of reality dominates the battlefield. It doesn't take a rocket scientist to figure out that the millions effectively spent by conservative think tanks have enabled them virtually to dictate the issues and terms of national political debates."[44] These foundations were successful for a number of reasons. First, they funded extremely aggressive and ideological institutions routinely committed to influencing budget and policy priorities. Second, they maintained an unusually strong focus on national public policy institutions. Third, they demonstrated a preference for the marketing of their ideas.

When President Reagan assumed office, the Heritage Foundation presented his transition team with a thousand-page document that described waste and fraud in the food stamp program, the school lunch program, and all the programs operated by the U.S. Department of Health and Human Services (including AFDC) — erecting, in the process, distinctions between the "worthy" and "unworthy" poor that have continued to serve as ideological guideposts within the welfare debate.[45] Further, Reagan's public policy initiatives were greatly influenced by three books positing that public assistance created immorality and dependency, undermined values, and increased poverty. Two of the books, *Losing Ground*, by Charles Murray, and *Wealth and Poverty*, by George Gilder, were funded by the Manhattan Institute. The third, *Mandate for Leadership*, was written and funded by the Heritage Foundation.[46] Obviously, this capacity for influencing the welfare policy debate has been matched by few — certainly not by African American churches.

Not only have structural barriers impeded African American church participation in the welfare policy process, but so have conflicting perspectives by black churchpersons on welfare policies. There were at least three clearly defined camps among African American churches throughout the discourse on welfare reform. The first camp was reluctant to be associated with welfare at all because of the stigmatization of welfare issues as a stereotypically black problem — however inaccurate that stereotype may be. The Reverend John Vaughn highlighted this view: "Many pastors mouthed a concern but were not ready to jump in. The issue was divisive. People had bought the rhetoric, and there were no proactive efforts to educate congregations about the real issues."[47] In many respects, this avoidance strategy was consistent with the posture of a number of black legislators. One well-informed source indicated that the New York State Black, Hispanic, and Puerto Rican Caucus would not issue policy statements on welfare reform and that members of the caucus refused to serve as the point persons on the subject. This may bear some relation to the decision of the Congressional Black Caucus not to exercise its option to hold separate meetings on welfare reform.

A second camp simply refused to participate in a welfare reform debate that it viewed as a misguided effort by government to abdicate its responsibility to the poor.[48] African American churches expressed concerns along these lines, stating that they were invited to participate in policy discussion only after the policy framework had already been constructed. Therefore, their participation in any discussions held under these circumstances would have amounted to tacit acceptance of the policy parameters already in place, including the shifting of responsibility for direct service delivery from the government to faith-based institutions. According to James Ferguson: "When you look at the severity of the legislation, it is not difficult to see the [overall] agenda. Black churches were not likely to be enthusiastic participants in a conversation framed by conservatives."[49]

A third camp saw the dismantling of the social safety net as a foregone conclusion and decided to position itself so as to benefit from, or to be minimally harmed by, the inevitable outcome. While, on the surface, this strategy may appear objectionable, interviewees provided compelling justifications for their position. As I have written elsewhere: "Churches have always fed the hungry, clothed the naked and given comfort to the distressed without public funds. Churches have been eligible for public funds for a long time. . . . Charitable Choice only codifies, formalizes and encourages what existed before."[50] Therefore, positioning one's institution to receive increased funding to better serve its constituents may be a sensible approach. A question to be asked, however, is whether such a strategy, however practical and well intentioned, robs the faith-based institution of its prophetic voice.

It is still true that whoever pays the piper calls the tune. The current reality is that many not for profits are reluctant to participate in public policy debates because of fear of reprisal in the form of reduced funding for critical programs. In fact, intermediary organizations have been formed to advocate for policy issues of concern to segments of the not-for-profit community while providing needed protections. All this suggests that the influx of public dollars to African American churches will have consequences, if not in the short run, then in the long run.

Looking Ahead

There is widespread recognition that the voices of African American churches are essential ingredients of any public policy being designed to affect black families and communities—if for no other reason than that they tend to be the primary direct social service providers for black families. As Andrew Billingsley states: "The Black Church knows the power of a holistic commitment by experience, for it was born of a vast schedule of needs that a nation committed to slavery could not, or would not address."[51] Lincoln and Mamiya similarly point out: "Black Churches gave spiritual refuge and reassurance, but they also spawned the first black banks, burial societies, insurance companies, schools, and homes for the aged as support services to the spiritual needs of their people."[52]

Nonetheless, there is also acknowledgment that times have changed, that the current public policy context requires resources and a high degree of strategic organization, and that African American churches cannot successfully engage in public advocacy without the necessary resources and structure. The successful strategies of the conservative foundations suggest seven valuable lessons for any group interested in influencing public policy: (1) understanding the importance of ideology and overarching frameworks; (2) helping build strong institutions by providing ample general operating support; (3) maintaining a national policy focus and concentrating resources; (4) recognizing the importance of media; (5) creating and cultivating public intellectuals and policy leaders; (6) supporting multiple social change strategies, including advocacy, leadership development, and constituency mobilization; and (7) preparing for the long haul.[53] These strategies are instructive for any group interested in influencing public policy, including African American churches.

In the case of African American churches, it is recognized that their role in the shaping of public policy is greatly limited by their lack of resources and the high demand placed on them by a population that is still largely poor and disenfranchised. As noted earlier, African American churches are involved in a myriad of activities to improve the spiritual, social, economic, and political status of the African American community. However, while increased resources are essential, other steps need to be attended to as well. For example, one of the lessons noted above is the importance of the link between the intellectual community and the policy formation process. Data-driven analysis is essential for influencing the current policy context, and this will require a close collaboration between scholars, African American church leaders, and professionals and clients in the social welfare field. There are some examples of this that are suggestive of the potential.

At the beginning of 2000, a partnership of more than fifty church leaders across the political spectrum launched the ten-year Campaign to Overcome

Poverty, the culmination of a half decade of organizing by Call to Renewal, an advocacy group based in Washington, D.C. Call to Renewal organized town hall meetings in sixteen cities around the country, produced a list of moral imperatives that could be used by congregants in evaluating local and national political candidates,[54] and issued (as part of a Washington meeting involving hundreds of representatives of religious organizations) the "Covenant to Overcome Poverty," which urged religious organizations to give a special priority to working on behalf of the poor.[55] In 1997, in response to the Welfare Reform Act, the Reverend James Forbes, the senior minister of the Riverside Church in New York City, launched the Emancipation from Poverty Project. According to the Reverend John Vaughn, the objectives of the project were to educate the congregation and others about the Welfare Reform Act and to deal with the myths. Project operatives also organized and advocated around issues in New York City, signed the Work Experience Program resistance pledge, and worked with other groups around health screenings. In addition, they started job-training and job-readiness programs that continue to remain active.[56]

Charitable choice has stimulated much discussion in a variety of arenas, including among African American churches, where much of the discussion focuses on whether to accept charitable choice dollars and the availability of funding to churches as well as whether and how to access these dollars. The question is whether these same churches will engage in advocacy to improve the social and economic conditions of the poor black children and families who are affected by these policies.

The conservatives who successfully crafted and passed the welfare legislation changed the debate in such a way that poverty is no longer viewed as a national problem. This is clearly antithetical to the interests of the African American community, which houses a disproportionate percentage of those in poverty. Economic issues such as wages and equity must be part of an agreed-on framework for advocacy on a variety of issues. The poor suffer more whatever the malady and, in most instances, suffer simply because they are poor. Don Browning suggests that, if religious institutions are to strengthen families, "churches and synagogues should become involved in public policy beyond the natural confines of their membership and immediate communities. . . . Religious institutions should explicitly support several economic strategies that can help families including the tax structure; child tax credit; Earned Income Tax Credit, shorter working hours for parents on welfare."[57]

The 2000 election stimulated the beginning discussions over reauthorizing PRWORA. Now is, therefore, an appropriate time for African American churches to strategize about increasing their role in the policy debate in order to promote their policy imperatives. As the debate relates to the reauthorization of TANF, African American churches must first understand what specifically is open for debate and, perhaps more important, what is not.

Welfare reform is a done deal. The federal government eliminated cash assistance and other services as entitlements and turned over large sums of money and authority to states in the form of block grants. This significant restructuring will not be revisited. Congress will, however, consider new funding levels for TANF. Specifically, funding cuts may be considered because some states have not used all their TANF funds or have used TANF funds to supplant state tax dollars. Congress will review requirements for states' maintenance of effort — including a review of the structure for bonuses and penalties, which influences the choices that states make in allocating funds from their block grants for work programs and social programs that lead to work. Congress will likely be receptive to analyses from evaluation studies and recommendations on critical issues such as the sixty-month time limit, immigrant exclusion, work requirements, education and training programs, and access to child care for working families. These are the areas in which African American churches can have immediate input, if for no other reason than that the relevant issues are open for discussion.

The next step toward effective participation is a realistic understanding of the strategies and organizational structures necessary to participate in policy discourse at the state and national levels. It could be argued that it is already too late for African American churches to form the necessary coalitions and the overarching framework required to engage in a national debate. But, even if it is not, some argue that this would not be the most effective strategy to pursue. Welfare reform was, and will continue to be, very much a state-driven issue. What state and local governments decide to fund from their block grants can be influenced through state and local legislators. Here is where African American churches have immediate access and influence.

As Dr. Sprigg noted: "I don't think a federal approach is the way to go. In order for churches to be more directly involved in affecting public policy, they have to feel connected to the faith-based and community nature of the issue. This can be more effectively achieved at the state level."[58] Barbara Blum agreed, indicating that, while a national coalition would also be an impressive presence, "religious representatives would be wise to unite and target state legislators as a short-term response." When asked why she thought that a state-targeted approach by African American churches would be effective, Blum responded: "What legislator does not listen to his or her clergy?"[59] This is more relevant in the context of charitable choice, through which the public sector is reaching out to establish formal partnerships with faith-based institutions.

While changes in the 1996 welfare reform law, TANF, may be limited and best addressed at the state and local levels, the broader and more significant issue of poverty and income security remain national issues. They are not as divisive as the narrower issue of welfare reform and are standard fare for African American churches.

Conclusion

The welfare system in the United States was dramatically transformed by the passage in 1996 of PRWORA, and, although large numbers of African Americans would be affected by the proposed changes to the welfare system, African American churches were largely absent from these policy debates. Structural impediments to citizen input within the policy process as well as a lack of black church resolve about the particulars of welfare reform and about systematic policy engagement in general help account for the marginality of African American churches to this process. Nevertheless, African American churches can still influence the direction of the welfare reform process through strategic input into the proceedings leading up to the reauthorization of various legislative components of PRWORA and through input into block grant distributions at the state and local levels. In fact, the state and local dimensions of welfare reform implementation may bring welfare reform within the reach of African American churches in a number of ways. For example, churches may likely find it easier to monitor legislative discussions and programmatic spending at the state and local levels rather than at the federal level. But, at whatever level the battles over welfare reform are fought, decisions about whether to join the battle can be made only by African American churches themselves.

Notes

1 Maulana Karenga, *Introduction to Black Studies* (Los Angeles: University of Sankore Press, 1993), 310.

2 Martin Gilens, *Why Americans Hate Welfare: Race, Media, and the Politics of Anti-Poverty Policy* (Chicago: University of Chicago Press, 1999), 3.

3 Ibid., 67.

4 Megan McLaughlin, "Toward Real Welfare Reform: Decoding Race and Myths," in *Removing Risks from Children: Shifting the Paradigm* (Silver Spring: Beckham House, 1997), 86, 98.

5 Neil Gilbert and Harry Specht, *Dimensions of Social Welfare Policy* (Englewood Cliffs: Prentice-Hall, 1974), 39–41.

6 Benjamin R. Barber, *A Place for Us: How to Make Society Civil and Democracy Strong* (New York: Farrar Straus Giroux/Hill and Wang, 1998), 4.

7 Ibid. 4–13.

8 E. J. Dionne Jr., *Community Works: The Revival of Civil Society in America* (Washington, D.C.: Brookings Institution Press, 1998), 5.

9 Harold Dean Trulear, *The African-American Church and Welfare Reform: Toward a New Prophetic Perspective* (Washington, D.C.: Center for Public Justice, 1999), ii.

10 Pub. L. No. 104-193, 110 Stat 2162 (1996).

11 John Ashcroft, "Summary of Charitable Choice Provision Expansion Act of 1999," 1999, available at www.johnashcroft.com (copy on file with author).

12 McLaughlin, "Toward Real Welfare Reform," 94–95.

13 Megan McLaughlin, "Reforming Welfare Reform" (paper presented at the tenth annual Bank Street College Infancy Institute, New York, June 25, 1997), 5–6.

14 Arloc Sherman et al., "Welfare to What? Early Findings on Family Hardship and Well-Being" (Washington, D.C.: Children's Defense Fund and National Coalition for the Homeless, December 1998).

15 Katherine Allen and Maria Kirby, *Unfinished Business: Why Cities Matter to Welfare Reform* (Washington, D.C.: Brookings Institution, Center on Urban and Metropolitan Policy, July 2000), 2.

16 Sherman et al., "Welfare to What?"

17 Tim Casey cites the following statistics on the impact of welfare reform in New York City: "Requests for emergency food grew 36% between January 1998 and January 1999; turnaways of hungry people grew 27% to 2,396 a day; 74% of providers cited

welfare and Food Stamp cutoffs and 63% welfare and Food Stamp application rejections as the main reasons that people need emergency food" ("Welfare Reform's Impact: Mounting Evidence of Hardship and Unmet Need" [paper presented at the meeting of the Welfare Reform Network at the Federation of Protestant Welfare Agencies, New York, August 1999], 3).

18   "Welfare Reform May Not Be Helping Minorities," Associated Press, 1 April 1999.

19   Allen and Kirby, *Unfinished Business*, 1–6.

20   Susan T. Gooden, "All Things Not Being Equal: Differences in Caseworker Support toward Black and White Welfare Clients," *Harvard Journal of African American Public Policy* 4 (1998): 23–33.

21   Susan T. Gooden, "The Hidden Third Party: Welfare Recipients' Experiences with Employers," *Journal of Public Management and Social Policy* 5, no. 1 (summer 1999): 69–83.

22   Susan T. Gooden, "Race and Welfare: Examining Employment Outcomes of White and Black Welfare Recipients," *Journal of Poverty* 4, no. 3 (2000): 23–44.

23   Cathlin Siobhan Baker, *Charitable Choice* (New York: Employment Project, 2000), 3–5.

24   Johnny Ray Youngblood, "Enough with the Piety," *New York Times*, 5 March 2000.

25   Reverend Dr. Calvin O. Butts III, senior pastor, Abyssinian Baptist Church, interview with author, New York, March 10, 20000.

26   C. Eric Lincoln and Lawrence Mamiya, *The Black Church in the African-American Experience* (Durham: Duke University Press, 1990), 398.

27   John Glover, a policy analyst with the Federation of Protestant Welfare Agencies, assisted with interviews and the review of legislative documents.

28   Reverend Dr. William Epps, Second Baptist Church, interview with author, Los Angeles, December 10, 1999.

29   Reverend Dr. Calvin O. Butts, interview with author.

30   Richard Roper, deacon, Bethany Baptist Church, and founder of the Roper Group, a public policy consultation group, telephone interview with author, January 12, 2000.

31   Barbara Blum, National Center for Children in Poverty, telephone interview with author, January 11, 2000.

32   Michael Laracy, Annie E. Casey Foundation, telephone interview with author, January 8, 2000.

33   Edward S. LaMonte and Michelle Coghlan, "Faith Communities and the Welfare Reform Act of 1996" (paper presented at the annual meeting of the Urban Affairs Association, Birmingham, April 1999), 5.

34   LaMonte and Coghlan, "Faith Communities," 5.

35   Dr. William Sprigg, National Urban League, telephone interview with author, January 9, 2000.

36 Sullivan Robinson, Congress of National Black Churches, telephone interview with author, February 4, 2000.

37 Andrea Martin, Congressional Black Caucus, telephone interview with author, February 5, 2000.

38 Another dynamic that may have contributed to the lack of African American participation in the debate over welfare reform was that African Americans invested a great deal of trust in President Bill Clinton and were often more inclined to give him leeway than to directly oppose him on his administration's policy agenda.

39 Anna Rhee, Children's Defense Fund, telephone interview with author, February 9, 2000.

40 Reverend Dr. Frances Manning, New Hope Baptist Church, telephone interview with author, March 1, 2000.

41 James Ferguson, Congress of National Black Churches, telephone interview with author, February 3, 2000.

42 LaMonte and Coghlan, "Faith Communities," 6.

43 Lucy A. Williams, "The Right's Attack on Aid to Families with Dependent Children," *Public Eye* 10, nos. 3/4 (1996): 3–4.

44 David Callahan, "$1 Billion for Ideas: Conservative Think Tanks in the 1990s," National Committee for Responsive Philanthropy Report (Washington, D.C.: National Committee for Responsive Philanthropy, 1999), 1, 5 (quotation).

45 Williams, "The Right's Attack," 11.

46 Ibid. See Charles Murray, *Losing Ground: American Social Policy, 1950–1980* (New York: Basic, 1984); George Gilder, *Wealth and Poverty* (San Francisco: ICS, 1993); and Charles Heatherly, ed., *Mandate for Leadership* (Washington, D.C.: Heritage Foundation, 1981).

47 Reverend John Vaughn, former minister for education and social justice, Riverside Church, and director, Peace Development Fund, Amherst, telephone interview with author, February 11, 2000.

48 Stanley W. Carlson-Thies, "'Don't Look on Us': The Negative Responses of the Churches to Welfare Reform," *Notre Dame Journal of Law, Ethics, and Public Policy* 2, no. 2 (1997): 667–89.

49 James Ferguson, telephone interview with author.

50 Megan E. McLaughlin, "Warnings to the Silent Church" (paper presented at the twentieth annual Ministers' Conference of the Federation of Protestant Welfare Agencies, New York, October 1999).

51 Andrew Billingsley, *Mighty Like a River: The Black Church and Social Reform* (New York: Oxford University Press, 1999), 111.

52 Lincoln and Mamiya, *The Black Church*, 12.

53 National Committee for Responsive Philanthropy, "Moving a Public Policy Agenda:

The Strategic Philanthropy of Conservative Foundation" (Washington, D.C.: National Committee for Responsive Philanthropy, July 1997).

54 For example, asking congregants to judge political candidates particularly by how their election would affect poor people.

55 Steve Manskar, "A Ten Year Campaign to Overcome Poverty," *Covenant Discipleship Quarterly* 15, no. 3 (July 2000): 2.

56 Reverend John Vaughn, telephone interview with author.

57 Don Browning, "The Task of Religious Institutions in Strengthening Families" (paper issued jointly by the Religion, Culture, and Family Project and the Communitarian Network, University of Chicago), available at www.uchicago.edu/divinity/family/communitarianpolicy.html (accessed March 2004; copy on file with the author).

58 Dr. William Sprigg, telephone interview with author.

59 Barbara Blum, telephone interview with author.

4

CONTESTANT, ADVOCATE, IMPLEMENTER:

SOCIAL SERVICES AND THE POLICY ROLES OF

AFRICAN AMERICAN CHURCHES

Michael Leo Owens

The potential for the African American faith sector to play an expanded role in social services has increased. The Personal Responsibility and Work Opportunity Reconciliation Act of 1996 (PRWORA) is the cause. The act changed welfare policy in the United States: welfare became a temporary grant, not an enduring entitlement.[1] It also sent a new message to the poor: "Welfare was to be a way station, not a way of life."[2] Aside from its message to the impoverished, PRWORA sent a signal to the pulpit: the government expects the faith sector to assist in reducing welfare dependence specifically and poverty generally, especially as public-funded providers of services to impoverished families. This signal came in the form of a set of new national laws. These laws, first passed by the U.S. Congress as part of PRWORA and expanded incrementally to encompass policy domains beyond welfare, constitute "charitable choice." They may radically change the relationship among private institutions, needy citizens, and the government, especially how states may relate to the faith sector in African American communities, for they position the faith sector to be the dominant sphere of action in the collective management of social problems in black America.

This essay identifies how the African American faith sector has responded to welfare reform and charitable choice. It clarifies how changes in public policy present the African American faith sector with political choices for involving itself in public policymaking as it relates to the interest, needs, and values of the poor. In doing so, it outlines the policy roles that members of the African American faith sector have assumed to serve best the needs of the poor in an era of devolved and decentralized public policy formulation and implementation.

Faith in Public Policy: The Changing Consensus

The national government transferred considerable public functions to sub-national levels of the federalist system. The general public, however, regardless of race or ethnicity, knows little about that transfer and how it changes the current policy context in which federal benefits are distributed to citizens.[3] Known as *devolution*, the process involves "a transformation internal to the state that alters the scale of activities, redefines government responsibilities for regulating civil society, transfers authority across levels and administrative units of government, redraws the map of government costs and benefits, and changes accessibility and entitlement to government services." In the case of social welfare policy, devolution involves the transfer of responsibilities for and the authority over the implementation of programs from state governments to private institutions, not public ones. That is, state governments depend on private institutions to execute public policy. The core of devolution is the contracting out of services delivery, not direct action through public organizations. State governments deliver social services through commercial organizations. Or they rely on nonprofit organizations to provide social services supported primarily by federal funding and state revenues. Either method "redefines the scope of government but does not eliminate its role altogether, because the state externalizes only selected functions to nongovernmental entities."[4]

The supply of social services by private — for-profit and nonprofit — organizations instead of services delivery by state or municipal workers shifts the provision of public services from a system based on public organizations to a system with an ever-expanding role for nongovernment organizations, especially nonprofits.[5] Since 1996, federal policymakers have attempted to transfer the provision of state services from a system based on secular nonprofits to a system with an ever-expanding role for faith-based organizations, particularly congregations. This is a major shift in domestic policy.

From the War on Poverty, begun in 1964, until welfare reform in 1996, policymakers emphasized secular solutions to public problems. Biased by

FIGURE 1 Faith in Public Policy, 1964–1996

The AFDC Regime: The Era of Social Welfare as We Knew It	Broad Federal Rules
No charitable choice	— Ban on money to congregations; required independent 501(c)(3) faith-associated nonprofits
Emphasis on secular solutions	— Ban on proselytism and evangelism as well as religious icons at service delivery sites — Nondiscrimination of beneficiaries
Assumption: secular programs work	

constitutional obstacles to church-state collaborations, and influenced by social experiments of the 1960s, the public consensus was that rational programs supported by public funding, rooted in secular humanism, and implemented by social welfare professionals worked best to reform the problems of the poor. Public policy allowed religious institutions (i.e., congregations and denominations) to assist, if they so chose, state and county public agencies in addressing public problems such as poverty, malnutrition, lack of affordable housing, and even safety in public housing.

If any religious institutions were to receive federal funding for their efforts, public policy required them to, among other things, establish separate faith-based nonprofits (see figure 1). They were to operate secular programs because the incorporation of religious doctrine with services that the public funded was unconstitutional. An undeterminable number of religious institutions chartered faith-based nonprofits. Legally distinct from and independent of religious institutions in their funding, expenditures, and governance, nonprofits such as Catholic Charities, Lutheran Social Services, and Jewish Boards of Family and Children's Services received substantial amounts of government money. At the government's request, the faith-based nonprofits removed religious symbols from service delivery sites. They abandoned, or at least downplayed, proselytism and mandatory worship in conjunction with the services that they delivered on behalf of public agencies at public expense.

During the public debate of the mid-1990s about reforming social welfare by ending the entitlement-based Aid to Families with Dependent Children (AFDC) program, policymakers railed against the expense of the welfare system. Jon Kyl (R-AZ), then member of the U.S. Senate Appropriations Committee, noted: "After trillions of dollars spent on welfare, it is obvious that Federal dollars alone will not solve the problems. . . . [A]t a minimum, the Great Society system has not worked; and, at its worst, it has actually contributed to the problem."[6] Aside from the expense, another criticism that dogged AFDC was that the government focused too much on the socioeconomic problems of the poor and not enough on the behavioral, moral, and spiritual causes of poverty and dependency. The policy story was that secular solutions alone were insufficient to reform the problems of the poor. Accordingly, some conservative activists, scholars, and policymakers contended that public policy should address other needs of the poor — spiritual renewal and faith.

The activist Marvin Olasky argued that, before there was government-given relief, there was congregation-provided assistance that served the poor well.[7] Olasky advocated for a return to the pre–New Deal practices in which the faith sector dominated the American regime of poor relief. Olasky insisted that contemporary congregations had the capability and the capacity to be major welfare service providers. He contended that increased private contributions and public money would enable the church to recover its role as the primary service provider to the needy, displacing government.

Simultaneously, public law scholars formulated a critique of American constitutional law to influence the thinking of policy elites concerning sectarian participation in public social services administration. Terming that critique *positive neutrality*, scholars made assertions along the lines of the following statement by Stephen Monsma: "Equal treatment says religious groups should have public benefits available to them on the same terms as all other groups. Being a religious group ought not put it at a disadvantage, so that it cannot use school facilities to which other groups have access, cannot rent a hall other groups are allowed to rent, cannot put up a display on public property where other groups are allowed to put up displays, or cannot receive subsidies that all other groups are receiving. Neutrality or evenhandedness of government policy is at the heart of the equal-treatment concept."[8] The notion of recognizing, accommodating, and supporting sectarian institutions at public expense appealed to some federal policymakers, especially Republicans such as then U.S. Senator John Ashcroft.

Ashcroft, who favored both a central role for the faith sector in addressing welfare dependency and a more permeable wall between church and state, accepted the positive neutrality standard. He determined that congregations should, and could, lead government agencies in reforming the conditions of the poor, particularly welfare recipients. He argued that government probably would have to accept and encourage the paid involvement of congregations, in addition to faith-based nonprofits such as Lutheran Social Services and the Salvation Army. Accordingly, Ashcroft introduced a policy alternative in a 1995 welfare reform bill that would permit public agencies to contract with all institutions of the faith sector. He described it as "a specific invitation to private charities, nongovernmental entities, even faith-based organizations to participate in the solution of [the] serious challenge to the success of this society in the next century."[9] Charitable choice was the policy alternative and invitation.

The proponents of charitable choice averred that congregations could be reliable partners with government agencies in addressing the problems of welfare recipients and other subgroups of the poor. They pointed to studies of the faith sector based on survey research that suggested that most congregations in the United States provided high rates of social services on their own, despite few volunteers and money; found that African American churches were most likely to offer services; and reported that the majority of their programs provided supportive services to adults and families, especially the working and unemployed poor.[10]

During the welfare reform debate, many clerics publicly opposed the abolition of AFDC. They cautioned that it was immoral to remove federal entitlements to public assistance and improper for the federal government to vest the faith section with greater responsibility for reducing welfare dependency and poverty. In a letter to Congress, forty-seven heads of congregations and faith-based nonprofits expressed reservations about charitable choice as a means for reforming the conditions of the poor and delivering public services to the needy. It was true, as others noted, that "actions on issues relating to soup kitchens, shelters for the homeless, care of battered women and children, counseling for families under siege, child care, international efforts to curb hunger and provide disaster relief [originally] were not initiated by government but to a large extent by people in congregations."[11] Yet the clerics voiced their reservation about the use of charitable choice and its potential effects:

> We are gravely concerned that some current proposals rely on the idea that the religious community can provide for those who will "fall through the cracks" of the safety net, cracks created by proposed reforms now in Congress. In fact, over the last decade, our social service providers have experienced a marked increase in the demand for our services, which are now operating at full capacity. . . . Since the present system severely challenges the religious community's ability to meet the needs of the country's poor, we fear that the current proposals would completely overwhelm the resources for serving the needy.[12]

Signatories included the Reverend Fred Kammer of Catholic Charities, USA, the Reverend Dr. Gordon Sommers of the National Council of Churches, Martin Kraar of the Council of Jewish Federations, and the Reverend Dr. Henry Lyons of the historically black National Baptist Convention, USA.

Aside from Reverend Lyons, institutional representatives of other national black church associations voiced their opposition to the abolition of AFDC and the devolution of social welfare to the states. In the fall of 1995, for example, Bishop John Hurst Adams of the African Methodist Episcopal (AME) Church and the Congress of National Black Churches (CNBC) opined: "Nobody objects to a reasonable and rational reform. But, the absurd, absurd, absurd agenda being promoted now deserves to be vetoed. It furthers the gap as it enriches the rich and devastates the poor, and we cannot subscribe to that."[13] A month later, Reverend Adams signed a joint statement of opposition to the abolition of AFDC. He agreed with his cosigners that "the very moral fabric of our nation would be torn" and that the end to AFDC would overturn the "60-year old promise to be protector of last resort for the poor, disabled, and abused children. . . . Unholy legislation that destroys the safety net must not be signed into law."[14] During the spring of 1996, the Reverend Michael Lemmons, then executive director of the CNBC, joined with secular national black organizations such as the National Association for the Advancement of Colored People and National Black Caucus of State Legislators to protest legislation supported by the National Governors' Association to switch from federal entitlements to state block grants for funding services to the poor.[15]

The appeals of the opponents of charitable choice were futile. Public disgust with the welfare system, advocacy by social conservatives, conceptual arguments by political theorists, support by policymakers, the presence of empirical research (albeit limited), and an election cycle pushed open a policy window that put welfare reform legislation, with its charitable choice provision, on the desk of then President Bill Clinton. Clinton signed PRWORA into law, despite his reservations that charitable choice construed the involvement of the faith sector in welfare reform too broadly.[16] Following the signing of the welfare reform law, Ashcroft remarked that government needed "to enlist our charitable institutions in the war on poverty": "America's faith-based charities and nongovernmental organizations, from the Salvation Army to Catholic Charities, have moved people successfully from [welfare] dependency and despair to the dignity of self-reliance. Allowing a 'charitable choice' will help transform the lives of those in need."[17] Charitable choice would also provide a social experiment for testing the efficacy of the faith sector to address public problems in an era of new social welfare.

Charitable Choice: The New Social Welfare Policy

Under the new regime of Temporary Assistance to Needy Families (TANF), at least until 2001, policymakers emphasized neither secular nor faith-based solutions to welfare dependency and poverty. The assumption was that effective programs, be they delivered by government agencies, secular nonprofits, faith-based nonprofits, or congregations, mattered most in affecting positively the lives of poor people and places. Therefore, if congregations wished to help states transition welfare recipients from public dependency to personal responsibility, charitable choice would allow them to do so without incorporating separate faith-based nonprofits (see figure 2). States could pay congregations directly with federal funds from the TANF program, as well as the federal Welfare to Work, Medicaid, supplemental security income, food stamp, Substance Abuse and Mental Health, and Community Services Block Grant programs, to foster work (job preparation, employment training, and vocational education), nutrition (emergency food distribution and subsi-

FIGURE 2 Faith in Public Policy, 1996–2000

The TANF Regime: The Era of New Social Welfare	Broad Federal Rules
Limited charitable choice via Section 104 of Welfare Reform Law and miscellaneous laws	— Money to congregations, without independent 501(c)(3) nonprofits be required — Money in the form of contracts and vouchers — Program limits — Welfare (TANF and welfare to work funds)
No emphasis on solution type	— Community services block grant — Substance abuse and mental health services funds — Supplemental security income, food stamps, and
Assumption: good programs work	Medicaid — Soft ban on proselytism and evangelism, with no ban on religious icons at service delivery sites — Nondiscrimination of beneficiaries, but mandated secular alternatives — Faith-based hiring discrimination

dized meals), healthy living (drug and alcohol treatment), and human care (adoptions, foster care, orphanages) among the needy, especially working-age, nondisabled heads of poor households and their children.

Charitable choice accommodates other institutions that share space with congregations in the faith sector, namely, faith-based nonprofits. They, too, may receive federal funds as contractors of social services. Consequently, congregations will probably continue to create and use faith-based non-profits to provide services. Some policymakers, both national and subnational, encourage the use of faith-based nonprofits to avoid constitutional challenges to their programs based on the Establishment Clause. Beyond preventing constitutional clashes, the use of faith-based nonprofits shields congregations from more mundane matters, protecting them from legal and financial liabilities.

Nevertheless, the emphasis of charitable choice, and much of the debate about it, is on the grant to states that allows congregations, particularly Protestant churches and other mainline houses of worship, to receive public

FIGURE 3 Elements of Charitable Choice

Six Elements of Charitable Choice Laws

---

1. States can, but are not required to, contract with congregations
2. When contracting out for services, states must consider the bids, proposals, and qualifications of congregations on an equal, nondiscriminatory basis against those of secular organizations and faith-based nonprofits
3. The use of federal funds for religious worship, instruction, or proselytism is prohibited, but congregations are permitted to retain their religious character (e.g., boards and sites)
4. Faith-based hiring discrimination is legal
5. Alternative secular providers of services to welfare recipients are required, but not guaranteed
6. There is no new public funding, nor are there guarantees that congregations will receive existing public funding, either directly or indirectly

---

money to deliver welfare-related social services. Nevertheless, public policy no longer mandates the creation and use of social enterprises by congregations and denominations. Instead, charitable choice allows states to use federal funds to contract directly with pervasively sectarian institutions to provide welfare-related services through purchase-of-service agreements with public welfare agencies.

As a policy tool, charitable choice is less a mandate for certain public action than a prescription for it (see figure 3). Charitable choice permits but does not require subnational governments to collaborate with congregations to deliver welfare and related services to the poor in their jurisdictions. States may also develop voucher systems to allow them to use federal funds to pay for health, human, and education services that welfare recipients may choose to receive from congregations. Additionally, charitable choice lifts the formal government ban on religious iconography at service delivery sites. Furthermore, the law softens the ban on proselytism and evangelism by permitting the use of worship, religious instruction, and proselytism in the delivery of services by religious organizations, as long as federal funds do not pay for it. That is, if their constitutions permit, states may choose to use their own money.

No state may decline to contract with congregations on the basis of the religious character of the organizations, for an aim of the law is to protect the governance and management process of congregations. This explains why the law explicitly upholds Title VII of the 1964 Civil Rights Act, which permits employment discrimination by the faith sector on religious grounds. States are obligated to assess and judge the abilities of congregations to deliver welfare and related services on the same basis as they would assess and judge nonsectarian institutions or preexisting faith-based nonprofits. If they select a congregation with which to contract for the delivery of public services, they are obligated by charitable choice to contract with a secular provider as well. This is to ensure that recipients of public-funded services have a choice in determining where they will receive assistance.

The Political Choices for the African American Faith Sector

Through public actions (e.g., the creation of the White House Office of Faith-Based and Community Initiatives), and in public statements, the Bush administration has attempted to shift the emphasis of faith in public policy, suggesting that states receiving public money should prefer sacred or "faith-based" solutions to others, with the explicit assumption that religious conversion and faith work best in addressing the problems of poor people and places. According to President Bush: "Much of today's poverty has more to do with troubled lives than a troubled economy. And often when a life is broken, it can only be restored by another caring, concerned human being. The answer for an abandoned child is not a job requirement—it is the loving presence of a mentor. The answer to addiction is not a demand for self-sufficiency—it is personal support on the hard road to recovery. . . . And any effective war on poverty must deploy what Dorothy Day [cofounder of the Catholic Worker Movement] called 'the weapons of spirit.' "[18] Public opinion surveys suggest that the Bush administration has a mandate for lifting up faith while in the bully pulpit and "rallying the armies of compassion" through its faith-based policy alternatives, at least in principle. National surveys report that 69 percent of adults believe that religion can better our behavior as individuals and as a society, and anywhere from 63 to 75 percent of adults favor the transfer of public money to congregations to achieve public purposes such as aiding the poor.[19] A large minority (44 percent) of adults favors public funding of congregations even if the money funds overt religious messages and pays for proselytism.[20]

Against a backdrop of presidential initiative and public support, the African American faith sector has multiple choices to make. Most of those choices are nonpolitical, at least as they relate to charitable choice. Will the African American faith sector expand its community outreach? Will congregations tithe to support new social ministries? What type of response—emergency relief or comprehensive development—to social problems will the faith sector address? These are fundamental questions for clergy, congregations, and faith-based nonprofits. They require choices as well as commitments of resources. Perhaps the most important choice is a political one: What role will the African American faith sector play in the current environment of governmental politics, the public debate of religion and public policy, and the adoption of charitable choice?

Theoretically, members of the African American faith sector can assume one of three roles—contestant, advocate, or implementer. Empirically, many in the African American faith sector have not adopted a role at all, opting to stand by and observe the policymaking process. Nevertheless, while there are those who do nothing, there are those who have assumed a policy role, preferring to be contestants, advocates, or implementers of charitable choice, instead of bystanders.

CONTESTANTS

Some members of the African American faith sector, particularly clergy, have assumed the role of policy contestant; they purposively challenge the implementation of welfare reform and/or oppose the receipt of public funds by congregations to deliver services on behalf of government, particularly Republican-led state and local governments. The extent to which African American clergy are contestants is unknown. However, data from the 1999–2000 Black Churches and Politics Survey suggests that most African American clergy favor contestation: a majority of black clergy opposes the core element of charitable choice and the general policy proposal of the Bush administration (see table 1).[21] Asked whether the current policy context that encourages congregations to seek and use public money to deliver human and health services is useful, 52 percent of African American clergy disagreed.[22]

TABLE 1 African American Clerical Opposition to Charitable Choice (%)

Question: Please state your level of agreement with the following:
It is helpful that the government is now encouraging churches to
apply for and use government funds to provide social services

Strongly agree	9
Agree	37
Disagree	19
Strongly disagree	33
Don't know/not applicable	1

Source: 1999–2000 Black Churches and Politics Survey.
Note: N = 324. Figures do not total to 100 percent owing to rounding.

Contestants from the African American faith sector have challenged welfare reform implementation in state capitols, city halls, and neighborhoods, rather than Congress and the White House. In Baltimore, Baltimoreans United for Leadership Development, an ecumenical, citywide grassroots organization of African American churches and other groups affiliated with the Industrial Areas Foundation, organized welfare recipients in 1999 and 2000 to challenge the administration of TANF in Maryland. It mobilized adult students on public assistance to rally in support of legislation to make educational opportunities count as work activities under the state's TANF program. In New York City, the Abyssinian Development Corporation (ADC) of Abyssinian Baptist Church has spent four years organizing TANF recipients around welfare reform. Funded by a grant from the Edna McConnell Clark Foundation, ADC hired professional community organizers to educate welfare recipients about their responsibilities and rights under TANF. It also published and circulated quarterly alerts notifying them of changes in the administration of benefits by the New York Human Resources Administration, especially pertaining to work requirements, opportunities for day care, and other issues relevant to families on public assistance.

Since the design of TANF programs and the effects of their implementation are local, not national, action by African American clergy at the state and local levels makes sense. Devolution obligates greater involvement and responsibility of state and local governments in the implementation of federal policy. It also permits state and local governments discretion over how they design and administer their programs. Consequently, organized opposition to welfare reform will be most successful at the subnational level. However, efforts by African American congregations to contest the implementation of TANF at the subnational level are rare. Furthermore, in those instances of activism by the African American faith sector, contestation occurs through clergy rather than congregations or faith-based nonprofits instead of congregations. Additionally, when clergy and social enterprises demonstrate against TANF implementation, activism is organized, but, in many cities, the African American faith sector is not organized and its response to policies more ad hoc.

At the national level, members of the African American faith sector, particularly its formal representatives, have not contested TANF implementation, even though many challenged the initial welfare reform law. They have, however, questioned charitable choice as legislation. Specifically, this segment of the sector has expressed qualms over various bills wending their way through Congress that would expand charitable choice. Chief among the contestants in Washington, D.C., is the CNBC, an ecumenical coalition of eight historically black denominations. Counting sixty-five thousand congregations with a combined membership of twenty million attendants, it is among the largest institutions in black America, let alone black faith sector. Despite opposition from some of its individual members, the organization has routinely played the role of contestant concerning charitable choice. Bishop Adams describes the content of a formal statement in the process of being prepared by the CNBC: "About a dozen questions are raised about the faith-based initiative and with what we know about it now, our position ranges from somewhere between alarm to caution to militant opposition."[23]

Beyond institutional responses are the responses of individuals from the faith sector contesting charitable choice. The Reverend Al Sharpton, who opposed the abolition of AFDC, has adamantly spoken against charitable choice and denounced its supporters from the African American faith sector. During a 2001 policy conference on the status of Afro-America, Sharpton contended that they were hypocrites and questioned why many of them anticipated the receipt of public funding to support their community outreach and ministries. His criticism was sharp: "One of the things that bothers me a lot of my colleagues in the clergy that just stopped accusing people of being poverty pimps are now going to become the ones that are applying for federal grants." He concluded that the African American faith sector has a "responsibility to be prophets to Pharaoh, not subsidized by Pharaoh."[24] At the same conference, the Reverend Dr. Michael Eric Dyson, the Avalon Foundation Professor in the Humanities at the University of Pennsylvania, buttressed Sharpton's remarks. Placing the charitable choice debate in the context of conservative efforts to reduce government activism and neglect the problems of the poor, Dyson argued that the policy "takes the focus off the government's responsibility towards those people itself." Furthermore, he admonished the pulpit and the public: "We must say to all of those who claim to know Jesus—like Jesus said—'Everybody that calls my name is not in my spirit.'"[25]

The prophetic voices of the contestants from the African American faith sector have been low during the debate over the expansion of charitable choice as well as the implementation of TANF. Media coverage of the debate generally has excluded the protestations of contestants, unless they come from those representing institutions from the civil liberties community such as Americans United for Separation of Church and State and the American Civil Liberties Union. A review of the opinion pages and letters to the editor of the *New York Times*, the *Washington Post*, the *Los Angeles Times*, and the *Wall Street Journal* from 1996 to 2001 shows that only three have come from members of the African American faith sector. The media have asked African American clergy who contest charitable choice and the faith-based initiative why they oppose them. However, since the end of 2000, the headlines in newspapers have downplayed the degree of opposition from members within the African American faith sector. The *Boston Globe* declared: "Black Clergy Back Bush Initiative." The *Atlanta Journal Constitution* proclaimed: "Bush's Faith-Based Initiatives: Black Clergy Could Add Surprising Support." "Black Ministers Reach Out to Bush" was the headline in the *Minneapolis Star Tribune*. And "Some Black Pastors See New Aid under Bush" ran in the *New York Times*.[26]

Additionally, the voice of concurrence from the white faith sector has muted the voice of dissent from the African American faith sector. The major national Christian institutions associated with historically white denominations have endorsed charitable choice and the Bush administration initiatives to expand it. These groups include the U.S. Catholic Conference, the Salvation Army, the United Methodist Church, the Episcopal Church, the Presbyterian Church, USA, the National Association of Evangelicals, and Habitat for Humanity International. Furthermore, Congress has excluded African American contestants from bearing witness before its legislative committees. Following the 1996 welfare reform, from 1997 to 2001, 549 testimonies were delivered before Congress related to charitable choice specifically or faith-based organizations generally.[27] Six testimonies came from members of the African American faith sector. All supported or advocated, rather than contested, charitable choice and/or the enactment of initiatives proposed by the Bush administration.

ADVOCATES

Unlike contestants, policy advocates of charitable choice from within the African American faith sector have received coverage and attention by the media and in policy circles. Among the foremost national advocates of public funding in the African American faith sector to address the problems of welfare recipients and other subgroups of the poor is the Reverend Eugene Rivers. Rivers, pastor of the Azusa Christian Community in Boston, which is affiliated with the Church of God in Christ, is also general secretary of the Pan African Charismatic Evangelical Congress. He has contended that pastors like him — black, Pentecostal, and disenchanted with traditional civil rights organizations and protest tactics — "are coming out strongly supporting Bush and the faith-based initiative."[28] On another occasion he noted: "We love our brothers in Christ, and we pray for them daily because, on this issue, they are wrong at the policy level, at the moral level, and at the theological level."[29] Another advocate, the Reverend Dr. Floyd Flake of Allen AME Church in New York City, endorses and supports charitable choice along with the efforts of the Bush administration to expand the law. Flake is one among the small set of African American clergy to testify before a congressional committee over the last five years concerning charitable choice. In 2001, he testified before the U.S. Senate Finance Committee that "charitable choice is a great idea. . . . I believe that it is possible for us, through this faith-based charitable choice initiative to address many of the problems that we have long ignored. Many of the problems that government has not been able to address [faith-based] organizations can . . . in a very compassionate, understanding way, meeting the needs of our society."[30]

Charitable choice and the proposed Bush policies represent, in the eyes of the Reverend T. D. Jakes, pastor of the Potter's House in Dallas, Texas, "an opportunity, rather than to scream at the darkness, to light a candle by getting control of our communities and creating our opportunity from this leveraged position to reach our own people and rehabilitate them through the auspices and economy that's provided from the government to the church."[31] Similarly, other advocates emphasize the potential of charitable choice to expand the capacity of the African American faith sector to deliver outreach services. They also question the actions of their peers who contest. Bishop Charles E. Blake of the West Angeles Church of God in Christ asks: "What good does protesting do now? . . . If you refuse to deal with [President Bush], the resources at his disposal will be given to others."[32] The Reverend Kirbyjohn Caldwell, pastor of Windsor Village United Methodist Church in Houston, Texas, considers African American support of charitable choice politically correct: "If . . . the money is going to be spent anyway, why deprive religious-based organizations . . . from this opportunity to participate?"[33] Bishop Harold Ray, pastor of Redemptive Life Fellowship Church in West Palm Beach, Florida, agrees. According to Ray: "Whether it is Democratic or Republican, good policies need to be embraced."[34] Believing that charitable choice is a good policy, he has committed his National Center for Faith-Based Initiative to lobbying on behalf of its adoption by the states.

The advocates from the African American faith sector are prominent in the media and policy debate because they are politically novel compared to most representatives from African American communities. Many self-identify as Democrats but support key elements of conservative social agendas associated with the Republican Party, such as school choice (e.g., vouchers and charter schools) and opposition to sex education and gay rights. Also, although they represent various denominations and theological perspectives, many, perhaps most, are Pentecostals. This is unexpected given the scholarship suggesting that black Pentecostals have historically avoided involvement in secular issues and public policy.[35] As David Daniels notes, there is a "minority for whom political activity is part of their African American Holiness and Pentecostal identity," "including those for whom political activity is a component of Christian ministry."[36] Furthermore, advocates have greater access to the White House and key Republicans in Congress than do their peers who assumed the role of contestants. Some, rooted in earlier policy and partisan campaigns, personally know President Bush. For example, Caldwell, who gave the benediction at Bush's inauguration, knew him from Texas. Flake, while falling short of a full endorsement, ostensibly threw some of his support behind the bid by then Governor Bush for the presidency. At an autumn 1999 campaign speech by Bush at the Manhattan Institute, Flake introduced the governor as his "homeboy" or compatriot in the politics to change public education through vouchers and charter schools. Others like Rivers are close to current and former political appointees (e.g., John DiIulio, the first director of the White House Office for Faith-Based and Community Initiatives).

Black public opinion supports the choice of advocacy by members of the African American faith sector. Although recent research suggests that the African American clergy generally oppose the policy idea of public funding for congregations, there is seemingly strong support for it by many of their congregants. In the main, African Americans are leery of the Bush administration and its policy proposals; 82 percent believe that it does not care about the needs and problems of blacks.[37] Nevertheless, blacks are among the most enthusiastic supporters of public funding of congregations: 81 percent of black adults, compared 68 percent of white adults, favor the idea.[38] It appears that, on the issue of charitable choice, the advocates, like President Bush, can claim a public mandate for their actions.

IMPLEMENTERS

Attention to either the advocates or the contestants from the African American faith sector gives the impression that the sector, generally, is reflective about and deeply involved in public policy. This is true for some members of it. However, the Black Churches and Politics Survey data suggest that 75 percent of African American churches are inactive concerning welfare policy. Generally, fewer than 10 percent of African American churches are "activist congregations" (i.e., deeply involved in public policy issues over the last ten years); fewer than 25 percent are directly involved with public policy issues in their communities.[39] Besides, many in the African American faith sector are opting to remain, not just outside the policy debate, but outside the arena of publicly funded social services completely. This is the case despite the assertions of some political scientists to the contrary. David Ryden, for example, has claimed: "Black churches have moved from staunch critics of welfare reform to collaborators in its administration."[40]

A majority of congregations are not involved in welfare reform as collaborators. The lack of collaboration with government agencies by African American congregations is historic. Few African American churches have received government assistance, other than tax relief granted to religious nonprofits generally. An earlier observation that a minority of urban African American churches (8 percent) participates in government programs that pay them continues to be true.[41] Whether African American churches lack the resources to develop social services programs is debatable. The data suggest that those with the resources prefer to operate independently of the government.

Nevertheless, within the African American faith sector are congregations seeking and accepting public funds and collaborating with public agencies to implement charitable choice. Although they are few, these congregations have purposively assumed the role of policy implementer. They have contracted with state and local governments to deliver services to the needy within their jurisdictions, in exchange for access to public funding. In California, the Alameda County Social Services Agency contracted with the Northern California Community Development Corporation, a social enterprise of the Glad Tidings Church of God in Christ, to operate its Institute for Success.[42] The institute, funded by the $632,318 contract, conducts job-readiness training and computer classes for welfare recipients. FAME Renaissance, a nonprofit subsidiary of the First AME Church in Los Angeles, received TANF funds to create a "welfare to wealth" program the elements of which include job training, employment placement, debt reduction, and financial-planning services.[43]

All Congregations Together, a faith-based nonprofit in San Diego whose members include Saint Stephen's Church of God in Christ, pastored by Bishop George McKinney, received a $316,000 contract in 1999 to use vans owned by churches to transport TANF recipients to their place of employment or to workfare locations.[44] Similarly, the Los Angeles County Department of Community and Senior Services contracted with a subsidiary of the Shield of Faith Church to deliver job-development and -placement services to TANF recipients using $250,000 welfare to work funds.[45] David Burr, operations manager of the initiative, explains why Shield of Faith deserved the contract: "We are reducing crime, reducing welfare rolls, reducing poverty. . . . We feel the government should pay us, because we're doing a good job."[46]

In New York City, the New York State Department of Labor and the New

York City Human Resources Administration contracted with a set of African American congregations (e.g., Memorial Baptist Church and Greater Bright Lights) and a faith-based nonprofit (i.e., Harlem Congregations for Community Improvement) to work with TANF recipients as part of a charitable choice demonstration project.[47] TANF recipients are sanctioned (i.e., lose portions of their welfare benefits) when they fail to participate in mandatory work assignments. For months, even years, despite the loss of benefits, a segment of the TANF caseload continued to avoid its work requirements. Recognizing that sanctions alone were insufficient to reform the behavior of TANF recipients and orient them toward work, the charitable choice demonstration project recruited the faith sector to apprise and counsel sanctioned TANF recipients of their responsibilities while receiving welfare. Edwin Reed of Allen AME Church, which participated in the demonstration project, summarizes well why members of the African American faith sector in New York City adopted the policy role of implementer in response to the devolution of social welfare and the adoption of charitable choice by the state and local government:

> We're willing, as a faith-based community, to work ourselves out of a job. We'd like to see people leave declining welfare rolls. We'd like to see people living healthier lives. We'd like to do less, in terms of social services, and, hopefully, get them to be whole people. So I don't mind working myself out of a job. I'm not a bureaucrat, not that that's a bad job. But, if I'm a bureaucrat and my job is a segment of the population, the last thing I want to see is that whole population disappear and I'm out of a job.[48]

As agents of the state and the city, the congregations and faith-based non-profits contacted TANF recipients to develop personalized plans for removing sanctions. The intent was to ensure that TANF recipients received their full benefits, that the city and state met their federal obligations under PRWORA, and that TANF recipients moved closer to self-sufficiency, if not out of poverty.

In Philadelphia, the Pennsylvania Office of Public Assistance awarded Cookman United Methodist Church $150,000 to move TANF recipients off the welfare rolls. Sherri Heller, commissioner of the Pennsylvania Department of Public Welfare, explains the state's action: "We learned that no matter what laws you pass, no matter what deadlines you set, what does it really take for a young single mother to get up at 6:00 in the morning and put a toddler in a snow suit, and stand at the bus, and go to an entry-level job? And the answer is they have to be inspired by something, by someone. For some people, it's a vision of a better future; for some people, it's caring about their children's future; for some people, it's faith in God."[49] The church provides women on TANF with daily classes in life skills development, literacy, mathematics, computers, and job placement. It does so on church property, but it maintains a separate account to keep church funds and state government funds distinct. According to Donna Jones, the pastor of the church, its job-placement rate is 87 percent.[50]

Accounting for the Decisions of the African American Faith Sector

Why do some members of the African American faith sector contest, even stand by, instead of advocate? Resistance to the receipt of public funding by congregations results from myriad reasons. For instance, there is a desire on the part of clergy and their congregations to maintain their independence and safeguard their missions. The acceptance of government funding by African American churches, even if under the auspices of affiliated non-profit organizations, potentially restricts public criticism of government and political elites by pastors. The Reverend C. Mackey Daniels, pastor of West Chestnut Street Baptist Church in Louisville and president of the Progressive National Baptist Convention, one of the denominational members of the Congress of National Black Churches, claims that the "[Bush] initiative can only be seen as another effort to muffle the prophetic voice of the African-American church. . . . I am convinced that charitable choice is akin to Judas accepting 30 pieces of silver to betray our Lord and Savior Jesus Christ. I say this because we cannot during these critical times in our history allow any program no matter how glamorous it seems to knock holes in the wall of the separation of church and state, especially when African Americans still remain at the bottom when it comes to receiving services and getting the opportunity to fully live the American dream."[51]

The Reverend William Augustus Jones of Bethany Baptist Church in Brooklyn, New York, clarifies clerical opposition to public support of the programs of African American churches: "I do not believe you can raise the voice of prophetic protest and at the same time eat of the King's meat. . . . I believe the church has to remain free from all encumbrances. Any financial support mutes the voice of the church, for he who pays the piper calls the tune."[52] In remaining independent of government, congregations avoid becoming secular minions of Caesar. As such, they may protest public decisions and challenge the actions of public policymakers without fear of reprisal.

Additionally, pastors may oppose charitable choice because they perceive public funding of congregations to contradict, ideologically and practically, a main tenet of black self-help—collective responsibility. "How can we say we're free and independent of white folks," observes the Reverend Timothy Preston Mitchell of Ebenezer Missionary Baptist Church in Flushing, New York, "if we go begging to government for relief. We must do for ourselves, with our own money, even if it means we don't solve all of the problems. We must maintain our dignity."[53] Furthermore, some clergy may believe that congregations that accept public money position themselves to become scapegoats for government retrenchment. Their point may be that the acceptance of public money to develop programs to address problems that they believe are the responsibility of government may cause the churches to lose credibility and incur liabilities if their programs fail to meet the expectations of policymakers and the public.

Perhaps members of the African American faith sector contest charitable choice because they are wary of becoming partners in an initiative that may result in dramatic reductions of government responsibility and funding. In the same vein, many clergy are aware that charitable choice does not necessarily mean that congregations will receive public funding. According to the Reverend Timothy McDonald, pastor of First Iconium Church in Atlanta: "It's a hoax, and it's a lie because there ain't no new money."[54] McDonald is correct about the absence of new money. Charitable choice encourages congregations to consider practicing or expanding faith-based community involvement, whether for money or voluntarily. It does not guarantee public funding of congregations, either directly or indirectly. Charitable choice does not provide new money for addressing social problems, whether by sacred or secular nonprofits. It invites more groups to seek public resources without expanding the pool of resources available for consumption.

Clergy may assume the role of contestant because they do not understand the public contracting process or have received poor advice concerning their pursuit and use of government funds to support the social ministries of their congregations. As well, pastors may not have the interest or resources for their congregations to seek public funds for social services delivery on their own. This may explain why few African American congregations receive public money for their social service programs. Then again, perhaps clerics oppose the public funding of faith-based social services on the basis of past bad experiences with government agencies. Perhaps pastors fear an influx of the disadvantaged through their doors. Scholars confirm this concern generally among clerics: "Many FBOS [faith-based organizations] and other charitable organizations are feeling as though the 'burden' of providing for the nation's poor is falling upon them. We keep hearing about the dramatic decline of the welfare rolls, so these groups are concerned that these thousands of people are simply going to move their dependency from the welfare office to their offices, and soup kitchens, and pantries, and homeless shelters."[55]

Why advocate, even implement, rather than contest? Like the explanations of opposition to charitable choice, the rationales for support of charitable choice by segments of the African American sector vary. Some advocates and implementers disagree with the notion that the receipt of public funding mutes the freedom of pastors to disagree with or condemn the actions of government officials publicly. The Reverend Wyatt Tee Walker of Canaan Baptist Church of Christ in Harlem is one of them. He professes that the acceptance of public funding does not restrict his advocacy. He counters:

> I've got all these [government-]funded dollars [and programs] around here — millions of dollars — and it has not kept me from saying anything I had to say. I have not had [my voice] squelched. So, what [they say] does not make any sense. There are a lot of ministers who make the claim that they need to [be] independent of government. They must protect their prophetic voice. It is an excuse. . . . It takes work to go after the [money for] these programs and to monitor them to see that the money is right. It has to do with how much work you want to do.[56]

Furthermore, other advocates and implementers contend that their practice of receiving public money does not conflict with black initiative or denote public dependency. Rather, the acceptance and use of public funding improve the self-help tradition of African American churches and gird the commitment of black people to initiative and enterprise. They may also assist African American churches in making black people more self-reliant. The

Reverend Calvin Butts of the Abyssinian Baptist Church in Harlem makes the "assisted self-reliance" argument best: "When we talk about self-help, what we are talking about is something we have been doing all along, and our pressure of government — on government — is another indication of our desire to help ourselves. . . . So you cannot say black churches, because they accept resources from folk other than black folk, are not involved in self-help. We, as black-led organizations, mix those resources with our own resources and try to better the condition of black people and help black people to better themselves, their families, and their communities."[57]

Pastors may acknowledge the potential for churches that receive public money to be in a position to assume the blame if government cuts the direct provision of social services by public workers and agencies, but they are still willing to take the risk. While they cannot control reductions in government budgets, they can use what money is available to provide their communities with services they may need. After all, as the advocates contend, the need in their communities is so great that not to seek and accept public funding would be ungodly. The Reverend Larry Fryer, director of the New Hope Community Center, a faith-based nonprofit in Augusta, Georgia, places his support for public funding, and possible regulation, in the context of poverty in his community: "These children are hungry. Now, I'm a minister, but if I have to remove the Bible, remove the cross from the wall, remove the Ten Commandments to get that government money, I'll do it. If God is in me, that's good enough."[58]

There is also a belief among clergy and their congregants that faith-based programs are better programs than any designed by government or secular nonprofits. Bishop Ray of the National Center for Faith-Based Initiative, for example, contends: "From coast to coast, and sea to shining sea, faith-based entities have overwhelmingly demonstrated their unequaled capacity to deliver community-based services . . . more efficiently . . . more economically . . . more inspirationally . . . and more comprehensively . . . because it is unequivocally the most practical and proximate relational link to grass-roots initiative."[59]

Additionally, some advocates may support charitable choice as a wedge issue for splitting the traditional black political leadership from their grass-roots supporters for the purpose of assuming mantles of leadership. This is the concern of some, such as the Reverend Julius Hope of New Grace Baptist

Church in Detroit and national religious affairs director of the National Association for the Advancement of Colored People. Hope observes that charitable choice in African American communities "could be like a Trojan horse, divide and conquer": "That's where we are now. You've got some clergy for it, some clergy against it."[60] Others have drawn the same conclusion, but go further, suggesting that charitable choice represents, along with other measures proposed by the Bush administration, an attempt to diminish the stature of the traditional black clerical leadership and support an alternative leadership, one dependent on federal public funding and supportive of Republican social, as well as fiscal, policies. In a letter to the *Washington Post*, Bishop Adams of the CNBC remarked that the organization was "disturbed because the leadership of the historic black churches was not invited, yet the meeting, which took place Wednesday, purported to represent the leaders of black churches. The persons listed by the *Post* as invited to the meeting do not represent our leadership."[61]

Finally, African American pastors may choose to advocate or implement charitable choice because they perceive themselves as quasi-political representatives of African American communities. Familiar with acting on behalf of black interests during election cycles, and assuming formal black government representatives to be of little effect concerning the allocation of public resources, some in the African American faith sector see charitable choice as a means to influence the use of taxpayer dollars on behalf, and to the advantage, of African American communities. For example, the Reverend Walker of Canaan Baptist remarks: "The people I preach to, they are citizens of the state, and I contend that, irrespective of their religious commitment, they have a right of access to the tax dollars that they provide. We don't get our fair share [as citizens or religious institutions]. Look at Catholic Charities and the tax dollars that go to them as compared to the numbers of blacks and Latinos in this community. The Catholic Charities probably gets fifty times the tax dollars that all of the black [church] enterprises like mine and the others might receive."[62] Clergy like Walker understand charitable choice in three ways. It is a means for equalizing, or at least improving, the chances of the African American faith sector to compete against nonblacks, even their peers in faith-associated institutions. It may allow them to influence what they consider political decisions concerning the distribution of public resources. And it might permit them to win a greater share of public funds for African American communities in need.

Conclusion

The devolution of public responsibility and authority from state governments to nonprofits is increasing.[63] As it does, the environment of governance changes. New interests are institutionalized in the government politics of who gets what, when, how, and where in the social welfare policy domain. Specifically, devolution increases the number of groups directly involved in public decisions and actions, policy formulation and implementation.[64] Consequently, according to Eddie N. Williams of the Joint Center for Political and Economic Studies: "African Americans must pursue their hopes and aspirations in the complex arena of public policy. . . . We must not rely on political and civil rights leadership, although they are vital. Today, as in other periods in our history, we must turn to the black church for the kind of overarching leadership that only it can provide as a rallying ground for activism."[65] Devolution via charitable choice may offer a supplemental means for black citizens, acting through the faith sector, to incorporate their interests, values, and needs into the public decisionmaking processes of governance. However, this will prove true only if members of the African American faith sector choose to participate politically.

Charitable choice is a tool of devolution that is influencing the involvement of the African American faith sector in policymaking. It requires the constituents of that sector to choose among a set of policy roles — contestant, advocate, or implementer. There is little, if any, disagreement that the majority of congregations, and perhaps most faith-based nonprofits, in African American communities have stood by, rather than assume one of the three roles. Nevertheless, a segment of the African American faith sector has chosen to transmit information and educate the public to mobilize it in opposition to devolution. Another segment has decided to enforce the decisions of policymakers and advocate for funding of the African American faith sector to deliver services. The remaining segment has selected to provide services in response to government-assessed public need, charging government a fee or even offering it free. Whether more members of the African American faith sector will adopt public policy roles, or assume the role of bystander, as devolution continues and states adopt charitable choice as public policy cannot be determined.

Notes

1 The seven general changes were as follows: (1) The individual entitlement to benefits provided by the Aid to Families with Dependent Children (AFDC) program, which provided targeted impoverished families with federal cash assistance for an unlimited duration, was abolished. (2) Impoverished families have a five-year lifetime limit on the receipt of federal cash assistance. (3) A new federal block grant — Temporary Assistance to Needy Families (TANF) — funds states to help families leave welfare. (4) States have increased discretion to spend federal welfare funds. (5) States must maintain a fixed percentage of their former spending effort to qualify for full block grant funding. (6) Increased proportions of welfare recipients must be in work-related activities. (7) States and welfare recipients face financial sanctions if recipients fail to meet work requirements. See Richard P. Nathan and Thomas Gais, *Implementing the Personal Responsibility Act of 1996: A First Look* (Albany: State University of New York, Nelson A. Rockefeller Institute of Government, 1998).

2 Isabel Sawhill, "From Welfare to Work: Making Welfare a Way Station, Not a Way of Life," *Brookings Review* 19 (summer 2001): 4.

3 David A. Bositis, *What Devolution Means to the American Public* (Washington, D.C.: Joint Center for Political and Economic Studies, 1997), 17.

4 Janet E. Kodras, "Restructuring the State: Devolution, Privatization, and the Geographic Distribution of Power and Capacity in Governance," in *State Devolution in America: Implications for a Diverse Society*, ed. Lynn A. Staeheli, Janet E. Kodras, and Colin Flint (Thousand Oaks: Sage, 1997), 81, 82.

5 Steven Rathgeb Smith and Michael Lipsky, *Nonprofits for Hire: The Welfare State in the Age of Contracting* (Cambridge, Mass.: Harvard University Press, 1993), 116.

6 Jon Kyl, "Welfare Reform: Common Sense Solutions to the Welfare Crisis," *Congressional Record*, 104th Cong., 1st sess., 1995, 141, pt. 16:22716.

7 Marvin Olasky, *The Tragedy of American Compassion* (Falls Church: Regnery, 1995).

8 Stephen V. Monsma, *When Sacred and Secular Mix: Religious Nonprofit Organizations and Public Money* (Lanham: Rowman and Littlefield, 1996), 177–78.

9 John Ashcroft, "The Welfare System," *Congressional Record*, 104th Cong., 1st sess., 1995, 141, pt. 18:25562.

10 Virginia Hodgkinson and Murray Weitzman, *From Belief to Commitment: The Activities and Finances of Religious Congregations in the United States: Findings from a National Survey* (Washington, D.C.: Independent Sector, 1993); C. Eric Lincoln

and Lawrence H. Mamiya, *The Black Church in the African American Experience* (Durham: Duke University Press, 1990), 151; Mark Chaves and Lynn Higgins, "Comparing the Community Involvement of Black and White Congregations," *Journal for the Scientific Study of Religion* 31 (1992): 425–40; and Stephen Thomas, Sandra Crouse Quinn, Andrew Billingsley, and Cleopatra Caldwell, "The Characteristics of Northern Black Churches with Community Outreach Programs," *American Journal of Public Health* 84 (1994): 576.

11 Virginia Hodgkinson, "The Future of Individual Giving and Volunteering: The Inseparable Link between Religious Community and Individual Generosity," in *Faith and Philanthropy in America: Exploring the Role of Religion in America's Voluntary Sector*, ed. Robert Wuthnow and Virginia Hodgkinson (San Francisco: Jossey-Bass, 1990), 285.

12 "Religious Organizations and Social Services Agencies Call on Congress to Remember the Poor in Making Decisions on Welfare Reform," *Congressional Record*, 104th Cong., 1st sess., 1995, 141, pt. 16:23203.

13 "Black Leaders Pressure Clinton on Social Programs," *Los Angeles Times*, October 21, 1995, A27.

14 Peter Steinfels, "Christian and Jewish Groups Call for a Veto of Welfare Bill," *New York Times*, November 10, 1995, A27.

15 Robert Pear, "Governors' Plan on Welfare Attacked," *New York Times*, February 16, 1996, A12.

16 Julie A. Segal, "A 'Holy Mistaken Zeal': The Legislative History and Future of Charitable Choice," in *Welfare Reform and Faith-Based Organizations*, ed. Derek Davis and Barry Hankins (Waco: Baylor University, J. M. Dawson Institute of Church-State Studies, 1999), 23.

17 John Ashcroft, "The Charitable Choice Expansion Act of 1998," *Congressional Record*, 105th Cong., 2d sess., 1998, 144, pt. 6:8554.

18 Remarks made by President George W. Bush during the commencement address at Notre Dame University, Notre Dame, Ind., May 21, 2001.

19 Pew Research Center for the People and the Press, *Faith-Based Funding Backed, but Church-State Doubts Abound* (Washington, D.C.: Pew Research Center for the People and the Press, 2001); and Public Agenda, *For Goodness' Sake: Why So Many Want Religion to Play a Greater Role in American Life* (New York: Public Agenda, 2001).

20 Pew Research Center, *Faith-Based Funding Backed*.

21 R. Drew Smith, "Black Churches within a Changing Civic Culture in America," in *New Day Begun: African American Churches and Civic Culture in Post–Civil Rights America*, ed. R. Drew Smith (Durham: Duke University Press, 2003).

22 This contradicts the National Congregations Study's finding that black clergy overwhelmingly favor the principle of charitable choice. See Mark Chaves, "Reli-

gious Congregations and Welfare Reform: Who Will Take Advantage of Charitable Choice," *American Sociological Review* 64 (1999): 836–46.

23 John Hurst Adams, "Forgotten Black Pastors," *Washington Post*, December 22, 2000, A32.

24 Remarks made by Al Sharpton during the conference "State of the Black Union: It's about Us — Black Think Tank II," Washington, D.C., February 3, 2001 (hereafter "State of the Black Union").

25 Remarks made by Michael Eric Dyson during the conference "State of the Black Union."

26 See Mary Leonard, "Black Clergy Back Bush Initiative," *Boston Globe*, March 20, 2001, A1; Ken Herman, "Bush's Faith-Based Initiatives: Black Clergy Could Add Surprising Support," *Atlanta Journal Constitution*, March 11, 2001, C7; Adelle Banks, "Black Ministers Reach Out to Bush," *Minneapolis Star Tribune*, January 27, 2001, B6; and John Leland, "Some Black Pastors See New Aid under Bush," *New York Times*, February 2, 2001, A12.

27 Information obtained from Lexis-Nexis Congressional Universe, *CIS Index*.

28 Laurie Goodstein, "A Clerical, and Racial, Gap over Federal Help," *New York Times*, March 24, 2001, A1.

29 National Public Radio, "All Things Considered: Bush's Controversial Initiative to Fund Faith-Based Social Programs," March 19, 2001.

30 Testimony of Floyd H. Flake, Allen African Methodist Episcopal Church, before the United States Senate Finance Committee concerning the Bush Tax Plan, in *Encouraging Charitable Giving: Hearing before the Committee on Finance*, Hearing no. 26, 107th Cong., 1st sess. (Washington, D.C.: U.S. Government Printing Office, March 14, 2001), 6–7.

31 Remarks made by T. D. Jakes during the conference "State of the Black Union."

32 Leland, "Some Black Pastors See New Aid," A12.

33 Remarks made by Kirbyjohn Caldwell during the conference "State of the Black Union."

34 Leland, "Some Black Pastors See New Aid," A12.

35 Hans A. Baer and Merrill Singer, *African-American Religion in the Twentieth Century: Varieties of Protest and Accommodation* (Knoxville: University of Tennessee Press, 1992).

36 David D. Daniels, "The Political Witness of African American Holiness and Pentecostal Churches in the Post–Civil Rights Era" (paper presented at the symposium "Social Witness, 'Prophetic' Discernment, and Post–Civil Rights Era Churches," Atlanta, March 2, 2001), 2.

37 Richard L. Berke and Janet Elder, "Bush Loses Favor, Poll Says, Despite Tax Cut and Trip," *New York Times*, June 21, 2001, A1.

38 Pew Research Center, *Faith-Based Funding Backed.*

39 Smith, "Black Churches within a Changing Civic Culture."

40 David Ryden, "Black Churches' Involvement in 'Charitable Choice' Programs: The Promise and Peril" (paper presented at the annual meeting of the American Political Science Association, Washington, D.C., August 31, 2000), 4.

41 Lincoln and Mamiya, *The Black Church*, 155; and Smith, "Black Churches within a Changing Civic Culture."

42 Amy Sherman, *The Growing Impact of Charitable Choice* (Washington, D.C.: Center for Public Justice, 2000), 26.

43 John Orr, *County Strategic Models: Los Angeles County—the Collaboration Council* (Los Angeles: University of Southern California, Center for Religion and Civic Culture, n.d.).

44 Sherman, "The Growing Impact of Charitable Choice," 25.

45 Orr, *County Strategic Models*.

46 Teresa Watanabe, "Mapping New Turf between Church, State," *Los Angeles Times*, February 4, 2001, A1.

47 JoAnn Rock and Richard Roper, *An Evaluation of the Start-Up Phase of the New York City Charitable Choice Demonstration* (Albany: State University of New York, Nelson A. Rockefeller Institute of Government, 2001).

48 Remarks made by Edwin Reed, Allen African Methodist Episcopal Church, during the symposium "Reforming Welfare through Charitable Choice," New York, May 17, 2000.

49 NewsHour with Jim Lehrer, "Faith-Based Welfare," November 11, 1999.

50 Testimony of Donna Jones, Cookman United Methodist Church, before the United States House of Representatives Government Reform Committee, 107th Cong., 1st sess., April 26, 2001.

51 Progress National Baptist Convention, "President of the Progressive National Baptist Convention, Inc. Compares Charitable Choice Initiative to 'Thirty Pieces of Silver,'" press release, February 14, 2001.

52 William August Jones, interview with author, Bedford-Stuyvesant, N.Y., April 22, 1999.

53 Timothy Preston Mitchell, interview with author, Flushing, N.Y., June 15, 1999.

54 Charles Yoo, "President's Religious Charity Plan Is Criticized; Panel of Clerics in Atlanta Finds Fault with Bush Initiative to Distribute Federal Money," *Atlanta Journal and Constitution*, April 18, 2001, D5.

55 Diana Etindi, *Charitable Choice and Its Implications for Faith-Based Organizations* (Indianapolis: Hudson Institute, Welfare Policy Center, 1999), 7.

56 Wyatt Tee Walker, interview with author, Harlem, N.Y., October 18, 1999.

57 Calvin O. Butts, interview with author, Harlem, N.Y., May 19, 1999.

58 Goodstein, "Clerical, and Racial, Gap," A11.

59 Bishop Calvin Ray, National Center for Faith-Based Initiative, press release, 30 Janu-

ary 2001, available at http://www.ncfbi.org/CapHillPressCnfText.htm (copy on file with the author).

60 Cited in Adelle Banks, "Bush's Faith-Based Initiative Divides Black Community," *Religion News Service*, May 2, 2001.

61 John Hurst Adams, "Forgotten Black Ministers," *Washington Post*, December 22, 2000, A32.

62 Wyatt Tee Walker, interview with author.

63 Richard P. Nathan, "The Nonprofitization Movement as a Form of Devolution," in *Capacity for Change? The Nonprofit World in the Age of Devolution*, ed. Dwight F. Burlingame, William A. Diaz, Warren Ilchman, et al. (Bloomington: Indiana University, Center on Philanthropy, 1996); and Todd Swanstrom, "The Nonprofitization of United States Housing Policy: Dilemmas of Community Development," *Community Development Journal* 34 (1999): 28–37.

64 Smith and Lipsky, *Nonprofits for Hire*.

65 Eddie N. Williams, "The Black Church, Building Communities," *FOCUS*, December 1998, 2.

5

SERVICE PROVIDER OR POLICYMAKER?

BLACK CHURCHES AND THE HEALTH

OF AFRICAN AMERICANS

Cathy J. Cohen

In many ways, health serves as an important marker for both the progress and the limits of a country's development. Over the years, as technology has come to "modernize" our lives, we have witnessed corresponding changes in important health indicators, such as consistent increases in life expectancy and similar decreases in infant mortality. Along the same lines, many have watched with awe as diseases previously thought untamable have been cured and eliminated from existence. And, even more recently, the announcement of the findings of the human genome project seems appropriately to symbolize the opening and unlimited possibilities of the twenty-first century. However, just as medical advances have been held up as examples of our progress, so too have the development of new diseases, the inability of scientists to find cures for continuing conditions, and the persistence and, in some cases, expansion of health disparities between groups been used to highlight the deficits in our country.

For example, many people point to escalating cancer rates as an indication that the price paid for our technological advances may be the health of, in particular, poor communities where the water or air has been polluted. Similarly, the emergence of HIV and AIDS has been explained by some as the unexpected consequence of medical and warfare experimentation. Most discouraging of all may be the continued disparities in health that exist between ethnic and/or racial communities in this country because they suggest that, even when progress is made, it is not made accessible to every person that is in need. Thus, while the health of the country serves as a marker of our progress, there may be no more explicit indicator of the country's persistent discrimination and racism than the lagging health status of African Americans.

Historically, and currently, African Americans exhibit health outcomes that diverge from the national average, and from the outcomes of white Americans in particular, in life-threatening ways. For example, black infants continue to die at twice the rate of white infants.[1] African Americans are disproportionately represented among those with AIDS nationally and in most major cities.[2] And, in certain poor areas like Harlem, black men suffer from mortality rates equal to those in developing countries.[3] In response to such disparities, there have been continued efforts from within African American communities to win some improvement. Whether the issue be the disproportionate impact of AIDS, hypertension, diabetes, or drug abuse in black communities, African Americans have initiated education and treatment programs as well as political campaigns to address the needs of those suffering.

Fundamental to such efforts has been the work of African American churches. Historically, it was African American churches that promoted public health practices to a newly emancipated black population. It was women's groups in African American churches that set up free clinics and launched public health campaigns. Furthermore, it was African American churches that served as an integral institutional partner with Booker T. Washington and the Public Health Service in their effort to implement the National Negro Health Week (NNHW).[4] In the light of this history and the documented activism of African American churches during the civil rights movement, many scholars have proclaimed the African American church the most politically active and important institution in black communities.[5] However, often missing from such analyses is, not only empirical evidence of the significance of African American churches since the 1960s, but also concern with domain-specific or issue-area variance in terms of commitment on the part of the church.

It is possible that, while African American churches were quite active during the 1960s, their political contribution has waned in recent years. Furthermore, the form of their activism may have changed over the years. For example, early church pioneers in the area of public health were concerned both with providing services and educational material to community members and with being involved in efforts to influence federal health policy. More recently, however, activity on the part of the church seems more restricted, focusing primarily on the provision of services for which there is funding. Additionally, while African American clergy and their congregations may be very active around certain issues such as poverty, they may be much less active around more controversial issues, those, for example, where questions of sexuality (teen pregnancy or AIDS) frame the discussion. No doubt part of the hesitation of African American churches to involve themselves in such issue areas stems from the stigma defining these topics as well as the perception that behaviors associated with these issues stand in contradiction to Christian practice and biblical teaching.

In this essay, I address the issue of health and black church activity in this area, exploring three examples of the church's work. As noted above, part of my analysis will focus on possible changes over time in the way in which African American churches respond to the health status of black Americans. Thus, my examples will highlight efforts on the part of the church to intervene in struggles around health issues confronting African American communities at different points in the history of African Americans. I am especially interested in the question of how African American churches fared as policy entrepreneurs. Specifically, while there are numerous examples of churches stepping forward to provide needed health services in African American communities, there is less evidence of churches or their national offices being active participants in the construction of health policy that would affect African American communities. Thus, unlike the work of Booker T. Washington and local African American churches in the early twentieth century that sought involvement in the policymaking process, today's African American churches and their denominational leaders seem content to implement policies designed by others.

The first section briefly sketches out the activities of African American churches in the area of health during slavery and Reconstruction. Although little has been written about the specific work of African American churches during this period, I attempt to outline the general health status of both enslaved and free blacks as well as the role of African American churches in providing supplementary services to a population in need. In part, I begin here because, during this period, when the needs of the black population were so great, we see the role of the church as service provider clearly established. This section is followed by a discussion of the participation of African

American churches in the national Negro health movement. A part of this discussion includes a gendered analysis that emphasizes the significant contributions made by African American women in this area, including the mobilization of African American women's clubs and church groups in response to black public health concerns.[6] This section also begins to illuminate the possibilities for African American churches as policymakers.

Once the historical role of African American churches in public health issues has been established, I turn my attention to more recent activity on the part of African American churches in the area of health and public health. I am interested in whether health or public health issues in this instance continue to receive attention from African American churches. Furthermore, if these issues are on the agenda of African American churches, what is their status, and are such issues perceived as a priority for African American clergy and their congregations? To more fully discuss this question, I turn to an exploration of the church's response to one health issue — AIDS. I have chosen AIDS as the case study for this section because I believe that the issues of HIV and AIDS, possibly more than any other, illustrate many of the challenges facing the African American church at the beginning of the twenty-first century. Specifically, HIV and AIDS are issues that are defined by stigma, tend to be more prevalent among the marginal segments of the black population, and for many stand in opposition to an interpretation of Christianity in which heterosexuality and sex only after marriage are two fundamental norms. By examining the church's response to HIV and AIDS, we can explore whether and how African American clergy and congregations navigate an apparently complex and contradictory calling — responding to the needs of their community while remaining true to Christian doctrine. AIDS is also a significant part of the national political agenda and, thus, provides us with an opportunity to test the ability and willingness of African American churches to influence national public policy.

Slavery Reconstruction and Health Care: African American Churches as Service Providers

Available data detailing pre-twentieth-century attempts to respond to black health needs in the United States are, as might be expected, sparse. In fact,

Susan L. Smith notes: "Historians date the start of organized public health work in the South to the 1870s, although there were some activities earlier in the nineteenth century."[7] Knowing this, we should not be surprised to find that information about the activity of African American churches in the area of health is even more limited. We do know, however, that, when blacks did receive health care, it came in the form of segregated services and facilities and, often, from those who would suggest that black sickness was evidence of the inferiority of the race. During slavery, health care for enslaved black Americans was made available largely because slaveholders sought to protect the labor and profit generated by healthy Africans and African Americans.

Most often, health care for the enslaved African and African American population was delivered by other enslaved black people. Using remedies passed down from their African heritage, enslaved blacks developed an elaborate system of care. Black women working as midwives and other blacks continuing in their roles as traditional African healers, priests, and root doctors came to constitute a black slave health system that was responsible for treating the sicknesses of most of the enslaved black population.[8] Fearing the ineffective and harsh treatment delivered by whites, most blacks not surprisingly preferred to receive treatment from other blacks and would, if necessary, hide their illness from those whites in positions of authority.

White slaveholders also participated in this slave health system. For example, some forms of treatment might be given by the slaveholder, by someone in his or her family, or by a designated person such as an overseer.[9] On larger plantations, one might even find health care dispensed through a plantation hospital. This system of "home" health care was the general rule in part because owners sought to hold down costs as well as because of a general cynicism that existed regarding the abilities of physicians. And, while with medical progress we have come to associate treatment with care, for enslaved blacks who received care (often from inexperienced whites) treatment could mean death if they were given the wrong medicine or no medicine at all. In fact, armed with the belief that enslaved blacks would do anything to get out of work, slaveowners sometimes ignored and left untreated threatening health conditions among blacks.[10]

As noted above, the use of physicians for the care of enslaved blacks was rare. If the condition was perceived as serious, then a white physician might be summoned. Not surprisingly, numerous physicians used their few personal interactions with blacks to develop and maintain theories of the genetic inferiority of the black race. Notions about the diseased nature of black people were often central to such ideas and were mounted in defense of slavery.[11] Such theories were cited, for example, as reasons for the differential treatment of blacks. It was the belief that blacks were less susceptible as a race to some of the same diseases killing whites, such as yellow fever and malaria, that was touted as justification for the nearly complete disregard of black communities during such epidemics.[12]

Unfortunately, it seems that, while some black individuals were allowed to provide care to the enslaved population, communal organizations such as African American churches, mistrusted as they were by whites, were prohibited from intervening in the health care of this group. Free blacks, however, were a different case. Free blacks during the antebellum period resorted to many of the same sources for treatment as did enslaved Africans and African Americans. Home treatment, self-treatment, and traditional folk remedies were the first line of defense, followed by consultation with local black healers in the area, leaving a visit to a physician as the last resort. Finally, in extreme cases, free blacks received medical care from white institutions and white doctors. Again, the availability of low-cost or charitable medical services was ensured, in large part, by the threat that illness in the black population, especially epidemic contagion, posed to the health and lifestyle of whites. Without free blacks to perform many of the menial tasks required for comfortable daily living among the middle-class white population, such responsibilities might have fallen to poor whites attempting to hold onto psychological distinctions between themselves and blacks.

The most prevalent black self-prevention and self-treatment strategies were aided by the informal and formal societies, religious groupings, and churches that free blacks established. For instance, the scholar Todd Savitt notes: "Black churches such as the First African Baptist Church of Richmond, one of the largest in the Old Dominion, supported community aid groups from weekly collections and large individual gifts. They provided nursing care and general assistance to diseased and aged blacks." However, beyond the material resources that churches could provide, prayer and support were among the most important offerings of African American churches during such times. Savitt describes extensive prayer meetings, presumably called by African American churches as well as individual blacks, in which the participants asked God for the ability to fend off diseases striking those around them.[13]

With the end of slavery came the end of any consistent concern on the part of the white planter class with the general health of the black population in the South. Not to dismiss those individual doctors and planters who continued to provide free medical care to the black population, the overall record is one of massive and coordinated neglect of this group, leaving blacks to once again care for themselves. The one major exception was the establishment of the Freedman's Bureau. In 1865, Congress established the Bureau of Refugees, Freedmen, and Abandoned Land. This agency was given responsibility for managing, and, on occasion, integrating into the Southern economy, the population of freed blacks in the South. And, while labor issues dominated the agenda of the Freedman's Bureau, the agency did attempt to provide and coordinate medical care to newly emancipated blacks. The medical division of the bureau used a number of institutions and programs, such as urban and rural hospitals, dispensaries, poor farms, infirmaries, and home-visitation programs, to care for this population. However, such work was severely impaired by the lack of staff and resources devoted to it. Despite such obstacles, the data suggest that the work of the Medical Division of the Freedman's Bureau had a significant impact on the health of Southern blacks, reducing their exposure and death from both endemic and epidemic diseases encountered in record numbers during and after the Civil War.

Although the Medical Division of the Freedman's Bureau proved to be an important institution in securing adequate health care for parts of the black population in the South, its efforts were only temporary, and, by 1869, most of its work had been eliminated. Once the bureau was no longer one of the primary providers of health care for blacks, the question arose as to who would fill that role. Some scholars have suggested that federal authorities were able to convince many local Southern communities to fill the vacuum of health provision.[14] Others argue that local acceptance of such responsibility was much more sporadic and often spurred less by government persuasion than by the threat of epidemic contagion.[15] The data seem to suggest that, while Southern localities played a part in the health care of blacks, other community-based institutions, such as African American churches, stepped up their efforts to fill this vacuum. Jude Thomas May writes explicitly about the work of African American churches during this period in Louisiana:

> Out of sheer necessity various kinds of medical care were generated from within the urban black community. The most significant of these was the health activities of religious and fraternal organizations. They were largely within the framework of conventional medical practice and their evolution provides an accurate reflection of the attempt to develop cohesion and sense of community among the black urban population. . . .
>
> A major part of the health and relief work in the urban areas was connected in some way with the black churches. As the most cohesive social organization within the community, the Negro church provided the best opportunity for mobilizing and coordinating self-help projects. In many instances health and relief programs which had grown up spontaneously were ultimately adopted or sponsored by a church.[16]

Thus, in the absence of significant federal and local initiatives to care for blacks, it would be indigenous institutions, including African American churches, fraternal organizations, and mutual aid societies that would attempt to provide such services. This should not be seen as a surprise since we know that one of the consequences of formal segregation is the development of autonomous black institutions as well as a black professional class intent on serving the needs of black people.[17] Institutions such as mutual aid and beneficial societies, institutions such as the National Medical Association (NMA), founded in 1895, and training centers like the Meharry Medical College all significantly contributed to building yet another alternative health care system for African Americans. Another central player in the provision of services and the development of this health care system was the black church.

As has been noted previously by scholars, churches were among the first and, possibly, the most important institutions to be fully controlled by African Americans.[18] The church has often functioned as one of the few safe havens for oppressed black communities. In black churches, African Americans planned and pursued a social justice agenda meant to provide for the survival and betterment of black life. In addressing issues ranging from education to employment, African American churches were central to the social progress and, in this case, the health of the black population. And, while the absolute numbers of those receiving medical care from such institutions were limited, their efforts to provide basic medical care to the black population during slavery and after emancipation were demonstrative of the black churches' important role as service providers. It was the churches' early, localized activity in the area of health that helped set the stage for their involvement in a national movement—NNHW. This time, however, the challenge would be to address black health urgencies, not only through local service provision, but also through federal policy.

Engaged, but Not with Policy: African American Churches and the National Negro Health Movement

The early twentieth century gave rise to a national effort on the part of African Americans to affect the health of their community as well as national health policy. In a departure from previous years, where the focus of institutions such as African American churches was primarily on health care provision, the emergence of NNHW signaled a new emphasis on local organizing and on engaging the national government on matters of black health. And, while this effort was largely identified with Booker T. Washington and the Tuskegee Institute, the black church (and, in particular, women parishioners and women's clubs within black churches) played a central role in its success.

It was at the beginning of the twentieth century that health disparities between blacks and whites began garnering the attention of national and local African American leaders. In large part, discussion of this topic was motivated by the enormity of the health crisis facing African Americans. As Phoebe Ann Pollitt argues, the health crisis facing black people was evident across most health indicators of the day:

> Tuberculosis killed African-Americans at three times the rate of whites in the early 1900s. Likewise, deaths from malaria, syphilis, and hookworm were also higher for the African-American population. In 1910 the average life expectancy for white females was 53.6 years and 50.2 years for white males. African-American females had a life expectancy of only 37.6 years and African-American males had an average life span of only 34 years. In cities such as New York, Richmond, Charleston, and New Orleans, the infant mortality rate for blacks was more than double that of whites. Given

the health inequalities between the races coupled with the relative lack of attention to African-American health concerns by the mostly white public health bureaucracies, African Americans initiated health programs and disease prevention programs in their own communities.[19]

As Pollitt notes, an indigenous response to such devastation would emerge from local communities. Correspondingly, national leaders and health professionals would also involve themselves in this pressing issue. For example, in 1905, the Men's Sunday Club of Savannah, Georgia, led by Monroe Work, started a program to educate the African American community about health and hygiene issues.[20] It was exactly this type of effort that organizers of the 1906 Atlanta "Conference for the Study of the Negro Problem" had in mind when they decided to highlight the need for "the formation of local health leagues among colored people for the dissemination of better knowledge of sanitation and medicine."[21] In an attempt to more systematically address such issues, in 1906 W. E. B. Du Bois edited a volume entitled *The Health and Physique of the Negro American* that included an exploration of health differences between black and white Americans. And, by 1909, the annual "Tuskegee Negro Conference" included among its workshop discussions the topic of health and Negro Americans.[22] Finally, at the 1914 conference, Monroe Work, then an employee of Booker T. Washington, used statistics to chart out the health disparities between blacks and whites. Susan Smith writes that Work's presentation was important because his numbers challenged "those whites who argued that these [health disparities] were a sign of inherent racial inferiority." His numbers also indicated "that nearly half of all black deaths were premature and could have been prevented through public health efforts."[23] Furthermore, Work's charts helped highlight the cost of such sickness to the economy as well as the possibility of contagion, both factors affecting the white population. As was noted in the last section, the prospect of contagion was a long-standing fear held among white Americans, who believed that the domestic workers who entered their homes might also bring diseases with them.

While each of these acts had some impact, most notably Work's presentation, a more organized movement of black lay- and professional people would lead the fight around health issues at the beginning of the century. Starting with small efforts in individual communities, a movement of na-

tional stature, the national Negro health movement, would result. Specifically, it was the Negro Organization Society of Virginia's statewide campaign
to encourage blacks to clean up their surroundings that would serve as the
model for NNHW. According to Smith: "The society was a coalition of over
250 black religious and secular organizations, representing 350,000 African
Americans in Virginia, about half of the state's black population."[24] In 1912,
the organization sponsored a cleanup day in black communities throughout
the state. Pollitt writes that, on this day, "approximately 130,000 African-
Americans in Virginia whitewashed buildings, discarded refuse, and generally cleaned up their homes, neighborhoods, and community buildings and
grounds."[25] The cleanup day was followed by cleanup weeks in 1913 and 1914.
The success of this program as well as the national attention generated from
Monroe Work's presentation at the 1914 annual "Tuskegee Negro Conference" prompted Booker T. Washington to initiate a national effort focused
on the public health of African Americans.

Believing that a program around black health could be mounted nationally, Washington, in 1915, asked the National Business League—an organization that he had founded—to issue a proclamation designating one week
National Health Improvement Week. This week, which would later become
NNHW, was the centerpiece of Washington's plan to highlight the devastating
health status of African Americans, enlisting local, state, and federal agencies and organizations in this effort. Increasingly, coming to understand that
his plan for the economic progress of African Americans would always be
threatened by the poor health of black people, Washington realized that only
a national response could begin to change this predicament.[26] In his speech
initiating National Health Improvement Week, Washington focused on the
high levels of death and serious illness in African American communities and
the cost of such illness in lost productivity to the country, in particular the
Southern economy.

Generally, this movement operated by establishing in local communities
health week committees that would be responsible for planning activities
aimed at educating community members in self-help techniques. To that end,
African American churches, long considered the most important institution
in black communities, played a central role in most local efforts across the
country. In fact, the structure of many local organizing efforts included a
special subcommittee dedicated exclusively to working with local churches.[27]

Women's groups in local churches were considered the backbone of and foot soldiers in this very important new project. They planned events, staffed exhibits, and provided hands-on training in preventive health measures.

However, beyond the efforts of individual parishioners, African American churches would take on a more centralized role in health week activities with, for example, Sunday deemed *mobilization day*. Additionally, during NNHW, African American ministers were encouraged to center their sermons on issues of health in the community. To this end, an official or model health sermon was written and distributed for educational purposes in black communities across the country. Churches were also asked to highlight issues of health in their gatherings later in the day on Sunday as well as hold special mass meetings throughout the week. The significance of the church to this movement is most clearly evident in the fact that health week began and ended on a Sunday. Quinn and Thomas note: "An eight day week, beginning and ending on Sunday was deliberately established to take advantage of the role of the church as a major convenor of community groups. The week culminated in a review of all activities and achievements intermingled with food, music and inspirational speeches."[28]

Not surprisingly, while most of the local level work was, Smith informs us, dominated by women (disproportionately working in or with church groups), much of the national attention and leadership was reserved for men. It was black doctors — almost always men — who took on increasing positions of power within the national leadership:

> The prominence of black male doctors, all active members of the NMA, and the paucity of black women in the executive committee [of NNHW] characterized national leadership patterns in the black health week movement. . . .
>
> The executive committee held the position that black doctors were best qualified to create health policy. In 1931 the committee concluded that even though local community organizations needed control over how they carried out the National Negro Health Week, doctors were the rightful national leaders.[29]

According to Smith, gendered orientations within families as well as the structure of many indigenous African American institutions like the church helped solidify the belief within African American communities and the nation that men should occupy positions of leadership while women took on the work of caretaking and health. Supporting these sexist beliefs was much of the work of black women's clubs, both religious and secular, which focused on improving the public health and social welfare of black communities, in particular the black poor. As Smith argues, the respectability concerns of middle-class black women would provide a strong impetus for their work in this area: "Black middle-class women felt a personal stake in the 'improvement' of the poor because of the potential effects on their own status. At issue for the middle class was the fact that white America did not recognize class differences among African Americans."[30]

Although much of the work for NNHW was conducted at the local level, a national advisory committee guided by Dr. Robert R. Moton, Booker T. Washington's successor, was established at the Tuskegee Institute, the national headquarters of the movement from 1915 to 1930.[31] The effectiveness of Moton's leadership was evident in the increasing numbers of participants in NNHW events. It is estimated that, in the health week's first year, sixteen states, primarily in the South, participated, a figure that would eventually grow to nearly twenty-five hundred communities in thirty-two states.[32]

While much of the success of this movement was due to national leaders like Moton and the work of such organizations as African American churches, local and national prominence would not have been reached without the assistance of willing local health departments, officials, and professionals as well as the initial seed money provided by the Anson Phelp Stokes Fund. The federal government, through the U.S. Public Health Service (USPHS), also became a major player in NNHW, increasing its participation during the 1920s largely at the urging of NNHW officials. For example, in 1921, the NNHW advisory board asked for the endorsement of the USPHS.[33] The USPHS responded by agreeing to take over responsibility for publishing the *National Negro Health Week Bulletin*, which eventually became the *National Negro Health News*. It also organized, in the same year, the first annual "NNHW Conference."[34]

The request from the advisory board was meant to secure more funding for the planning and promotion of this national event as well as generate more involvement from local public health officials. Organizers also sought assistance in transforming the week into a yearlong effort. Through such an expansion, black leaders involved in the movement hoped to put the issue of black health squarely on the national policy agenda. Black leaders also sought to diversify the agenda considered by both national policymakers and participants in NNHW events. Beyond mere self-help techniques, the issues that participants and planners began to address ranged from the training of black medical personnel, to the registration of African American births and deaths, to the spread of venereal diseases, to the availability of housing.[35]

Over the years, the USPHS would continue to increase its involvement in the work classified as NNHW. For example, not only did the USPHS enlist local institutions such as African American churches to communicate with potential black participants, but it also used radio broadcasts, posters, and special newspaper articles to spread the message. Eventually, almost all control of the week would fall under the auspices of the USPHS, with financial support coming from a number of sources, including the Rosenwald Fund, the Tuskegee Institute, Howard University, and the NMA.[36] This formal arrangement was most clearly manifested in the creation in 1932 of the Office of Negro Health Work, headed by Dr. Roscoe C. Brown. During its years of operation, the office served as a clearinghouse for projects dealing with black health and coordinated the yearlong effort around black health that came to be known as the national Negro health movement. With the move toward integration, however, African American leaders such as Walter White of the National Association for the Advancement of Colored People and Dr. Montague Cobb of the NMA argued that a separate Office of Negro Health Work was outdated and sent the wrong message to the nation.[37] In agreement, the federal government decided to abolish it and ended the movement in 1951.[38]

During its heyday, the national Negro health movement demonstrated once again the ability of African American communities to come together using their own indigenous resources as a base on which they could attempt to influence federal policy. And, while institutions such as African American churches may not have been directly involved in policymaking, they were a critical piece of the infrastructure that made this effort a success. In this instance, we see the church, not only attending to the issue of health, but, just as important, also mobilizing to build a national effort in response to the devastation faced by black people. African American churches helped define the health of black Americans, not only as a medical issue, but also as a public health issue that affected the political, economic, and social condition of African Americans. The church demonstrated the importance of designing programs and policies that did not circumvent but utilized the power and centrality of such institutions.

This example also reminds us, however, of the limits of the black church's control over such efforts. In this case, the church was on the margins of policymaking with regard to the health status of African Americans. Unlike the role that they played during slavery, where most often they independently augmented the failing health services available to both enslaved and freed blacks, during the national Negro health movement African American churches were an integral player in the effort. Their role was, however, again largely one of delivering services designed by others. The question that must, therefore, be asked is: When will African American churches make forays into the policymaking process themselves?

Contemporary Issues in African American Church Work around Health and Public Health—AIDS

The beginning of the new millennium finds many African American communities continuing their struggle for equality and justice. Unfortunately, in the way of achieving this progress are many of the same problems that black people have struggled against for some years. Continued poverty, residential segregation, the disappearance of living-wage jobs, and substandard education in poor communities and communities of color once again top the list of problems. However, while activists, leaders, and members of the community mobilize to deal with these issues, other new battles have emerged. An intensified effort to incarcerate young members of the African American community is but one example of this new repression on the part of the state. And, while struggles around the criminalization of black youths, affirmative action, and police brutality take center stage on the agendas of many African American leaders and elected officials, an equally terrifying and sinister crisis has emerged and taken root in African American communities. This one has received much less outcry and action. The crisis is HIV and AIDS, a public health threat that has increasingly become an epidemic of people of color, in particular African Americans.

As noted earlier, recent data from the Centers for Disease Control and Prevention (CDC) indicate that African Americans are disproportionately represented among those reported as having AIDS. For instance, African

Americans constitute 35 percent of all those designated with AIDS since the beginning of the epidemic. AIDS is the leading killer of African American women aged twenty-five to forty-four and African American men aged thirty-five to forty-four. African American women account for a more astonishing 57 percent of women with AIDS. And a similar pattern is found among black children, with 56 percent of all pediatric AIDS cases being found among African American children. Shockingly, while these statistics indicate the severity of the problem, they do not convey the hard reality that, proportionally, the situation is getting worse in African American communities. For example, of those AIDS cases reported in 2001, half (50 percent) were from the African American community. The depressing news associated with that statistic is made even more clear when it is remembered that black Americans account for only 12 percent of the population. Furthermore, a recent ten-city study by the CDC reported that nearly 30 percent of black gay men are believed to be HIV positive. Thus, no matter how we frame the AIDS crisis, there is no mistaking the havoc that it is wreaking on black communities.

However, while African American leaders are increasingly more willing to talk about, for example, inequities between those neighborhoods hardest hit by the epidemic and those neighborhoods and groups receiving the bulk of the government money, the question still remains: What are these same leaders doing to actively confront this crisis? Reassuringly, the answer has changed over the years, from largely nothing, to now pushing an important legislative agenda focused on the funding issue. For example, in 1998, the Congressional Black Caucus (CBC) finally took on the leadership that many black AIDS activists had been demanding of them throughout the epidemic, pressuring the government to declare AIDS a state of emergency in communities of color and to designate over $150 million dollars for a response to the particular needs of people of color affected by HIV and AIDS. Although this money has greatly aided efforts in communities of color to fight this epidemic, some activists are concerned that the programs being funded do not effectively target and highlight those individuals most at risk — gay men, men who sleep with men, and injection drug users. These activists suggest that, still beholden to a "politics of respectability," the CBC is unable to truly embrace those most at risk and stigmatized in communities of color for fear of tainting the public image of the larger community.

It is in the light of what appear to be some important but still tentative moves on the part of traditional leadership in African American communities to address the issues of HIV/AIDS that I ask: What have African American churches done in this area? As I noted earlier, I believe the black church's response to AIDS to be critical, not only because of the centrality of this institution to most African American communities, but also because AIDS represents the type of socially stigmatizing and divisive issue that increasingly is confronting African American communities. Thus, unlike racial discrimination, which has been framed largely as a consensus issue, relevant and threatening to the entire African American community, AIDS is what I have termed elsewhere a *cross-cutting* issue. By *cross-cutting issues* I mean those issues that appear to be rooted in or built on the often-hidden differences, cleavages, or fault lines of marginal communities. Cross-cutting issues are perceived as being contained to identifiable subgroups in African American communities, especially those least empowered. Furthermore, cross-cutting issues "bring into question how traditional black leaders and organizations will respond to issues that no longer manifest themselves strictly as racial consensus issues, but instead stratify along the lines of class, gender, and sexuality."[39]

The role of African American churches in responding to AIDS has been debated nearly since the beginning of the epidemic. Those involved in the church contend that its response has evolved over the years, moving from glaring absence to the development of AIDS ministries and service provision across the country. In contrast, some black AIDS activists contend that the church was slow to get involved, largely because of those segments in African American communities most at risk—black gay men, black men who sleep with men, and black injection drug users. They argue, further, that it is the church's uncompromising attitude toward sin, in particular the sin associated with homosexuality, that has allowed it to look the other way as thousands in African American communities die. Finally, while some activists will concede that the response of African American churches has been mixed, with recent signs of progress, they still argue that the observed movement has been toward the provision of services, not toward a political activism that would embrace and empower those community members most at risk. These activists are, therefore, not willing to applaud the church's activism, for they see this change in position as a limited one, constrained by the judgmental Christian model of "love the sinner, hate the sin"—especially the sin of homosexuality.

Without a doubt, both those close to the church and those critical of its activities in response to this epidemic are in part accurate in their assessment. There has been movement, but, in most cases, we have not witnessed the radical change that would allow black congregations to fully deal with those most at risk in African American communities and the behaviors involved in transmission of HIV. Specifically, until African American ministers and their congregations can discuss such topics as sexuality, homosexuality, and drug use in an open and candid manner, they will never be able to truly confront the crisis of AIDS in African American communities. Moreover, if African American churches do not attain some real understanding of the complexity of this epidemic as well as all the ideological and political issues that define it, their effectiveness will be hampered if they are given access to the policy arena. It is specifically on the question of African American churches as policymakers around AIDS that I want to center the rest of my examination in this section. For, while the debate still rages about the role of African American churches in the AIDS epidemic, there are those who are engaged in a daily struggle to push the church into the role, not only of service provider, but also, and more prominently, of policymaker. Let me talk briefly about one such organization—the Balm in Gilead.

THE BALM IN GILEAD

The Balm in Gilead was founded in 1989 by Pernessa Seele. Working at the time at Harlem Hospital, Seele questioned why the African American community was not responding more forcefully to AIDS. She says that it was revealed to her "that what was missing was the faith imperative—the directive from religious leaders to their congregations to learn, act and care as their Lord would expect of them in the age of HIV/AIDS."[40] Armed with that insight, Seele proceeded to build an organization that would dramatically attempt to engage African American clergy in the struggle against AIDS. The first event to be implemented by the new organization was the Black Church Week of Prayer for the Healing of AIDS. This program, designed to engage even the most sheepish clergy, is modeled after the successful Harlem Week of Prayer for the Healing of AIDS established by Seele in 1989. Now in its twelfth year, the Black Church Week of Prayer is this year expected to garner the support of and prompt activity in over ten thousand churches across the country, with African American ministers using their pulpits to educate their congregations about HIV and AIDS. In addition to the success of the Black Church Week of Prayer, the Balm in Gilead has expanded into other areas. For instance, it now holds a biannual skills-building conference entitled "The Black Church National Education and Leadership Training Conference on HIV/AIDS." It has also established a network of eleven national organizations to educate and disseminate information to churches about AIDS. In tandem with that effort is the resource center and clearinghouse that it instituted. Correspondingly, it also does the important work of educating, publishing and distributing materials that can engage, educate, and mobilize African American congregations. One of the more courageous publications produced was the 1997 reader *Though I Stand at the Door and Knock: Discussions on the Black Church Struggle with Homosexuality and AIDS*.

While the accomplishments of the Balm in Gilead are impressive, Seele is the first one to point out that there is still much more work to do. Specifically, she argues that, while African American churches are moving in a direction where many have AIDS ministries and some provide direct services, few are actually involved in the policy process. This is her next goal. She wants African American ministers involved in local funding decisions about where government resources are directed. As she explains, now is the time to push for involvement in policy decisions. With new guidelines associated with money from the CDC and the Ryan White Care Act directing communities to establish community-planning structures that include representatives from those communities most affected by the epidemic but previously excluded from decisionmaking, the door is, she believes, opening for greater policy involvement on the part of faith-based leaders in African American communities. She suggests that all the work of the Balm in Gilead can be viewed as a continuum that seeks first to familiarize African American clergy with the issue of AIDS, then help them establish their own AIDS ministries, then engage them in the bigger dialogues that must inform effective AIDS work—discussions of sexuality, morality, and drug use—and, finally, move them into the policy arena.[41] No doubt, Seele has an ambitious outlook on what African American churches can do in response to AIDS, but her track record suggests that most of her goals will be accomplished.

The question still remains: Should African American clergy be involved in policy decisions regarding AIDS, or, even more minimally, should they be the first ones to take a previously absent seat at "the funding table"? Lost in some of our vigor to include the representatives of African American churches in policy decisions is how their sometimes conservative notions of the epidemic — even those ministers who have AIDS ministries — might affect policy outputs. There seems to be little understanding, or at least recognition, of the heterogeneous nature of those groups previously excluded. Rarely is the fact explored that different segments of African American communities bring different interests to the table. Do we really expect black gay men or black injection drug users of color to have the same perspectives or concerns about AIDS as faith-based practitioners from African American communities? Thus, when we embark on a mission to include the excluded, a more complex understanding of the excluded must be at work. There must be some recognition of the differential access to power even in African American communities and a commitment to include all those voices in the discussion. Only by radically challenging and changing those with access to power within and outside African American communities can a goal of true inclusion be reached. Thus, beyond asking whether the church will be involved in policy matters, we must now ask how it will be involved. Do African American clergy represent the many within African American communities who are denied access to decisionmaking, or are they the representatives only of those in their congregations? This seems to be the next political question that the church must confront.

Finally, it is important to remember that the Balm in Gilead is not the only organization engaged in this type of work with African American churches. For example, the National Black Leadership Commission on AIDS also has a program to work with African American clergy across the country. It reports facilitating the distribution of over $5 million to African American churches and clergy organizations for direct service provision. Similarly, the AIDS National Interfaith Network (ANIN) — a nonprofit coalition representing thousands of local and regional AIDS programs — "brings together nearly 20 major national religious denominations and organizations, each of which oversees its own national organization of AIDS programs and services."[42] Interestingly, none of the seven historic African American denominations are actual members of ANIN's Council of National Religious AIDS Networks. Instead, these seven, as well as the Full Gospel Fellowship of Churches and Ministers International, are represented on the council by the Balm in Gilead.

Throughout the country, one finds national, regional, and local organizations attempting to engage with clergy, including African American clergy, around the issue of HIV/AIDS. Leading this work has been the Balm in Gilead. For example, it is the only black AIDS organization endorsed by every major African American church denomination and caucus. Its effectiveness stems from the dynamic leadership of Pernessa Seele and from the organization's ability to respond to the questions and concerns of the faith-based leaders with which it works, but also from its willingness to continue to encourage clergy to think more broadly and openly about the underlying issues of this epidemic, in particular sexuality and homosexuality. This is an organization that has the ability to help African American churches move into the policy arena in a manner that will lead, not only to additional material resources in African American communities, but possibly also to the redefinition of the epidemic and those most at risk in these communities.

Conclusion

One need only glance at the newspaper or talk to a community member to get a sense of the continued importance of African American churches in the lives of many African Americans. Similarly, in the arena of public health, one is often reminded of the numerous programs across the country headed by the faith-based institutions in African American communities to combat everything from cancer, to high blood pressure, to drug addiction, to teen pregnancy. And, while the church has established itself as a central institution, not only in the spiritual life of, but also in the provision of direct services to many African American communities, we must ask whether this is enough and whether it is appropriate.

With government contracts available to community-based institutions interested in servicing marginal communities, African American churches are now being paid for doing the type of work that they have pursued for years. However, in many cases, the church is being paid to manage segments of African American communities thought to be morally and behaviorally out of control. Not too unlike contagion fears that fueled white attention to the health status of black Americans earlier, one must wonder whether the work of black faith-based institutions will truly empower those in need or simply help keep them out of the sight of, and, thus, keep them from threatening, more privileged white and black Americans. Furthermore, as efforts are made to include black faith-based leaders in the public policy process, should we consider this involvement an unequivocal success? Recognizing the differentiated interests that exist in African American communities and the often socially conservative Christian ideological orientation of African American clergy, one might wonder whether these disciples are best situated to empower and represent those most marginal and morally stigmatized in African American communities.

These dilemmas suggest that, in addition to pushing for the inclusion of faith-based leaders in policy decisions, we must also develop mechanisms, like those practiced by the Balm in Gilead, that will engage clergy around such issues politically. Some attention must be paid to the political education of African American clergy even in the area of public health. As was evident during the civil rights movement, engaging the consciousness of the clergy is a necessary precursor to their participation in, let alone leadership of, progressive and liberatory struggle. In the absence of a movement, and with the unprecedented access to decisionmaking that numerous African American middle-class organizations have acquired today, the systematic attention to the political education of the clergy may be the difference between these individuals functioning simply as service providers or policy entrepreneurs and their functioning as collaborators with an oppressive state or progressive leaders for social change and justice.

Notes

1 National Center for Health Statistics, "Infant Mortality Rates Vary by Race and Ethnicity," *Fact Sheet*, August 5, 1999.
2 *HIV/AIDS Surveillance Report* (Centers for Disease Control) 10, no. 1 (1998): 1.
3 C. McCord and H. P. Freeman, "Excess Mortality in Harlem," *New England Journal of Medicine* 322 (1990): 173–77.
4 Sandra Crouse Quinn and Stephen B. Thomas, "The National Negro Health Week, 1915 to 1951: A Descriptive Account," *Journal of Wellness Perspectives* 12, no. 4 (1996): 172–79.
5 Aldon D. Morris, *The Origins of the Civil Rights Movement: Black Communities Organizing for Change* (New York: Free Press, 1984).
6 Susan L. Smith, *Sick and Tired of Being Sick and Tired: Black Women's Health Activism in America, 1890–1950* (Philadelphia: University of Pennsylvania Press, 1995).
7 Ibid., 3.

8 See Michael W. Byrd and Linda A. Clayton, *An American Health Dilemma: A Medical History of African Americans and the Problems of Race: Beginnings to 1900* (New York: Routledge, 2000). It is also important to note that the use of traditional healers and folk remedies as well as witchcraft was a central component of the health care practices of blacks long after the formal end to slavery. Similarly, in black churches, one can find a reliance on the Holy Spirit as a force for healing. All these traditions migrated north with black communities and can be found in use today.

9 Todd L. Savitt, *Medicine and Slavery: The Diseases and Health Care of Blacks in Antebellum Virginia* (Urbana: University of Illinois Press, 1978), 150.

10 Ibid., 152.

11 James H. Jones, *Bad Blood: The Tuskegee Syphilis Experiment* (New York: Free Press, 1993), 17.

12 Todd L. Savitt, "Black Health on the Plantation: Masters, Slaves, and Physicians," in *Sickness and Health in America*, ed. J. W. Leavitt and R. L. Numbers (Madison: University of Wisconsin Press, 1985), 314.

13 Savitt, *Medicine and Slavery*, 217 (quotation), 239.

14 Michael Anthony Cooke, *The Health of Blacks during Reconstruction, 1862–1870* (Ann Arbor: University Microfilms International, 1983), 209.

15 Jude Thomas May, *The Medical Care of Blacks in Louisiana during Occupation and Reconstruction, 1862–1868: Its Social and Political Background* (Ann Arbor: University Microfilms, 1971), 147.

16 Ibid., 171–72.

17 Cathy J. Cohen, *The Boundaries of Blackness: AIDS and the Breakdown of Black Politics* (Chicago: University of Chicago Press, 1999).

18 E. Franklin Frazier, *The Negro Church in America* (New York: Schocken, 1964); C. Eric Lincoln and Lawrence H. Mamiya, *The Black Church in the African American Experience* (Durham: Duke University Press, 1990); Andrew Billingsley, *Mighty Like a River: The Black Church and Social Reform* (New York: Oxford University Press, 1999).

19 Phoebe Ann Pollitt, "Commentary: From National Negro Health Week to National Public Health Week," *Journal of Community Health* 21, no. 6 (December 1996): 401–2.

20 Quinn and Thomas, "National Negro Health Week," 173.

21 W. E. B. Du Bois, *The Health and Physique of the Negro American* (Atlanta: Atlanta University Press, 1906), 110.

22 Smith, *Sick and Tired*, 37.

23 Ibid.

24 Ibid., 36.

25 Pollitt, "Commentary," 402.

26 Roscoe C. Brown, "The National Negro Health Week Movement," *Journal of Negro Education* 6, no. 3 (1937): 554.

27   Quinn and Thomas, "National Negro Health Week," 177.

28   Ibid., 175.

29   Smith, *Sick and Tired*, 34, 65 (quotation).

30   Ibid, 18.

31   Brown, "National Negro Health Week," 553.

32   Smith, *Sick and Tired*, 39.

33   Ibid.

34   Quinn and Thomas, "National Negro Health Week," 175.

35   Smith, *Sick and Tired*, 45.

36   Brown, "National Negro Health Week," 560.

37   Smith, *Sick and Tired*, 58, 76.

38   Quinn and Thomas, "National Negro Health Week," 177.

39   Cohen, *The Boundaries of Blackness*, 9.

40   *The Black Church Week of Prayer for the Healing of AIDS: March 4–10, 2001* (New York: Balm in Gilead, 2001), 1.

41   Pernessa Seele, interview with author, New York, October 15, 2000.

42   Public Media Center and the AIDS National Interfaith Network, *Faith and AIDS: American Faith Communities Respond to the AIDS Epidemic* (San Francisco: Public Media Center, 1997).

6

AFRICAN AMERICAN CHURCHES AND

REPRODUCTIVE HEALTH RIGHTS

Emilie M. Townes

Several issues have traditionally fallen within the domain of women's rights: reproductive health and rights; affirmative action; child care; domestic and sexual violence; education; health care; economic justice; media portrayals; sexism; sexual harassment; sex role stereotyping; welfare; and women in prison. These issues are not, however, associated with women's rights exclusively, as other essays in this volume demonstrate. Yet, initially, those who have been and continue to be active in women's rights often do so out of a concern for more justice-based relationality in these areas and from the standpoint of the particular impact that these issues have on the lives of women and children.

Nevertheless, African American churches have not generally addressed women's rights as issues of public policy. Although this absence of support for women's rights is not entirely unique to African American churches, it is glaring among them. Official journals, magazines, and proceedings of African American denominations reveal little discussion of issues directly affecting black women's rights. Results from the 1999–2000 Black Churches and Politics Survey, reported on by Smith (chapter 1 in this volume), show that only 17 percent of respondents indicated that their congregations were involved in women's rights issues. Indeed, the record of black church involvement on these issues is so bare that only one issue, reproductive health and rights, can be examined in any depth. However, as a rule, African American churches understand this issue to be one, not of public policy, but of morality. African American denominations and churches have maintained a profound silence concerning domestic and sexual violence, sexism, sexual harassment, sex role stereotyping, and women in prison. This does not follow the pattern that these churches have established when dealing with other forms of civil rights, such as racial discrimination and voting rights.

I do not intend to speculate on the matrix of rationales and theoethical arguments that conspire to create such a lacuna concerning women's rights among post–civil rights movement black churches. Rather, I focus on reproductive health and rights, with a concern about why issues with a direct impact on African American women (and a collateral impact on African American children and men) are generally not viewed by African American churches as issues of public policy.

Reproductive Health and Health Care

Black women in the United States have, historically, endured a systematic, institutionalized denial of reproductive health services. From the slave master's economic stake in black women's fertility, to the racist connotations of early birth control policy, to sterilization abuse in the 1960s and 1970s, to the current campaign to inject Norplant and Depo-Provera in the arms of black teenage women and welfare mothers, African American women have endured a nearly relentless onslaught on the reproductive capacities of our bodies.

Public policies concerning reproductive health affect women of color disproportionately. For example, national prochoice organizations have incorporated slowly (if at all) the full spectrum of reproductive health care issues that continue to have a significant impact on women of color and African American women in particular—for example, infant mortality, sterilization abuse, and cesarean section abuse. Figures complied in 1989 revealed that the infant mortality rate was 18.3 percent among African Americans but only 9.3 percent among whites. Eighty percent of women who are forced to have cesarean sections are women of color.[1] Economics is a key factor in these instances. Those who have financial resources can choose to purchase the health services they need or want, while those lacking financial resources have fewer choices and rely heavily on a federal government that has slashed funding for family planning and public health. For instance, the Hyde Amendment restricts the use of Medicaid funds for abortion services.[2] This has had a direct impact on the lives of more than twenty-two million people living in poverty—five of ten of whom are women of color. Many women of color who are affected by the restrictions of the Hyde Amendment are also the ones most susceptible to health risks, nutrition deficiencies, and limited access to adequate health care. These conditions contribute to problem pregnancies or unintended pregnancies.[3]

Women of color suffer disproportionately from a variety of serious health conditions that may be exacerbated by pregnancy—hypertension, diabetes, sickle-cell anemia, and HIV/AIDS. In the case of hypertension, the incidence is 82 percent higher among women of color than among white women. Even more alarming is the fact that it affects more than 25 percent of African Americans in general. When these two statistics are combined, chronic hypertension is associated with up to 30 percent of maternal deaths and up to 22 percent of perinatal deaths. Hypertension has also been linked to strokes during pregnancy, and childbirth poses a greater risk of death than abortion.[4] One in 165 black people is born with the sickle-cell trait. Pregnant women with sickle-cell anemia are more prone to miscarriages, aggravated circulatory problems, and depression. Seventy-five percent of all female AIDS cases are women of color—80 percent of their children are affected. These are sobering realities that African American women and men must face when it comes to issues of reproductive health.

Closely related to these medical realities are social policies and attitudes that blame poor black mothers for perpetuating social problems by transmitting defective genes, irreparable crack cocaine damage, and a deviant lifestyle to their children. The legal scholar and law school professor Dorothy Roberts notes a *Philadelphia Inquirer* editorial arguing that the United States could reduce the number of children born to poor black women. The editorial drew its specious intellectual arguments from Charles Murray and Richard Herrnstein's *The Bell Curve*, in which it is claimed that social disparities come from the higher fertility rates of the genetically less intelligent groups—most colored racial ethnic groups.[5] African American women have not been indifferent to such efforts to curtail these impositions on their reproductive rights. In a 1991 study, 83 percent of the black women surveyed favored access to abortion and birth control.[6] Key here is the word *access*. The general tone in the study is that women felt that, without the right or ability to decide whether to continue a pregnancy, a woman cannot achieve full control over her fertility and cannot, therefore, exercise a degree of control over her destiny.

Forty-three percent of women in the United States will have at least one abortion by the age of forty-five. Among American women, black women between the ages of eighteen and twenty-four are most likely to have an abortion. These black women are usually separated or unmarried with an annual income of less than $15,000 or have Medicaid assistance. All in all, women of color are approximately twice as likely to have an abortion as white women. Legally induced abortion is one of the most frequently performed surgical procedures in the United States. In 1997, the most recent year for which statistics are available, 1,184,758 legally induced abortions were reported to the Centers for Disease Control (CDC).[7] In 1972, there were 586,760 legally induced abortions, of which 23 percent were performed on black women. In 1997, of the nearly 1.2 million legal abortions performed, nearly 36 percent were on black women — an increase of 31 percent.[8]

As of June 17, 1999, the CDC put the average deathrate for African American mothers at 19.6 per 100,000 live births.[9] This is about the same as the rates for Nicaragua or Vietnam. The rate for white women was 5.3 per 100,000. Black women are dying from complications related to pregnancy at four times the rate of white women. From 1979 to 1999, the leading causes of pregnancy-related deaths have been massive bleeding, high blood pressure, blood clots in the lungs, infection, and heart disease. African Americans are disproportionately vulnerable to high blood pressure. Poverty also has an impact in that it generally leads to a less healthy lifestyle, poorer nutrition, poor or nonexistent medical care, lack of prenatal care, and a lack of knowledge about the early warning signs of illness and disease. However, the causes of pregnancy-related deaths sustain themselves across the economic spectrum of black women's lives. Black women, regardless of income and status, die at inordinate rates during pregnancy.

Various medical and justice-related organizations have focused on infant health. However, Julia Scott, president and CEO of the National Black Women's Health Project notes: "The time has come to act upon the reality and understand that healthy babies come from healthy mothers."[10] Genuine reproductive health and rights are possible only when healthy mothers and healthy babies are able to flourish. Genuine reproductive health is achieved when there is access to all the necessary information and services — from adequate health care and housing to education and employment. Genuine rights are achieved when decisions are made free from coercion, from actual or threatened violence, from addictions — and having full access to the resources necessary to support those decisions. These are crucial at a time in the life of the United States when the overall deathrate for mothers of all races is 7.7 per 100,000 live births — a rate that has been relatively consistent for two decades. However, it is sobering to realize that twenty other countries have lower deathrates than the United States does.

Responses by African American Churches

Clearly, reproductive health is a public policy issue that has a profound impact on the African American community and, by extension, on black churches. However, reproductive health receives neither the attention nor the concern that many other public policy issues addressed in this volume receive. This was graphically illustrated at a neighborhood church forum entitled "Civil Rights under Attack: Recent Supreme Court Decision" sponsored by several civil rights organizations. Dorothy Roberts was counseled by a black male audience member to "stick to traditional civil rights concerns, such as affirmative action, voting rights, and criminal justice" when she focused on the Supreme Court's decision in *Webster v. Reproductive Health Services*. Roberts linked the court decision, which weakened *Roe v. Wade* by denying the right to abortion at publicly funded hospitals, to a series of current attacks on black women's reproductive autonomy. The black male respondent charged that she risked solidarity around racial issues by interjecting the controversial issue of reproduction.[11]

A 1992 study by Mark Chaves and Lynn Higgins showed that black congregations are significantly more likely to participate in meals services, civil rights activities (antiracism focused), community economic development initiatives, and public education programs concerning disease than are white congregations.[12] White congregations were significantly more likely to participate in recreational programs for youths, right-to-life actions, and refugee-related programs. The fact that African American congregations are more active in civil rights and social services activities than on issues such as the right to life suggests, among other things, that African American churches may view women's reproductive health and rights issues as related to private morality and unrelated to problems of structural inequality faced by African Americans as a group.

Jacquelyn Jackson gives, perhaps, the best overview of the tenor of African American church responses to reproductive health and rights. She notes that the conversations and pronouncements in this area center, not on health or rights, but on abortion and illegitimacy.[13] She goes on to note that most African American churches seem to oppose abortion for reasons that range from concerns about black genocide to religious beliefs about murder. She also observes that one problem in dealing with abortion and illegitimacy is that the moral pronouncements are usually made by males, typically blame females for pregnancies and for abortions, and rarely connect the question of abortion with supporting the infant. Jackson's insights about the misgivings of African American churches about the moral ends of abortion are key to understanding why African American churches do not have a strong public policy voice on the issue of reproductive health and rights.

Reproductive health and rights have been discussed in a few specific African American church contexts. The *A.M.E. Zion Quarterly Review* and the monograph *What A.M.E.'s Believe* shed light on the silence of African American churches and on the religious and ethical issues that they often attach to reproductive health and rights. This broad spectrum of concerns is often collapsed into one issue—abortion.

THE *A.M.E. ZION QUARTERLY REVIEW*

In general, searches through official African American denominational journals and magazines uncover very little public discussion about reproductive health and rights. The only African American denominational journal carrying any such discussion has been the *A.M.E. Zion Quarterly Review*—and this has been limited to two articles published in 1991.[14] The first article, written by Claude Christopher (a pastor and member of the Board of Evangelism of the African Methodist Episcopal Zion [AMEZ] Church), covers a variety of issues, including drugs, gambling, and the family. When dealing with reproductive health and rights, Christopher links teen sex and abortion. For Christopher, teen pregnancy is a growing problem that is spiritual in nature. For him, the solution is increased attention to spiritual values—which he believes to be the domain of churches, not the government or the school system. He notes, however, that churches have not been successful because they fail to influence the majority of teenagers. He goes on to state that most children are allowed to stop attending church when they get into their teens, that many families do not introduce their children to the church, and that many teens who do attend church can be influenced more by their peers than by religious teaching. Christopher pushes for further church involvement on these issues where he states: "The nation is in a dilemma over the abortion issue. It is of interest to both married and single women. . . . The church is involved, whether we want to be, or not, because many of the people getting abortions are members of the church."[15]

For Christopher, teen sex, teen pregnancies, premarital sex, and abortion are not "simple moral issues but are related to our spiritual well being," and he argues for greater church consistency on these issues: "The message of the church must be based on the scriptures that command us to abstain from fornication and not to destroy life. The church must not argue like the secular world over when a fetus becomes a person and other technicalities, a process that ensure[s] no solution to the problems. The church must take a definite stand backed by the Bible, always showing the love of Christ." In the concluding section of his article, "Moral and Moral Living," Christopher comes close to making a case for the engagement of churches in public policy formation, broadly conceived. Here, he brings together a muted public policy voice with a strong call for individual morality and values but leaves the implementation of the value system that he advocates in the public arena largely unaddressed:

> Many people reject the right of the church to establish a value system for the whole community. But the church must continue to assert its right to establish our value system and it must work to strengthen the family as an institution through which a good value system can be maintained. . . . Cultural changes might require some changes in methods of ministry but the purpose or goal remains the same. Different racial or cultural groups might have different attitudes toward ministry. Their attitudes toward ministry will demand adjustments in methods of ministry. As knowledge increases, culture changes. But ministry only changes methods, not purposes. The A.M.E. Zion Church must find ways to speak to the minds of black men and women, boys and girls, and then the rest of the world, conveying the message of repentance, forgiveness, and discipleship that leads to eternal salvation. It might be necessary to change some of our age-old methods of ministry. It might be necessary to change some organizational structure.

The things that must not be changed are our interpretation of scripture, our faith in God, and our purpose.[16]

The second article, by Reginald D. Broadnax (a pastor and seminary student at Chicago Theological Seminary at the time), focuses on a distinction between morality and law, with the two regarded as mutually exclusive given that morality cannot be legislated. After noting a diversity of opinion on abortion among African American churches, Broadnax suggests that the strongest inclination among African American churches is in a "pro life" direction. By placing *pro life* in quotation marks, he poses a challenge to assumptions that "those who support abortion rights are 'Pro Death.'" He poses a further challenge to the denial of choice, stating that "to remove one's choice, even the choice of sin, is against the plan of God." Broadnax argues, on scriptural grounds, that God gives us a choice through the concept of free will in which we each enter into a process of decisionmaking. From this stance, he argues that, because abortion is not an end in itself (it is an effect, not a cause), the question of abortion is not where the church should focus its attention. Rather, the real moral question is the sex act prior to abortion (which he considers to be the cause). In language that appeals to the individual rather than to public policymaking, Broadnax states: "The Church is clouded by this issue and I believe that this is the work of the Adversary [Satan] in causing confusion and deterring the Church from its primary task, attacking the causes of sin, not its effects."[17]

Like Christopher, Broadnax highlights the way in which African American churches place the behavior of women at the center of the problem. He provides a larger context for the discussion of public policy issues — but these issues are centered, not on reproductive health and rights, but on the traditional civil rights issues that African American churches tend to address as public policy issues: "What will the Church say to a generation of young women who have reached maturity without ever having felt loved? Where is the voice of the Church concerning adequate health and prenatal care for the poor; conditions which contribute to abortion being an option for some women? Where is the voice of the Church concerning unemployment in our communities which causes concern for being able to support a child? If the Church allows such circumstances to persist, it must necessarily suffer the consequences of its effects." He then returns to an argument that centers on individual morality rather than on abortion and the whole range of issues found in reproductive health and rights:

> While I believe that this is a person's right, the freedom to make decisions concerning both that which is good and that which is evil, I do not believe that this should be the position of the Church. In fact, the Church should not have a position at all but rather it should take up its responsibility. . . . [I]t is the Church's responsibility to teach its people how to make responsible choices: choices based upon the Word of God. Those who are of the world will always choose the things of the world, but it is the responsibility of the Church to teach its people the things of God, that they may not follow the ways of the world. . . . It is not the responsibility of the Church to speak out against or join the argument for the effects of sin. It is the responsibility of the Church to teach its people how not to choose sin, therefore, eliminating both cause and effect.[18]

Clearly, Broadnax and Christopher approach sexual and reproductive health issues as matters to be arbitrated through *appropriate* interpretation and application of Scripture rather than through public policy — which has the effect of providing, knowingly or unknowingly, tacit support for public policies that would limit women's sexual and reproductive health rights. Given that these articles are among the few treatments of these issues to be found in the *A.M.E. Zion Quarterly Review*, and absent formal denominational statements to the contrary, we must assume that they are not entirely unrepresentative of the AMEZ Church perspective on these issues.

WHAT A.M.E.'S BELIEVE

What A.M.E.'s Believe was developed for the African Methodist Episcopal (AME) Church by the Seventh Episcopal District under the supervision of Bishop John Hurst Adams.[19] This monograph comprises brief position papers designed to help equip AME churches. In the foreword, Bishop Adams notes: "It is only as we are absolutely clear about who we are and what we believe that we will have the spiritual, ethical, intellectual, and emotional capacity to govern and manage the awesome complexities and the scientific and technological advances destined to face us in the 21st century."[20]

As in the AMEZ Church materials, the focus here is on abortion. Again, this is seen as a moral debate, but it is argued somewhat differently in that the framers of this response state: "Questions arise as to whether a woman should have control over her body and the right to choose whether to have children." For them, the moral question is: "Does life begin in the first trimester of conception, when survival outside of the womb would be literally miraculous."[21]

The committee invokes Jeremiah 1:5, Matthew 1:18–25, Luke 1:26–38, and Luke 1:39–45 to state:

> The Scriptures point to the existence of life before birth, and speak of no circumstance that justifies the taking of an unborn life. As such, we hold that abortion is the taking of a life and is contrary to the word and will of God. We further hold that abortion should in no wise be used as a means of birth control, as abstinence is the Christian means of birth control. Additionally, the A.M.E. Church does acknowledge that medical science has found value in fetal tissue research, but cannot sanction securing such fetal tissue by any means initiated by humankind and not by God.

Further, it addresses illegitimacy by stating that any life created by God cannot be judged as impure or illegitimate. In a blending of personal morality and muted social policy, it states that "we must see that our children are held to and taught a standard of Christian morality" and that adoption must be promoted as a "positive alternative to abortion."[22]

Echoing Jackson's findings, the committee remarks:

> While we hold [antichoice/prolife activists'] view of abortion as the taking of a life, we must be circumspect in joining their protests. Many of those who most stridently march and resort to confrontation for the rights of the unborn also support political positions — such as welfare reform, the abolition of public education, and cruel prison reform — that trample upon the rights of those already born. As such, the A.M.E. Church does not stand with those who make abortion a political issue, unless they in turn embrace a wider political agenda that affirms and secures the well-being of the living, as well as that of the yet unborn.

Additionally, it found that, while abortion is an undesirable option for church members, it acknowledged the potential for such circumstances as jeopardy to the mother's life, stillbirth, rape, or incest to necessitate abortion. Nevertheless, it ends by reasserting the desirability of adoption and affirms birth parents that choose this option. This is one of the rare occasions that the role and place of men in reproductive matters are alluded to in black church pronouncements related to abortion.[23]

The Women of Color Partnership and the Black Church Initiative of the Religious Coalition for Reproductive Choice

Since 1996, the Religious Coalition for Reproductive Choice (RCRC) has been headed by Carlton Veazey, a National Baptist Convention, USA, minister and the pastor of the Fellowship Baptist Church in Washington, D.C.[24] RCRC understands that one of its many roles is to attempt to shape public policy decisions. As a public policy advocacy and education group, and specifically through its work with the Women of Color Partnership and the Black Church Initiative, RCRC provides a coalition structure through which African American clergy and churches can address reproductive health and rights from a prochoice stance. The Women of Color Partnership was organized in 1985 to give women of color a voice in the decisionmaking process of the prochoice movement. Through the Women of Color Partnership, RCRC has established partnerships with clergy, faith groups, and grassroots community organizations serving Latino, African American, poor, and other underrepresented women.

The Black Church Initiative, established with Veazey's leadership, helps African American clergy and laity address teen childbearing, sex education, unintended pregnancies, and other reproductive health issues within the context of African American culture and religion. In addition to the educational models "Keeping It Real!" and "Breaking the Silence" (see below), the initiative hosts the annual National Black Religious Summit on Sexuality, at which African American clergy and laity discuss such issues as teen pregnancy, sexuality and religion, domestic violence, HIV/AIDS, and other issues of reproductive health. In addition, the initiative sponsors two-day Regional Black Religious Summits on Sexuality that help prepare clergy and laity to introduce community- and faith-based programs addressing teen pregnancy.

The Black Church Initiative, intentionally and strategically, addresses the issue of reproductive choice (one aspect of reproductive health and rights) by addressing issues of sexuality. Its educational model "Breaking the Silence" is "a faith based sexuality education model developed to assist local congregations, parents, guardians, and clergy address sex and sexuality to assist teens in making healthy life choices." This model seeks to address issues of sexuality as it engages African American Christian educators, pastors, Sunday school directors, adult discipleship directors, deacons and deaconesses, and congregations in biblical, ethnological, and theological reflection. "Breaking the Silence" recognizes that most black church members are unclear about the meaning of sexuality "and where it fits in their lives as believers," and it goes on to note: "Quite often the only time the Church responds to the subject of sexuality is when judging and or condemning individuals."[25]

The Black Church Initiative also has an educational model geared toward African American youths between the ages of thirteen and seventeen entitled "Keeping it Real!" Its aim is to prepare youths to make healthy and responsible decisions as sexual and spiritual human beings. In explaining this material, the initiative spells out some of the HIV/AIDS statistics from the CDC that make it necessary to provide a resource for black churches and black youths.[26] It notes: "As parents, guardians, ministers, church educators, we are called to lead youth with prayer, Bible study, and honest dialogue." And it stresses the need for the full support of the pastor, parents or guardians, and ministry leaders as crucial to the success of the program.[27]

These two programs from the Black Church Initiative serve as educational tools to help black clergy and laity begin to address issues of reproductive health and rights by intentionally proceeding from the pedagogical stance that African American Christians cannot address reproductive health until they have a clear understanding of sexuality. These programs also help contextualize and provide foundation for "Black Ministers Support Your Right to Choose," a statement issued by nine African American men and women pastors that notes: "It's your body. It's your life. It's your choice. We encourage you to choose what is best for you and your family today. As you make your decision, meditate on God's mercy and love." The statement ends: "We are Black ministers, and we are writing to remind you that God loves you— no matter what! You are always a part of the caring community of Black people."[28]

A companion statement is "We Remember: African American Women Are for Reproductive Freedom."[29] This statement outlines clearly what reproductive freedom means in this instance: access to comprehensive, age-appropriate information about sexuality and reproduction; freedom to choose to have a child; good, affordable health care to assure a safe pregnancy and delivery; access to health services to help the infertile achieve pregnancy; freedom to choose not to have a child; access to the full range of contraceptive services and appropriate information about reproduction; freedom to end an unwanted pregnancy; access to safe, legal, affordable abortion services; freedom to make informed choices; easily accessible health care that has been proved safe and effective; and reproductive health and freedom to make one's own reproductive choices.

Summary

African American religious bodies draw a clear distinction between religious and political issues when discussing reproductive health and rights, resulting in a great reticence on their part relative to these public policy issues. Rather than seeing reproductive health and rights as a broad area encompassing abortion, sterilization abuse, mortality, and cesarean section abuse — issues that black women name as crucial — African American churches tend to equate reproductive health and rights with abortion. This leads black denominational bodies and many individual black churches to argue from a prochoice or prolife stance. The few denominational statements concerning abortion rely heavily on scriptural interpretations.

It appears that the only public policy voice in which some individual black churches, clergy, and laity may participate when it concerns women's rights is the interfaith initiative of the RCRC. It must not be lost, however, that, while many denominations and denominational judicatories are RCRC members, historically black denominations are not. This lack of black church voice on public policy matters concerning women's rights is troubling. Overcoming the failure to maintain a consistent witness in all categories of civil rights will continue to be an ongoing challenge for African American churches in the coming decades.

Notes

1 Sabrae Yulonne Jenkins and Chung C. Seto, "Women of Color Address Abortion," *The Witness* 72, no. 6 (June 1989): 9.

2 The Hyde Amendment was passed by Congress in 1976. It excludes abortion from the comprehensive health care services provided to low-income people by the federal government through Medicaid. To date, Congress has annually renewed the ban on federal funding for abortion through amendments to annual appropriations bills. Congress has made some exceptions to the funding ban, exceptions that have varied over the years. Currently, Medicaid mandates abortion funding in cases of rape or incest and when a pregnant woman's life is endangered by a physical disorder, illness, or injury. Most state legislatures have followed the federal government's lead in restricting public funding for abortion. At present, fifteen states fund abortions for low-income women on the same or similar terms as other pregnancy-related and general health services. Three of these states (Hawaii, New York, and Washington) provide funding voluntarily; twelve (California, Connecticut, Idaho, Illinois, Massachusetts, Minnesota, Montana, New Jersey, New Mexico, Oregon, Vermont, and West Virginia) provide funding under court order. Courts in four states (Kentucky, Michigan, North Carolina, and Pennsylvania) have refused to accord independent state constitutional protection to the right of reproductive choice for the purpose of ordering the nondiscriminatory public funding of abortion. The thirty-five states that do not provide funding either voluntarily or under court order all pay for abortions for low-income women in cases of life-endangering circumstances, rape, or incest, in accordance with federal law. Some states pay as well in cases of fetal impairment or when the pregnancy threatens "severe" health problems. These states do not, however, provide reimbursement for all medically necessary abortions for low-income women.

3 Provisions adopted by Congress in 1997 may further burden access to abortion services for Medicaid recipients, including those in states with nondiscriminatory funding. Federal law now requires states that use managed-care organizations to administer health benefits to have a contract with those organizations for the added abortion coverage, a contract that is held as distinct from the contract covering other Medicaid services. This adds both an administrative burden and cost to the coverage. In states that fund abortion independently, low-income women's access to abortion may be curtailed by a provision of the Balanced Budget Act of 1997 that permits health maintenance organizations serving Medicaid recipients to refuse to provide counseling or referral for services, such as abortion, to which the organization objects on moral or religious grounds.

4 Jenkins and Seto, "Women of Color Address Abortion," 10; National Black Women's Health Project, "WBWHP Factsheet: African American Women and Abortion," available at http://www.nbwhp.org/abortwom.htm (copy on file with the author). Fewer than 1 percent of pregnant women experience major complications with abortions.

5 See Dorothy Roberts, *Killing the Black Body: Race, Reproduction, and the Meaning*

of Liberty (New York: Pantheon, 1997), 3. See also Charles Murray and Richard J. Herrnstein, *The Bell Curve: Intelligence and Class Structure in American Life* (New York: Free Press, 1994). Murray and Herrnstein take 845 pages to present their arguments on such unreliable premises as that intelligence can be depicted by a single number, the IQ score; that the IQ score can be used to rank people in linear order; and that the score is genetically based and cannot be changed. They claim that race and class differences are largely caused by genetic factors and are not capable of or susceptible to change — they are immutable.

6 Julia R. Scott, "Why Are Black Mothers Dying?" National Black Women's Health Project, available at http://www.nbwhp.org/safemom.htm (copy on file with the author).

7 Lisa Koonin and Jack Smith, "Abortion Surveillance: Preliminary Analysis — United States, 1997," Centers for Disease Control, January 7, 2000, available at http://www.cdc.gov/eop/mmwr/preview/mmwrhtml/mm4851a.htm (copy on file with the author).

8 A more discrete breakdown of the statistics reveals that, of women having abortions in 1972, white women constituted 77 percent (451,805) and black women 23 percent (134,955) and that, of women having abortions in 1997, white women constituted 58.5 percent (693,083) and black women 35.8 percent (424,143).

9 Scott, "Why Are Black Mothers Dying?"

10 Ibid.

11 Roberts, *Killing the Black Body*, 5.

12 Mark Chaves and Lynn M. Higgins, "Comparing the Community Involvement of Black and White Congregations," *Journal for the Scientific Study of Religion* 31, no. 4 (1992): 433.

13 Jacquelyne Johnson Jackson, "Contemporary Relationships between Black Families and Black Churches in the United States: A Speculative Inquiry," in *Families and Religions: Conflict and Change in Modern Society*, ed. William V. D'Antonio and Joan Aldous (Beverly Hills: Sage, 1983), 205.

14 The *A.M.E. Zion Quarterly Review* is an official journal of the African Methodist Episcopal Zion (AMEZ) Church, (AMEZ) which was founded in 1796 in New York City because of the dissatisfaction that blacks felt regarding their mistreatment at John Street Methodist Church. In United Methodist Church, "Our Common Vision" (available at http://www.umc.org/faithinaction/unity/one_voice.htm [copy on file with the author]), it is noted: " 'Zion' was added to distinguish the A.M.E.Z. Church from other African-American Methodist organizations. The church's commission is to witness to the world. The best sermon, act of worship, pastoral care, instruction, theology or charity has no value if it is done in the isolation of a self-congratulating community. A truly Christian church must be dedicated to mission, world evangelism, perfection and human liberation."

15 Claude Christopher, "The Church and Its Social Responsibility," *A.M.E. Zion Quarterly Review* 103, no. 2 (April 1991): 29.

16 Ibid., 29–30, 30–31.

17 Reginald D. Broadnax, "A Biblical Foundation for Choice and the Fallacy of Mortality," *A.M.E. Zion Quarterly Review* 102, no. 4 (October 1991): 39–42, 39.

18 Ibid., 42.

19 The AME Church was formally organized in 1816 from a congregation formed by a group of Philadelphia-area slaves and former slaves who withdrew in 1787 from St. George's Methodist Episcopal Church in Philadelphia because of discrimination. In 1799, Richard Allen was ordained minister of the church by Bishop Francis Asbury of the Methodist Episcopal Church. In 1816, Asbury consecrated Allen bishop of the newly organized AME Church. The AME Church was confined to the Northern states before the Civil War and spread rapidly in the South after the war.

20 *What A.M.E.'s Believe* (Nashville: AMEC Publishing House, 2000), v.

21 Ibid., 43. The committee for this position statement was made up of the Reverends Gregory Grooms, Stephen Singleton, Judy Paul, and Ronnie Brailsford and Miss Gayle Wilson.

22 Ibid., 43–44.

23 Ibid., 44.

24 Established in 1973, RCRC is the voice of prochoice people of faith in the United States. The coalition is made up of more than forty national organizations from eighteen denominations, movements, and faith groups, including the Episcopal Church, the Presbyterian Church, USA, the United Church of Christ, the United Methodist Church, Unitarian Universalist Association, and the Conservative, Humanist, Reconstructionist, and Reform movements of Judaism. It is the only national interfaith coalition for choice. It professes to represent the views of mainstream people of faith, and it seeks to counter what it terms *antichoice* religiously based arguments. It addresses, not only abortion, but also unintended pregnancies, the spread of HIV/AIDS, and adequate health care and economic opportunities for women and families.

25 Religious Coalition for Reproductive Choice, "Breaking the Silence: A Faith Based Model for Adult Dialogue on Sex and Sexuality," available at http://www.rcrc.org/bci/breaking.html (copy on file with the author).

26 For example, a 1997 survey of black youths aged 13–19 reveals that they accounted for 58 percent of adolescent HIV/AIDS cases but only 15 percent of the adolescent population overall. Again, a 1998 survey of students in grades 9–12 revealed that blacks (31.4 percent) were significantly more likely than whites (18.1 percent) or Hispanics (19.6 percent) to have begun having sexual intercourse before age thirteen. That same survey also revealed that blacks (42.4 percent) and Hispanics (31.4 per-

cent) were significantly more likely than whites (22.7 percent) to have been pregnant or to have gotten someone else pregnant.

27 Religious Coalition for Reproductive Choice, "Keeping It Real!" available at http://www.rcrc.org/bci/keeping.html (copy on file with the author).

28 Religious Coalition for Reproductive Choice, "Black Ministers Support Your Right to Choose," available at http://www.rcrc.org/woep/blackpas.html (copy on file with the author). The statement was signed by Edgar L James (AME Church), Carlton W. Veazey (National Baptist Convention, USA), Walter Fauntroy (Progressive National Baptist Convention), Myrtle Francis Hatcher (United Methodist Church), Alma Faith Crawford (United Church of Christ), the Right Reverend Barbara Harris (Episcopal Church), Bernice Powell Jackson (United Church of Christ), Elenora Giddings Ivory (Presbyterian Church, USA), and Daniel Webster Aldridge (Unitarian Universalist Association). It is important to note that only James, Veazey, and Fauntroy are from predominately black denominations.

29 Religious Coalition for Reproductive Choice, "We Remember: African American Women Are for Reproductive Freedom," available at http://www.rcrc.org/pubs/speakout/remember.html (copy on file with the author).

7

AFRICAN AMERICAN CLERGY AND

URBAN SCHOOL REFORM

Desiree Pedescleaux

In a segregated America that denied educational opportunities to African Americans, African American churches provided kindergartens, established libraries, and offered basic classes in reading and writing. More recently, they spearheaded movements to improve the quality of education for black students and to hire black teachers. Fueled by research showing that low expectations held by white middle-class teachers and administrators caused poor performance, black political and church leaders demanded greater control over their children's education. Carmichael and Hamilton strongly stated the case in *Black Power*: "Control of ghetto schools must be taken out of the hands of 'professionals,' most of whom have long since demonstrated their insensitivity to the needs and problems of black children. These 'experts' bring with them middle-class biases, unsuitable techniques and materials; these are, at best, dysfunctional and at worst destructive."[1]

In cities like Atlanta, Baltimore, Detroit, and Washington, D.C., African American ministers played prominent roles in addressing this education crisis. Their involvement was important, for example, in negotiating the compromise that desegregated the Atlanta public schools and provided for the hiring of substantial numbers of African American teachers and the first black superintendent. In Baltimore, African American clergy fought for the hiring of the first black superintendent and mobilized the African American community when he came under attack by a segment of the white community. In Detroit, African American ministers pressed for the desegregation of public schools and fought for the removal of incompetent and racially prejudiced white educators from black schools. And, in Washington, it was African American clergy who mobilized the African American community in opposition to educational tracking and other detrimental practices that disadvantaged black children.

This legacy of involvement in education reform indicates that African American ministers were, indeed, major players in securing black control of these school districts and providing quality education for black youths. However, education reform, particularly urban education reform, is still on the public agenda. Present calls for school reform ring with an urgency not heard since the 1960s:

> Our Nation is at risk. Our once unchallenged preeminence in commerce, industry, science, and technological innovation is being overtaken by competitors throughout the world. . . . [Education is] only one of the many causes and dimensions of the problem, but it is the one that undergirds American prosperity, security, and civility. We report to the American people that while we can take justifiable pride in what our schools and colleges have historically accomplished and contributed to the United States and the well-being of its people, the educational foundations of our society are presently being eroded by a rising tide of mediocrity that threatens our very future as a Nation and a people. What was unimaginable a generation ago has begun to occur — others are matching and surpassing our educational attainments.
>
> If an unfriendly foreign power had attempted to impose on America the mediocre educational performance that exists today, we might well have viewed it as an act of war. As it stands, we have allowed this to happen to ourselves. . . . We have, in effect, been committing an act of unthinkable, unilateral educational disarmament.[2]

This new crisis in education, particularly as it affects black youths, should be of grave concern to all segments of the African American community. In an earlier era, the battles for civil rights and community control of schools prompted African American church leaders to mobilize black communities in cities around the United States. The legacy of involvement by African American ministers and the standing of the black church in the community suggest that African American ministers may, indeed, still be players in education reform. In the current wave of reform, the mobilization of families and communities by African American ministers is crucial in determining the success or failure of school reform. Drawing on interviews conducted in four black-led cities—Atlanta, Baltimore, Detroit, and Washington, D.C.—during the course of the Civic Capacity and Urban Education Project, this essay assesses the role of African American ministers in urban education reform.[3] In each city, interviews were conducted with three types of respondents. *General influentials* (ninety-seven) were individuals who, by position or reputation, were likely to be important actors in local decisionmaking across a range of policy issues not limited to education.[4] *Community-based representatives* (forty-seven) were individuals active in children's advocacy groups, minority organizations, neighborhood organizations, religious organizations, and PTAS.[5] *Education specialists* (sixty-nine) were persons especially knowledgeable about the implementation of school system policies and programs.[6] The essay is also based on detailed analysis of newspaper articles and other secondary sources. Where appropriate, comparisons will be made between the four black-led cities and seven other cities, referred to as *comparison cities*, from the Civic Capacity and Urban Education Project.

The Challenge of Urban Education Reform

American schools are widely regarded to be in serious need of reform. Since the National Commission on Excellence in Education warned in *A Nation at Risk* that "the educational foundations of our society are presently being eroded by a rising tide of mediocrity that threatens our very survival as a nation and a people," numerous reports, articles, speeches, and campaign platforms have declared that an education crisis exists requiring action on a large and dramatic scale.[7] Much of that concern is expressed as a relatively undifferentiated lack of confidence in the performance of public schools. This portrayal of a broad systemic failure—Myron Lieberman goes so far as to insinuate the need for an "autopsy" of public education—is linked to calls for radical structural change, including state takeovers, privatization, and school vouchers.[8] According to another influential analysis, the problem *is* the system; Chubb and Moe argue that the most fundamental causes of poor educational performance "are, in fact, the very institutions that are supposed to be solving the problem: the institutions of direct democratic control."[9]

Such broad-brush critiques of American education and such sweeping dismissals of recent reform initiatives as symbolic or pitifully incremental bolster the claim of conservative analysts that only a radical introduction

of market forces can save education from the stifling confines of public bu-
reaucracy, professional domination, and political manipulation. Yet the data
that Chubb and Moe rely on also make it clear that many American public
schools are doing a good job at providing conditions that are generally conducive to high performance.[10] Since the release of *A Nation at Risk*, American public schools have made substantial progress in exposing students to
more demanding course requirements, and there is accumulating evidence
that steps like these are resulting in improved performance on standardized
national and international examinations.[11] It is plausible to suggest that it is
both possible and important to acknowledge such progress without settling
into complacency or losing sight of the significant problems that remain.

While some public school systems are providing rigorous academic programs and recording achievement gains that allow them to rival private
schools, others clearly are not, and these others are disproportionately con-
centrated in large urban areas with racially and ethnically more heterogeneous populations. Children in urban school districts perform much more
poorly than do children in nonurban school districts on standardized tests
designed to measure educational achievement, and, within urban districts,
minority children and children in high-poverty schools perform more poorly
still. About two-thirds of nonurban students scored at the "basic" level or
higher on the National Assessment of Educational Progress reading, math,
and science tests. In contrast, only about 40 percent of all urban students,
and fewer than one-third of those in high-poverty schools, met this minimal standard.[12] This uneven performance is reflected in public assessments
of education that find that blacks are more likely than whites to say that the
nation's schools overall are doing a good to excellent job but are less likely
than whites to say that about their local school.[13] Two of three blacks and one
of two whites believe that limited access to good education is an important
reason for persistent racial gaps in jobs, income, and housing.[14]

This problem of poor school performance in predominantly black and
Hispanic school districts has troubling implications. Black and Hispanic
youths are a growing proportion of our population. Between the years 2000
and 2020, the white population between the ages of five and thirteen is expected to decline by about 11.2 percent, while the black population between
those same ages is expected to increase by 15.4 percent and the Hispanic
population by 47 percent.[15] While the nation's economy is growing and many

Americans are faring well, large segments of the minority population are in danger of being left behind owing to changes in the economy that fall disproportionately on those who lack high school diplomas and basic employment skills. As Blank observes: "Fundamentally, the demand for less-skilled workers appears to be declining faster than the number of less-skilled workers, and their wages are therefore drawn downward. This trend is related to the increasing internationalization of the U.S. economy, which places less-skilled U.S. workers in competition with less-skilled (and typically lower-paid) foreign workers, and to technological changes that have accelerated the demand for more-skilled workers."[16]

Research on student performance makes it clear that one of the factors important to an individual student's performance is the socioeconomic background of the other children in the school. Nearly two of every three (65 percent) black children in the United States attends a high-poverty school, compared to less than a third (27 percent) of white children, making it clear that the odds are stacked against the educational success of black children.[17] While poor schools are not the sole reason that urban minority youths may lack requisite skills, and while lack of requisite skills is not the sole reason that minority youths might have difficulty finding decent jobs, the evidence, according to Blank, points to the fact that "the best long-term response to the declining demand for less-skilled workers is policy that promotes skill training and effective schooling for today's children."[18]

Human Capital Development and Civic Capacity

Schools are seen as an investment in human capital, that is, as public action to enhance opportunities for less privileged individuals to obtain the knowledge, skills, and discipline needed for full participation in the economic, social, and political arenas of modern life. Although public education is the primary means for developing human capital, families, neighborhoods, churches, and peer groups all provide individuals with opportunities to develop social skills, knowledge, insights, and other forms of information that can enhance their ability to find a place in the mainstream labor market and secure gainful employment. Thus, educational opportunities must be understood, not simply in terms of what transpires in the traditional classroom, but also in terms of the cooperative and complementary activities that enhance a community investment in its youths.[19] According to Stone, once student performance is linked to a broad and informal human capital formation process, a case can be made for realigning the school-community relationship: "In order for the performance of disadvantaged students to be improved, the community needs to contribute to the process, devising specific efforts to enhance the informal development of human capital and facilitate the official educational process." Schools need to reciprocate by enlisting the help of various elements of the community. Indeed, because of schools' limited jurisdiction and capacity, only a conscious and broad-based effort can enrich an otherwise diffuse and deficient process of human capital formation as it works for disadvantaged students.[20]

This emphasis on human capital points to the usefulness of the concept that Clarence Stone has termed *civic capacity*. Building on the regime literature,[21] Stone intends the term to refer to the ability to build and maintain effective alliances among a broad cross section of stakeholders—representatives from the government, business, parents, educators, churches, child advocacy groups, and nonprofit/community-based organizations—that will work toward a collective goal, in this case urban education reform. He also means the term to refer to the extent to which various sectors of the community have developed formal and informal means with which to define common objectives and pursue common goals. Civic capacity does not emerge spontaneously or in response to a single issue; rather, it evolves out of shared experience, purposive interaction, and mutual trust. Indeed, civic cooperation requires trust that all participants will fulfill their obligations. The assumption underlying this concept is that, as institutions, organizations, and individuals in different sectors learn to cooperate and trust one another, they can by acting together accomplish goals that could not be accomplished if they acted separately or competitively.[22]

Civic cooperation can, of course, be built and maintained around purposes other than developing human capital. Such things as economic growth, historic preservation, and addressing homelessness are among the many aims that could be pursued. Stone found, for example, that Atlanta's downtown redevelopment regime was strong because the city's business community formed alliances among themselves, giving them a powerful voice in redevelopment issues. Likewise, the business community formed alliances with the city's black community, especially black elected officials and prominent church leaders.[23]

The concept of civic capacity offers a systemic means with which to pursue education reform. That is, schools must be seen, not as organizations detached from the larger community, but as a collection of relationships. Schools and school reform are unlikely to succeed without the support of and interaction among a broad cross section of stakeholders.[24] And what that means is that, if education is to compensate for social and economic disadvantage, then deliberate efforts must mobilize appropriate resources from a wide range of community sources. Reform must be sustained and systemic.[25]

The concept of civic capacity also emphasizes the importance of politics and coalition building in determining the viability of reform endeavors. The deemphasis of politics is manifested in an overfascination with educational ideas and organizational form. Many proponents of broad structural reforms seem to believe that the solution involves little more than bringing into town an entrepreneurial superintendent with an attaché case full of hot new concepts and a gunslinger's readiness to face down recalcitrant bureaucrats.[26] Similarly, the market metaphor that animates many of the proposals for systemic reform dismisses the importance of collective action in favor of a narrow focus on the behavior of individual households acting as rational consumers.[27] It is reasonable to suggest, however, that there is no route *around* politics. To the contrary, the concept of civic capacity suggests that the prospect for meaningful and sustainable reform depends on lines of conflict and cooperation among a wide array of actors, both inside and outside the educational arena. Building civic capacity—the capacity collectively to set goals and effectively pursue them—calls for exercising political leadership and mastering political skills.

Black Teachers and Black Preachers

African American church leaders continue to play an important role in school issues. Interview data from the larger Civic Capacity and Urban Education Project show that church leaders were more likely to be seen as major players in both general politics and education decisionmaking in black-led cities than in the other cities. Respondents in Atlanta, Baltimore, Detroit, and

TABLE 1 Major City Stakeholders and Players in Education Politics

	Black-led Cities		Other Cities	
	Stakeholders in City Politics	Players in Education Politics	Stakeholders in City Politics	Players in Education Politics
Mayors and country executives	52.9	33.9	46.5	26
City government	56.6	50.8	64.3	47.5
City council	15.4	15.3	15.5	9.0
School board	19.1	42.7	35.7	50.3
School superintendent	14.0	22.6	9.4	20.3
Educators	13.2	10.5	15.5	29.4
Business community	73.5	50	70.0	53.7
Community groups	29.4	25.8	36.6	27.1
Nonprofit community	19.9	18.5	10.3	10.2
Parent organizations	14.0	16.9	10.3	21.5
Unions	9.6	9.7	4.2	3.4
Church groups or church leaders	18.4	11.3	6.6	2.8

Note: This is a condensed version of a table presented in Jeffrey R. Henig, Richard C. Hula, Marion Orr, and Desiree S. Pedescleaux, *The Color of School Reform: Race, Politics, and the Challenge of Urban Education* (Princeton: Princeton University Press, 1999). It reports the percentage of respondents agreeing that actors are either "key stakeholders" or "players" in education politics. Respondents were asked: "What are the key groups in the county . . . by that I mean those that play a major part in decision making? Sometimes people talk about stakeholders. Who would they be in X?" Total adds to more than 100 percent since respondents were allowed to name up to five stakeholders. Respondents were then asked whether education was a specialized arena or had several important players. Those who felt that there were several players (68 percent in black-led cities, 58 percent in other cities) were asked "who they were." Again, total responses add to more than 100 percent since each respondent was allowed to name up to five players.

Washington, D.C., were four times more likely to identify church leaders as major education stakeholders than were respondents in comparison cities (see table 1).

While the particular role played by clergy varies with issue and city, the African American religious community usually opposes school reform if the proposed change is seen as a threat to local control and jobs. Asked why the broader African American community is not more active in demanding

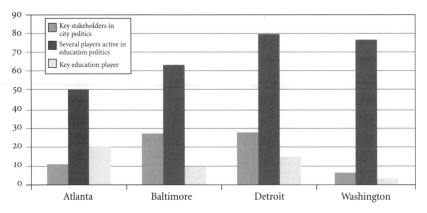

FIGURE 1 Role of Church Groups in City/Education Politics
Note: Figures are given in terms of percentage of respondents identifying church leaders as key stakeholders in city politics, agreeing that education politics has several key players, and, if they agree that education politics has several key players, seeing church groups as key players.

school reform, a Baltimore education consultant suggests: "They ain't mobilized because the preachers ain't gonna let them. See, the preachers got to have their cut. And if the preachers are not adorned then they don't help get their people revved up about any one issue. That's the problem; you got too many of them [who are] corrupt."[28] While this commentator sees corruption and venality as the cementing force, it is plausible to suggest that the failure of the religious community to play a stronger role in demanding better school performance can be traced to a bond between black preachers and black teachers that has deep roots in local history and racial experience.

Figure 1 presents respondents' perceptions of the role of church groups and religious leaders as general stakeholders in local politics and as key players in education-specific decisionmaking. Note that an interesting pattern begins to emerge in which perceived influence in general politics and perceived influence in education politics are not closely linked. Respondents in Atlanta were less likely than were those in Detroit or Baltimore to mention religious leaders when asked about general stakeholders in local politics, but, of those who indicated that education was an open arena with multiple interests involved, they were the most likely (20 percent) to name church organizations and religious leaders as being major players in school affairs.

In Atlanta, churches and ministers were ranked just below business leaders as the most active nongovernment group in education matters. In Detroit and Baltimore, where churches were much more likely to be named as general stakeholders, their involvement in education-specific decisionmaking is relatively less pronounced, only 14 percent of Detroit respondents and 9 percent of Baltimore respondents identifying church leaders as major education players. That lack of involvement is most pronounced in Washington, D.C., where only 3 percent of respondents viewed the clergy as playing a major role in education decisionmaking.

Role of Church Leaders in Education Politics

The data on the proportion of respondents identifying clergy as important actors in general city politics probably understate indirect impact. Katherine Tate's analysis of black electoral behavior indicates that religious institutions are an important organizational resource for disseminating information about elections, encouraging church members to vote, providing individuals a base from which to work with political campaigns, and allowing individuals to contribute to political candidates financially.[29]

Politicians in all four cities recognize the capacity of the churches to mobilize voters. In his study of Atlanta, Clarence Stone found that African American ministers were "important gatekeepers for the black electorate in citywide elections" and "an integral part of the city's electoral politics."[30] A Detroit business leader described African American ministers in the Motor City as "extraordinarily powerful," adding: "I would say the single most powerful organization in Detroit is the Baptist church." In Baltimore, "unified support" from African American church leaders is considered a must for success in any citywide election.[31] "They [i.e., church leaders] may not be able to elect you but they can keep you from being elected," explained a Baltimore business leader. And, in Washington, African American ministers have played a central role in Mayor Marion Barry's electoral coalition.

The key African American preachers in Atlanta, Baltimore, Detroit, and Washington are not only political figures and leaders in the African American community; they are also spiritual leaders and personal friends of black teachers, principals, and school administrators. There is a kind of "holy communion" between prominent African American clergy and the members of their churches whose livelihood is schooling and for whom the school system is a source of wages, professional development, and economic advancement.

In Baltimore, Union Baptist Church, Saint James Episcopal Church, and Bethel African Methodist Episcopal (AME) Church are three of Baltimore's most prominent African American churches, and their congregants include principals, teachers, administrators, and other school system personnel. In Detroit, the Hartford Memorial Baptist Church is a seven-thousand-member congregation whose minister, the Reverend Dr. Charles Adams, was described by one respondent as "a black minister of a huge middle-class church in Detroit, which is supported by many city and school employees." Black professional educators tend to be prominent members of many such churches.

Thus, in Atlanta, Baltimore, Detroit, and Washington, the politics of school reform is not simply a matter of resisting the efforts of business and other civic leaders. An important third party—the black church—typically supports the position of public educators, who are, at best, politically marginalized and, at worst, direct obstacles.[32]

AFRICAN AMERICAN CLERGY AND SCHOOL REFORM IN DETROIT

Detroit's African American ministers play a central role in electoral politics. For example, in the 1970s, through his church, now called the Shrine of the Black Madonna, Rev. Cleage (now known as Jaramogi Abebe Agyeman) created the Black Slate—a list of candidates for elected offices endorsed by the leaders of the church—as a political arm of his church.[33] The other important African American religious organization in Detroit is the Council of Baptist Pastors, its 250 members acknowledged by many observers to be "the most powerful religious leaders" in Detroit.[34] Candidates for mayor, city council member, school board member, and other offices submit eagerly to the Council of Baptist Pastors and the Shrine of the Black Madonna's Black Slate, seeking an endorsement.

African American church leaders in Detroit have supported education-related programs such as Each One, Reach One, an effort by churches to link with schools in their community by opening their buildings to young students before and after school. African American church leaders were also strong proponents of the African American Male Academies. Nevertheless,

Detroit's African American preachers have not used their political clout to push for systemic change within the Detroit Public Schools.

Indeed, a number of Detroit respondents questioned the black clergy's commitment to reforming the public schools. The sentiment seems to reflect that of a former member of the HOPE team[35] who told us that the black clergy were "not necessarily positive." Another school activist described the Reverend Jim Holley, a former president of the Council of Baptist Pastors and a major player in schools and related issues, as "controversial because everybody says he's politically tied in and then some of his motives are not pure." In 1988, shortly after the reform-minded HOPE team won election to the school board, the lame-duck board members attempted to appoint Holley (who opposed the HOPE team) to fill out the remaining term of a school board seat that had become vacant shortly before the elections. According to Rich: "Holley was promoted as the grass-roots candidate [for the vacant post] but seen by the HOPE supporters as a defender of the status quo."[36] Holley's effort failed.

Many of the key members of the Council of Baptist Pastors—Charles Adams, Jim Holley, Frederick Sampson, and Charles Butler (the late Mayor Coleman Young's personal minister)—all lead churches whose members include schoolteachers, principals, school administrators, and others who work for the school system. These ministers opposed many of the reforms instituted by the HOPE team. In the 1992 Detroit school board elections, many African American church leaders joined the Detroit Federation of Teachers and opposed the reelection of the HOPE team. "I knew we were going to lose the election; we were not allowed to come into the churches to campaign," recalled a former HOPE team member.

AFRICAN AMERICAN CLERGY AND SCHOOL
REFORM IN WASHINGTON, D.C.

In Washington, the involvement of the religious community in school politics has been episodic and reactive. While respondents acknowledged that African American ministers played an important political role in the city, they only occasionally mentioned them in terms of education issues. The religious community is seen as being most involved with school issues relating directly to values and behavior. A key foundation executive indicated that, although she worked with them on occasional projects, she did not have a close relationship with leading religious leaders and did not think of them as key actors when it came to generating political support for human capital issues: "Well, I think certainly in D.C. politics, the role of prominent ministers and their ability to deliver votes is absolutely critical to win an election or it used to be. I think in my world here I sort of vaguely know of the power of the church. . . . I sort of know who you would put in a room, but I don't have chatty relationships with any of them and I would almost bet that these, of the other players that we mentioned, don't either." According to an African American minister who *does* want to see the religious community become more involved in school issues: "From the political side, the religious community has always been viewed as a place to get votes, not a place to implement change. Okay. When politicians who would run for office, they sought out the church. But in the implementing of policy, day-to-day policy, it never included the church, or synagogues, or mosques, in any planning or any forethought of that."

African American ministers have spoken out in an organized manner on issues of school prayer, the distribution of condoms in public schools, and the general need to curb violence among the city's youths. Many churches have had a long history of involvement in direct service provision to low-income children and their families, often under contract with the city government; in alliance with other local nonprofits, African American ministers have also spoken out about the need to maintain public funding for such efforts. But, with relatively few exceptions, the organized religious community has not been a force in proactive measures to reform the city's schools. More often, it has led opposition to reforms that are seen as a threat to local control and local jobs. As one African American minister sees it, the religious community found it difficult to maintain the activist role that it adopted in the battle for civil rights and home rule once power was transferred into local hands:

But I think for the black church, major emphasis in the past was put on civil rights, and it was a major, major drive. And due to the composition of the color of the District of Columbia, once home rule stepped in, I mean, we had major, we had mostly African Americans in position. That wasn't such a huge issue, so the church actually kind of sat back after that. . . . And then there's also a notion that grew up with, which was, which has hurt us as African Americans, there was a notion of, there was an unspoken rule that you couldn't criticize your own we can't really say anything about it because it looks like we're fighting amongst ourselves. . . . They gave us, you know, an invitation to their house for a picnic now and then, they gave us a photo opportunity, and that was sufficient. And that was sufficient. We went back and preached the gospel. Communities never got better, the education system went down, and we never held them accountable. So, I, but I think that's changing . . . the churches were very strong in the civil rights movement here, but I think what's happening now is the churches are beginning to say, "we're going to hold you accountable, be 'you' black or white, male or female."

While many Washington, D.C., residents either welcomed or acquiesced in the Control Board's involvement in local and school affairs, a few African American ministers have been the focal points for sharp efforts to resist. Most visible was the Reverend Willie Wilson, leader of the six-thousand-member Union Temple Church. A major Barry supporter, Wilson organized a prayer vigil outside the Control Board offices in June 1996, where he criticized congressional Republicans for "whipping and beating" the city, suggesting that, on the basis of their actions, "maybe their names ought to be Ku Klux Klan." Another key protest figure was George Stallings, the archbishop of the African American Catholic Church, a group he started after breaking away from the Catholic Church in 1989. In announcing his ultimately unsuccessful bid for the Sixth Ward city council seat in December 1996, Stallings linked schools and the race issue indirectly through a powerful symbol of black culture and pride: "Our schools are under siege. Our financial structure is under siege. Home rule is under siege. . . . We need a voice that is forceful on the city council . . . a voice of truth. A voice that will, as Spike Lee said, 'Do the Right Thing.' "[37] While Washington's religious leaders feel that they can speak out forcefully on moral issues, many find that their congregations have much less tolerance for their involvement in more controversial issues. When, for example, the Reverend Albert Gallmon decided to run for the school board, many members of his church, Mount Carmel Baptist, objected. Prompted by the church trustees — some of whom felt he had neglected his duties and failed to consult with the congregation before taking public stands — Gallmon stepped down.[38]

A spokesperson for a coalition of churches noted that the narrow and diverse agendas of many of the city's religious leaders make it difficult for them to take a united stand on complicated issues:

> Clear-cut issues . . . are easier then, clear-cut issues, issues of the moment. It's hard to keep them [the city's religious leaders] focused and sustained on more complicated issues. Unless it's very clear, easy issues, it's hard for them to stay focused and organize. Death penalty. Those are clear and moral issues for the churches. Gambling. . . . Clear and moral issues are easier for them to deal with than long-term, economic, fundamental, bureaucratic change. Obviously, it's easier to galvanize a winning coalition with something that's coming to a vote with definable ends and definable results than long-term neighborhood change, bureaucratic change, governmental change. That's a lot harder. . . . We stay with social, neighborhood, service issues. We avoid some of the larger philosophical debates. All the debates that go on that I couldn't get a consensus on, they don't affect the local. So I keep the churches focused on local issues, and it helps, a lot, to gain consensus.

The failure of African American churches to unite around school reform proposals is also a reflection of division within the religious community. It is hardly surprising that there are some very strong personalities among the district's most visible ministers. Often, these leaders find it difficult to work together. Indeed, some charge that personal ambition rather than the public good motivates them.

AFRICAN AMERICAN CLERGY AND SCHOOL REFORM IN BALTIMORE

African American church leaders in Baltimore continue to be influential in school issues. The fact that only 9 percent of Baltimore respondents named ministers as being key stakeholders in school issues almost certainly understates the role that church leaders play in school issues. A number of respondents indicate that African American clergy were critical in mobilizing for a policy goal. When asked how he would go about building support for an education reform program, a Baltimore Urban League official immediately stated: "I would present it, first of all, to the preachers in this town. The black clergy are a very, very, critical force of mobilizing. The preachers are critical." Black clergy's role in Baltimore's school affairs remained important into the 1990s.

Despite their widely recognized influence, however, church leaders in Baltimore are viewed as being unreliable partners in a school reform coalition. More often, key church groups and influential African American ministers have allied with the school unions and opposed most major school reform initiatives, especially those that threaten local control and jobs. For example, when the decision was made to award EAI (Educational Alternatives, Inc.) a five-year contract to manage nine Baltimore schools, Baltimore United in Leadership Development (BUILD) held a meeting attended by about six hundred supporters to express to city officials its opposition to the experiment.[39] The Interdenominational Ministerial Alliance (IMA) an organization representing approximately 166 black ministers, also opposed EAI. What is instructive is that BUILD and IMA opposed EAI from the outset, long before any independent evaluation of the impact of Tesseract, EAI's innovative curriculum and approach to instruction, on the students and their performance. Indeed, the thrust of the African American church leaders' opposition was similar to that of the Baltimore Teachers Union (BTU): Tesseract represented a potential loss of jobs. An active and influential black minister affiliated with BUILD suggested that EAI could destabilize the city's employment base: "It destroys some of the employment base in the city. Tesseract then has the authority to hire and fire, to reallocate, to reassign employees at will, that's very threatening to a person. That's their livelihood in the school system." When asked about his position if a credible and independent evaluation confirmed that the quality of education and student achievement in the EAI-operated schools improved appreciably, he responded: "We'd still be leery of privatization of a traditional government function."

In 1997, the Maryland legislature adopted a five-year school aid package that would send a billion dollars to the Baltimore schools. The legislation also greatly increased the state's role in the management of the schools. Mayor Schmoke, reluctantly, endorsed the legislation, believing that the increased funds would ultimately benefit the city's youths. The legislation was also supported by a majority of Baltimore legislators. The BTU and the Public School Administrators and Supervisors Association (PSASA) denounced the partnership as a usurpation of local control. BTU opposed provisions in the legislation allowing the restructured school board to reopen contract talks. BTU and PSASA leaders objected to the requirement that certain central office supervisors reapply to the new school board for their old positions.

Baltimore's African American ministers, however, were the loudest critics of the legislation. The Reverend Arnold Howard, president of the IMA, noted that the ministers opposed the legislation because they believed that the amount of additional funds was "not enough" to warrant state oversight of Baltimore's largest municipal department.[40] The Reverend Frank Reid, pastor of Bethel AME (and Mayor Schmoke's stepbrother), also spoke out against the legislation. Paraphrasing a verse from Scripture, Reid asked: "What does it profit a city to gain $254 million and lose its soul?"[41]

For many of the African American ministers, sharing administrative authority of the school system with state officials was the central reason for opposing the legislation. In an open letter to state legislators, the ministers and other community leaders denounced the school aid package as "anti-democratic" and "racial paternalism": "We will not accept Baltimore becoming a colony of the state, with its citizens having no say in the education of their children. African Americans, in particular, have fought a long, hard battle for equality. Over the years, too many paid the ultimate price for community empowerment. We will not stand and allow the gains those people sacrificed and died for to be given away. We have earned the dream of quality education for our children, and local autonomy in decision-making."[42] Howard "Pete" Rawlings, an African American Baltimore legislator who sponsored the school aid package, lambasted the ministers for putting the concerns of adults before the concerns of children: "These folks are being led and fed information by people who do not have the interest of Baltimore children at heart. The interest of the children should be the bottom line."[43]

In June 1997, the new Board of School Commissioners was jointly announced by Mayor Schmoke and Governor Parris Glendening. It is too soon to develop conclusions about student performance. However, the new school board developed a long-range reform plan that includes reducing class sizes in grades 1–3 and establishing "after-school" academies to improve student achievement. The Baltimore City Public Schools (BCPS) launched a major effort to recruit new teachers, including raising the salaries of starting teachers. To help reduce class sizes and staff the after-school programs, hundreds of retired teachers were hired on a part-time basis to tutor students in read-ing and math. In May 1998, following a nine-month search, the school board named Robert Booker, the top financial officer for San Diego County, Cali-fornia, as BCPS's first permanent CEO. An African American, Booker previ-ously worked for the Los Angeles Unified School District as its chief business and financial officer. Booker's experience in financial management reflects the school board's and state officials' desire to improve the management of BCPS dramatically. Booker assumed office on July 1, 1998, promising to in-stitute a series of management and financial changes designed to make the system run more efficiently.

AFRICAN AMERICAN CLERGY AND SCHOOL REFORM IN ATLANTA

Church leaders in Atlanta have been the least engaged in the overall political process of education reform. More often, churches have forged partnerships with specific schools. For some churches, this has been a long-term commit-ment, one that generally entails direct educational services such as tutoring, mentoring, after-school programs, and the like. Systemwide church efforts are virtually nonexistent.

Concerned Black Clergy (CBC), a coalition of 125 churches and mosques representing more than 100,000 congregants, lists some of Atlanta's most prominent ministers as members, including the Reverend Timothy McDon-ald, cofounder of Erase the Board (a grassroots, community-based orga-nization created in 1993 to unseat obstructionist school board members), past president of CBC, and pastor of First Iconium Baptist Church, and the Reverend Gerald Durley, current president of CBC and pastor of Provi-dence Baptist Church. Other ministers noted by respondents include the Reverend Joseph Roberts, Ebenezer Baptist Church, the Reverend Joseph Lowery, former pastor of Cascade United Methodist and past president of the Southern Christian Leadership Conference (SCLC), the Reverend Barbara King, Hill Side Church, and the Reverend C. T. Vivian, a civil rights activ-ist, to name a few. However, the primary focus of CBC and others has been homelessness.[44] Ministers do, however, use their pulpits to get people out to the polls — often without targeting black incumbents.

Some systemwide efforts looked promising after the 1993 school board elections. The Reverend R. L. White was elected president of the local Na-tional Association for the Advancement of Colored People chapter. He alone has a congregation of just over seven thousand. Likewise, the Reverend Joseph Lowery of the SCLC called for a "movement akin to the civil rights struggle of the 1960s to focus attention on the plight of 'miseducated' black youths." Citing tracking and low test scores, he said: "We recognize now what has happened. Until we free our children to have access to quality and meaningful educational opportunities, we will not be able to overcome social ills that plague our communities."[45]

In addition to these promising efforts in 1994, a new interfaith, biracial organization was formed to deal with the city's social ills. ABLE (Atlantans Building Leadership for Empowerment) — composed of seventy congregations and more than nine hundred people — gathered for training sessions and small group meetings to build relationships aimed at developing grassroots political power.[46] The organization had several primary foci, including homelessness, education, and employment. The education focus group worked to develop a curriculum for the Atlanta public schools that highlighted diversity in Atlanta.

Nevertheless, systemwide ministerial- and/or church-organized efforts are virtually nonexistent. For instance, at its "action agenda" meeting in November 1994, ABLE leaders failed to mention the efforts of its education group and focused its efforts primarily on jobs and homelessness. Currently, ABLE has virtually no presence in the movement for education reform. Likewise, the SCLC failed to mobilize the movement it called for. It continues to emphasize a direct service approach to education reform by offering a number of mentoring and after-school programs.

Conclusion

The Atlanta, Baltimore, Detroit, and Washington, D.C., experiences show that, to understand why school reform is elusive, it is necessary to view the politics of reform as a complex multiactor game in which efforts to mobilize or neutralize important third parties play an important role. African American clergy, for example, have personal relationships with many schoolteachers, principals, and school administrators, relationships that encourage them to align with black teachers even when their stance seems at variance with generally accepted notions of good school policies. These bonds between black preachers and black teachers allow school unions to draw on an especially broad and powerful constituency that also includes African American politicians and other black community leaders. The resulting coalition of teachers' unions and organizations representing school administrators and African American churches is very powerful indeed.

Race and racial consciousness sometimes make it easier for teachers and school administrators to rally community support even when their stance seems narrow and reactionary. Often, there is reluctance on the part of many African Americans to criticize other black leaders publicly. Before the schools underwent a racial transition, African American clergy were some of the most vocal advocates for improved educational opportunity for African American youths and for holding teachers and administrators accountable. But, as the political scientist Wilbur Rich has observed, "when blacks took over City Hall, it was difficult to rally people against the black establishment."[47] Indeed, in his study of the development of black social capital and school reform in Baltimore, Marion Orr recently noted: "Given a history of white domination and control, today's African American leaders view recent gains, especially black administrative control over the school system, as long in coming. Past experiences encourage these leaders to cooperate with each other and to guard against losing power they do have. . . . [W]idespread identification with the past struggles of the African American community is a source of power. The distrust these struggles have engendered . . . hamper[s] the formation of significant intergroup social capital."[48]

Prospects for coalition building for school reform in Atlanta, Baltimore, Detroit, and Washington, D.C., are affected by the broader economic and employment environment. Where quality private-sector jobs are increasingly scarce and racial discrimination is still a reality, the employment opportunities available to blacks in the public schools are vital to the stability of the African American community.[49] If jobs are leaving and employment opportunities bleak, the perception that reform initiatives could threaten wages and fringe benefits in the public sector is heightened and likely to engender greater resistance from teachers, principals, and other school system employees. Moreover, the ability of teachers to rally African American clergy, politicians, community activists, and other non–teachers' groups to their side may be greater. School reformers cannot ignore the fact that, in many black-led cities, the public school systems are an important source of jobs, economic opportunity, and social status for African Americans. An important issue in

Atlanta, Baltimore, Detroit, and Washington, D.C., that must be addressed is whether school reformers can improve systemwide performance without destabilizing the historical and racial legacy of the school systems' employment base.

A major obstacle to education reform is, not a lack of ideas or initiatives, but the challenge of building and sustaining a broad coalition for positive change. Case material strongly suggests that racial tension and mistrust have hampered the development of the necessary conditions to support such coalitions. Some of this tension is in part generated by a continuing concern in the African American community over issues of control. Broad-based reform alliances with powerful partners (such as area business elites) are seen as interjecting an element of risk and uncertainty. African Americans may have an unspoken fear that, if power is shared, it will eventually be lost.

Limited experience in Baltimore and Detroit with business-sponsored school compacts gives evidence that such coalitions can function around education initiatives.[50] In each of these cities, a much greater capacity has been activated and sustained in the area of economic development. Atlanta, for example, has a tradition of high and sustained civic capacity as it relates to physical development — the bricks and mortar of the development of the downtown district.[51] However, the involvement of the larger community in systemic education reform has been sporadic. Given the tension and mistrust that are generated by race, there must be a candid and continuing dialogue among all stakeholders. Systemic reform requires an open and frank discussion about issues driven by race. Farkas sees this need in terms of defining a new politics: "There is a critical need for a different kind of political process, one that allows the general interest of communities to prevail over the narrow interests that currently dominate. And more importantly, all parties must never lose sight of the underlying purpose. . . . What we must do to help the children learn. And how we will work together to do it."[52]

In an earlier era of school reform, African American clergy took the lead and mobilized many segments of the black community. Today, they must again take the lead to stimulate the cooperative interactions and build the alliances that are conducive to systemic education reform.

Notes

This essay relies heavily on Jeffrey R. Henig, Richard C. Hula, Marion Orr, and Desiree S. Pedescleaux, *The Color of School Reform: Race, Politics, and the Challenge of Urban Education* (Princeton: Princeton University Press, 1999). I am grateful to my colleagues for the use of this material.

1   Stokeley Carmichael and Charles V. Hamilton, *Black Power* (New York: Vintage, 1967), 59.

2   Ernest Boyer, *High School: A Report on Secondary Education in America* (New York: Harper and Row, 1983), quoted in Marilyn Felt, *Improving Our Schools* (Newton: Educational Development Center, 1985), 1–3.

3   The Civic Capacity and Urban Education Project was an eleven-city study of urban education reform funded by the National Science Foundation. Conducted by a team of political scientists, the study had as its principal investigator Clarence Stone and as its coprincipal investigators Bryan Jones and Jeffrey Henig and was funded by the Education and Human Resources Directorate of the National Science Foundation (grant RED9350139). The team leaders were as follows: for Atlanta, John Hutcheson (Georgia State University), Carol Pirannunzi (Kennesaw State College), and Desiree Pedescleaux (Spelman College); for Baltimore, Marion Orr (Duke University); for Boston, John Portz (Northeastern University); for Denver, Susan Clarke and Rodney Hero (University of Colorado); for Detroit, Richard Hula (Michigan State University) and Alan DiGaetano (Baruch College, City University of New York); for Houston, Thomas Longoria (University of Wisconsin, Milwaukee); for Los Angeles, Fernando Guerra (Loyola Marymount University); for Pittsburgh, Robin Jones (University of Pittsburgh); for Saint Louis, Lana Stein (University of Missouri, Saint Louis); for San Francisco, Luis Fraga (Stanford University); and, for Washington, D.C., Jeffrey Henig (George Washington University). The full results of the Civic Capacity and Urban Education Project were published as Jeffrey R. Henig, Richard C. Hula, Marion Orr, and Desiree S. Pedescleaux, *The Color of School Reform: Race, Politics, and the Challenge of Urban Education* (Princeton: Princeton University Press, 1999).

In Atlanta, Baltimore, Detroit, and Washington, D.C., the formal institutions of local governance have come under the control of African American officials. Blacks became a majority of the population in Washington, D.C., during the 1950s and in Atlanta, Baltimore, and Detroit by the 1970s. By the mid-1970s, black mayors had been elected in Atlanta, Detroit, and Washington. Baltimore, which was the latest of the four to turn into a predominantly black city, was also the latest to elect a black mayor—Kurt Schmoke, who entered office in 1987. All four cities have African American school superintendents, and faculty and administration in the public schools are largely African American.

4 Researchers were instructed to attempt to arrange interviews with the following individuals or their representatives: the mayor; two city council members (if mixed at-large/district, one from each category); city manager or chief administrative officer; two school board members; president or executive director of the chamber of commerce or other major business organization; CEO or personnel director of one of large private employers or officer of a local bank or utility; minority business executive; private industry council (PIC) chair; head of education committee of chamber of commerce or counterpart in another business organization; member of city future commission or strategic planning body; head of teachers union/organization; executive director of United Way; board chair of Black United Fund or other minority charity; board chair or executive director of local foundation; editor/publisher of local newspaper or reporter who covers city hall or education; state legislator from city, preferably on education committee; judge or attorney on desegregation case/issue. Here, as elsewhere, each research team was given considerable discretion in adapting its quota to the idiosyncrasies of its city.

5 Researchers were instructed to attempt interviews with the following individuals or their representatives: head of community-based organization with some concern in area of education and children's issues, preferably from an umbrella organization; two influential religious leaders, at least one of whom should be from a coalition or alliance of religious groups; systemwide PTA officer; head of another parent advocacy group or, if there is no such group, a second PTA officer; education committee chair or other specialist from a good government group (such as the League of Women Voters); three minority organization representatives, spread as appropriate to the city's demographic base, and including at least one from a nonmainline organization; two heads of children's advocacy organizations or day-care advocacy groups.

6 Researchers were instructed to attempt interviews with the following individuals or their representatives: the superintendent; two assistant school superintendents or equivalents; Headstart administrator; Chapter One administrator; police department official with responsibility to address school violence; social services individual who liaisons with schools (e.g., JOBS or preschool); two principals in innovative school or heads of innovative education programs; economic development administrator with education portfolio; school board staff member, preferably someone with institutional memory; education compact administrator or counterpart for school/business partnerships; PIC staff member with education responsibilities; United Way or similar staff member (with preschool or youth development responsibilities); lobbyist for school district in city hall or state capitol.

7 National Commission on Excellence in Education, *A Nation at Risk: The Imperative for Educational Reform* (Washington, D.C.: U.S. Government Printing Office, 1983), 1. Besides *A Nation at Risk*, some of the other commission, foundation, and

public interest group reports include Boyer, *High School*; Education Commission of the States Task Force on Education for Growth, *Action for Excellence* (Denver: Education Commission of the States, 1983); National Governor's Association, *Time for Results: The Governors' 1991 Report on Education* (Washington, D.C.: National Governors' Association, 1987); Research and Policy Committee of the Committee for Economic Development, *Investing in Our Children: Business and the Public Schools* (New York: Committee for Economic Development, 1985); and Twentieth Century Fund, *Making the Grade* (New York: Twentieth Century Fund, 1983). Some of the important analyses by education scholars are Mortimer J. Adler, *The Paideia Proposal* (New York: Collier, 1982); John I. Goodlad, *A Place Called School* (New York: McGraw-Hill, 1984); and Theodore R. Sizer, *Horace's Compromise: The Dilemma of the American High School* (Boston: Houghton Mifflin, 1984). For a good overview of many of the reform proposals, see Philip G. Altbach, Gail P. Kelly, and Lois Weis, eds., *Excellence in Education: Perspectives on Policy and Practice* (Buffalo: Prometheus, 1985).

8   Myron Lieberman, *Public Education: An Autopsy* (Cambridge, Mass.: Harvard University Press, 1993).

9   John E. Chubb and Terry M. Moe, *Politics, Markets, and America's Schools* (Washington, D.C.: Brookings Institution, 1989), 2.

10 Chubb and Moe argue that constraints imposed by higher-level administrators are the critical factor leading to ineffective school performance. While, as Chubb and Moe emphasize, private schools are much less likely than public schools to experience such administrative constraints, their own analysis shows that almost half the schools with low constraint are publicly controlled and that suburban public schools, in particular, often combine low levels of bureaucratic control and high performance (ibid., 170–71). Using much the same data, Valerie E. Lee, Julia B. Smith, and Robert G. Croninger ("Another Look at School Restructuring," *Issues in Restructuring Schools*, Issue Report no. 9 [fall 1997]: 10) make a much more emphatic case that public schools can undertake reforms that will improve achievement.

11 Jeffrey R. Henig, *Rethinking School Choice* (Princeton: Princeton University Press, 1994), chap. 2; David C. Berliner and Bruce J. Biddle, *The Manufactured Crisis* (Reading: Addison-Wesley, 1995); Division of Research, Evaluation, and Communication, Directorate for Education and Human Resources, *Indicators of Science and Mathematics Education, 1995* (Arlington: National Science Foundation, 1996).

12 "Quality Counts '98," *Education Week* 17 (January 8, 1998): 12.

13 Stanley M. Elam, Lowell C. Rose, and Alec M. Gallup, "The 28th Annual Phi Delta Kappa/Gallup Poll of the Public's Attitudes toward Public Schools," *Phi Delta Kappa* 78 (September 1996): 41–59.

14 Lee Sigelman and Susan Welch, *Black Americans' Views of Racial Inequality* (New York: Cambridge University Press, 1991), table 5.3.

15 U.S. Department of Education, *National Center for Education Statistics, Youth Indicators, 1996* (Washington, D.C.: U.S. Department of Education, 1996), indicator 2.

16 Rebecca M. Blank, "The Employment Strategy: Public Policies to Increase Work and Earnings," in *Confronting Poverty*, ed. Sheldon H. Danziger, Gary D. Sandefur, and Daniel H. Weinberg (Cambridge, Mass.: Harvard University Press, 1994), 173.

17 National Center for Education Statistics, *The Social Context of Education* (Washington, D.C.: U.S. Department of Education, 1997), 15.

18 Blank, "The Employment Strategy," 200.

19 See James Comer, *School Power* (New York: Free Press, 1980), and "Home-School Relationships as They Affect Academic Success of Children," *Education and Urban Society* 16 (1984): 323–37; and B. L. Jones and R. Maloy, *Partnerships for Improving Schools* (New York: Greenwood, 1988). For a more thorough discussion of the development of social capital, see James Coleman, *Foundations of Social Theory* (Cambridge, Mass.: Harvard University Press, 1990); and Robert Putnam, *Making Democracy Work* (Princeton: Princeton University Press, 1993).

20 Clarence Stone, "Civic Capacity and Urban Education: A Progress Report on the Second Year of Activity" (George Washington University, 1995, typescript), 3.

21 Clarence Stone is probably the most prolific scholar on regime theory. See, e.g., Clarence Stone, *Regime Politics: Governing Atlanta, 1946–1988* (Lawrence: University Press of Kansas, 1989); and Clarence Stone, Marion Orr, and David Imbroscio, "The Reshaping of Urban Leadership in U.S. Cities: A Regime Analysis," in *Urban Life in Transition*, ed. M. Gottdiener and C. Pickvance (Newbury Park: Sage, 1991).

22 For a more thorough discussion of the concept of civic capacity, see Stone, "Civic Capacity and Urban Education"; and Jeffrey Henig, "Defining City Limits," *Urban Affairs Quarterly* 27, no. 3 (March 1992): 375–95. See also Henig et al., *The Color of School Reform*.

23 Stone, *Regime Politics*.

24 Stakeholders include any group or organization that has a significant interest or stake in public education.

25 Clarence Stone, Jeffrey Henig, and Bryan Jones, "Urban Human Investment and Civic Capacity: A Proposal" (George Washington University, n.d., typescript).

26 One manifestation of this viewpoint is the extraordinarily high turnover among urban school superintendents, whose average tenure lasts only about three years. Most recently, this notion that reform can be readily imposed by a tough-minded outsider has been reflected in attempts by some states (and, in the case of Washington, D.C., the U.S. Congress) to disempower local school boards and superintendents in favor of externally imposed intervention teams.

27 Henig, *Rethinking School Choice*.

28 Unless otherwise indicated, all direct quotations of informants are drawn from tran-

scripts of the interviews conducted in Atlanta, Baltimore, Detroit, and Washington, D.C., for the Civic Capacity and Urban Education Project. All interviews were conducted in person between June 7 and December 1, 1993.

29 Katherine Tate, *From Protest to Politics: The New Black Voters in American Elections* (Cambridge, Mass.: Harvard University Press, 1993). See also Frederick C. Harris, "Something Within: Religion as a Mobilizer of African American Political Activism," *Journal of Politics* 56 (February 1994): 42–68; and Ronald Brown and Monica Wolford, "Religious Resources and African American Political Action," *National Political Science Review* 4 (1994): 30–48.

30 Stone, *Regime Politics*, 167–68.

31 Kevin O'Keeffe, *Baltimore Politics, 1971–1986* (Washington, D.C.: Georgetown University Press, 1986), 95.

32 Henig et al., *The Color of School Reform*, esp. chap. 4.

33 Wilbur C. Rich, *Coleman Young and Detroit Politics* (Detroit: Wayne State University Press, 2003), 82.

34 Carol Hopkins, "Pulpit Power," *Detroit Monthly* (December 1990), 57–61.

35 Three school reformers running in the 1988 Detroit school board elections and their supporters were dubbed the HOPE team—short for Frank Hayden, David Olmstead, and Larry Patrick for Education.

36 Wilbur Rich, *Black Mayors and School Politics* (New York: Garland, 1996), 46.

37 Debbi Wilgoren, "Stallings Seeks Ward 6 Seat," *Washington Post*, December 9, 1996.

38 Laurie Goodstein, "Pastor Quits to Follow Political Call," *Washington Post*, September 1, 1993.

39 Mark Bumster, "Schmoke Facing Challenge Tonight on School Reform," *Baltimore Sun*, July 20, 1992.

40 Jean Thompson, "Ministers Join PTA Group in Opposition to Giving Up Control of Baltimore Schools," *Baltimore Sun*, March 26, 1997, C5.

41 "Two Ministers Join Effort to Defeat City Schools Deal," *Baltimore Sun*, April 1, 1997, B3.

42 The open letter ran on p. A1 of the April 5, 1997, edition of the *Baltimore Sun*.

43 Tony White, "Community Leaders Oppose School Settlement," *Baltimore Afro-American*, April 5, 1995.

44 See Harvey Newman, "Black Clergy and Urban Regimes: The Role of Atlanta's Concerned Black Clergy," *Journal of Urban Affairs* 16 (1994): 23–33.

45 Hollis R. Towns, "A New Movement: Lowery Calls for Education Reform," *Atlanta Journal Constitution*, May 13, 1996, B7.

46 "New Interfaith Group Begun," *Atlanta Journal Constitution*, March 16, 1994.

47 Rich, *Black Mayors and School Politics*, 150.

48 Marion Orr, *Black Social Capital: The Politics of School Reform in Baltimore, 1986–*

1998 (Lawrence: University Press of Kansas, 1999), 192. See also Henig et al., *The Color of School Reform*; and Clarence Stone et al., *Building Civic Capacity: The Politics of Reforming Urban Schools* (Lawrence: University Press of Kansas, 2001).

Note that civic capacity can be thought of as a category of social capital.

49 William Julius Wilson, *When Work Disappears: The World of the New Urban Poor* (New York: Knopf, 1996).

50 See Richard Hula, Richard Jelier, and Mark Schauer, "Making Educational Reform: Hard Times in Detroit, 1988–1995" (paper presented at the meeting of the Urban Affairs Association, Portland, Oreg., May 3, 1995).

51 See Stone, *Regime Politics*.

52 S. Farkas, "Divided within, Besieged Without: The Politics of Education in Four American School Districts: A Report from the Public Agenda Foundation, Prepared for the Charles Kettering Foundation" (New York: Charles Kettering Foundation, 1993).

8

END OF A MIRACLE? CRIME, FAITH, AND

PARTNERSHIP IN BOSTON IN THE 1990S

Christopher Winship

The 1990s was a remarkable decade for Boston. Not only was it a period of nearly unprecedented economic prosperity, but it was also one of historically low crime rates and unusually good police-community relations. Most dramatically, the number of homicides plummeted over the decade. Whereas there had been 152 homicides in 1990, there were only 31 in 1999. Much of the drop occurred for individuals twenty-four years of age and younger. Whereas in this age group there were 73 homicides in 1990, there were only 15 in 1999 and 2000. For the twenty-nine-month period ending in January 1998, there were no teenage homicide victims.[1] Thus the so-called Boston Miracle.

Much less discussed, though perhaps equally miraculous, is that in the 1990s the police department formed a partnership with a group of inner-city black ministers—the Ten Point Coalition—directed at dealing with the problem of youth violence. This is remarkable at two different levels. First, the relationship between the department and one of three core ministers in the coalition, the Reverend Eugene Rivers, was, in the early 1990s, openly and highly inimical. Second, and more generally, Boston's race relations have historically been highly antagonistic. The fact that the police and any group of black citizens would be willing to work together is extraordinary.[2]

Not surprisingly, Boston's achievements have received considerable national attention, cumulating in a cover story in *Newsweek* on June 1, 1998. The cover of that issue pictured one of the Ten Point Coalition's key leaders, Reverend Rivers. The story inside detailed both how a group of black inner-city ministers had first come to work together as a coalition and then come to work with the police in dealing with the problem of gang-related youth violence.[3]

To date, the new century has not been so kind to Boston. The number of homicides there rose to thirty-eight in 2000 and sixty-eight in 2001, an increase of over 100 percent since 1999.[4] An obvious question, then, is whether the so-called Boston Miracle has, in fact, ended.

I answer this question by breaking it down into several pieces. I first examine whether anything miraculous did, in fact, occur in Boston during the 1990s. The conventional wisdom is that what was miraculous was that homicide rates dropped 80 percent over the decade. Although this drop was historically unprecedented, other cities and the nation as a whole experienced large drops in their homicide rates as well. This, then, raises the question whether the policies of the Boston Police Department were specifically responsible for the decline. I will argue that, although the evidence is mixed, the weight of the data strongly supports the contention that those policies have been important.

Next, I present a brief overview of the historical context of the events of the 1990s, examining the police and crime situation as well as race relations more generally. I then consider the events of the 1990s themselves, focusing on, not only trends in crime, but also changes in the relationship between the police and inner-city residents. Specifically, I discuss the partnership that developed between the police and the Ten Point ministers as well as how racial politics in Boston changed over the decade. Then I move on to the causes of the drop in Boston's homicide rate and whether the achievements of the 1990s have been lost. I conclude by discussing Boston's prospects for the future.

Historical Context

Like many major cities, Boston saw a rapid surge in drug activity in the late 1980s with the development of crack markets. As also occurred elsewhere, the new drug markets brought increased violence as gangs sought to establish control over their geographic areas and to maximize their market shares.[5] Not surprisingly, the number of homicides in Boston erupted during the 1980s, going from a previously stable level of approximately 80–100 per year to 152 in 1990. This increase was due almost entirely to increased youth violence, with the number of homicides involving individuals under twenty-four going from approximately 30 per year in the mid-1980s to 72 in 1990. The increase

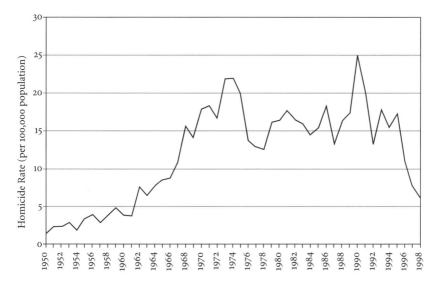

FIGURE 1 Trends in Homicide Rates, Boston, 1950–98

was also almost entirely due to gun-related homicides. Most of this increase also appears to be gang related, though further analysis is needed.[6]

Figure 1 shows the long-term trends in the homicide rate from 1950 to the late 1990s. At first, police department policy was to deny that Boston had a gang problem. However, the fact that shots were being fired on a nightly basis, and that there were multiple shootings and a host of funerals, eventually made it impossible for the department to continue to deny that there was a gang problem. After the number of shootings peaked in 1990, Boston adopted a heavy-handed strategy of policing. The homicide rate dropped, but, because of events in the immediate past, the policy could not be sustained.[7]

In 1989, Carol Stuart, a pregnant white woman, was shot and killed as she and her husband returned from Lamaze class. The husband was also shot and nearly died of his wounds. He described the assailant as a young black male. Given the tensions surrounding the sharply escalating levels of youth violence in the city, it is perhaps not surprising, though certainly not acceptable, that the police aggressively investigated the crime, constantly stopping young black males for questioning. At one point, the police had even arrested a suspect. In the end, however, it turned out to be the husband, not a black assailant, who had murdered Carol Stuart. The primary motivation had been an insurance policy. The husband had shot himself in order to cover up the crime. He jumped off Boston's Tobin Bridge before he could be arrested.[8]

Any event such as the Carol Stuart murder and its mishandling by the police would have the potential to inflame racial tensions in any city. Because of Boston's particular history, this particular murder had dramatic effects. First, Boston was still in the process of recovering from the previous decade of racial protest and violence that erupted over court-mandated school busing. Busing had split the city in two as the courts and the white school board fought over whether the policy would ever be implemented. When it was put into effect, there were frequent racial confrontations, and black children were repeatedly attacked on their way to school. Although by the mid-1980s efforts were being made to heal the racial divide, the wounds were still deep.[9]

In the mid-1990s, Boston also had to deal with a series of potentially volatile racial issues. With respect to the police department itself, there were at least three difficult situations. First, in March 1994, there was the death of a retired black minister, Accelyne Williams. In the process of carrying out a drug bust with a SWAT team, the police broke into the wrong apartment—Reverend Williams's. Williams became hysterical, had a heart attack, and died.[10] During the following year, Anthony Cox, a black undercover cop, was mistaken for a fleeing suspect and caught and beaten by a racially mixed group of police.[11] Also in 1995, an assistant district attorney, Paul McLaughlin, was shot and killed as he sat in his car at a subway stop on his way home from work.[12] Eventually, it was determined that the killer was a notorious black gang member. Each of these incidents received considerable attention in the press. Each could have resulted in racially explosive situations. Instead, the police department and the Ten Point ministers worked together to ensure that each case was properly investigated and that those responsible were held accountable.[13]

More broadly during the 1990s, Boston had to deal with other racially sensitive issues. When the Boston City Hospital was sold to Boston University, there was considerable concern that it would no longer adequately serve the needs of Boston's inner-city community.[14] Most potentially contentious was a 1996 effort supported by one of Boston's key black politicians, Diane

Wilkerson, among others, to have Boston's school board revert back to being elected. The school board had been the locus of the fiery busing controversy of the previous decade.[15] In 1989, the then mayor, Ray Flynn, at the insistence of a different group of black ministers, had led a legislative effort to have the school board be appointed. In the subsequent eight years, although Boston's schools were still quite weak and faced many challenges, education issues had not been defined primarily in racial terms. In both the case of Boston City Hospital and that of the school board, the Ten Point Coalition played a central role in working out a resolution in a way that minimized racial hostility and that was beneficial to Boston's inner-city minority community. In each case, consensus was reached by avoiding defining the issue as essentially racial.[16]

In sharp contrast to the situation prevailing in the 1970s and 1980s, in the 1990s political and policy issues were not defined and debated in racial terms. Boston changed from a city with a reputation for being one of the most racist in the country to a city with a working multiracial coalition. Some might argue that the Ten Point ministers have sold out and that there are many issues in Boston that should be racially contested. For better or worse, however, Boston has gone through a radical transformation in how it deals with race and politics. A second dimension of the Boston Miracle, then, has been the development of a multiracial coalition between the Ten Coalition ministers, the police, and city government more generally and the resulting dramatic transformation in the way in which Boston deals with racially sensitive political issues.

Another challenge faced by Boston at the beginning of the 1990s was the competency of the police. As had been true throughout much of Boston's history, the upper levels of the police department had been staffed through cronyism. The department lacked professionalism and had a reputation of being unconcerned with improvement.[17] The Carol Stuart murder was the catalyst needed to set off a public outcry over the quality of the department. An eight-part series disparagingly entitled "Bungling the Basics" that ran in the *Boston Globe* April 7–10, 1991, unmercifully critiqued the department's day-to-day procedures. Further pressure was put on Mayor Flynn to act when, in the summer of 1991, a Dorchester teenager was fatally shot by a Boston police officer and the department was slapped with a $1 million wrongful-death suit.[18] The mayor was then forced to appoint a commission to investigate the police department.[19] This commission, headed by a Republican, the former Nixon Watergate counsel Charles St. Clair, issued a broad-ranging and very damning report stating that the only way to reform the department was to fire the police commissioner, Mickey Roache.[20]

Roache was not, in fact, fired.[21] Rather, in February 1992, William Bratton was brought in as Roache's second in command and given the mandate to create a professionally oriented police department. Bratton did become commissioner in July 1993, but, by October of that year, he had effectively left to become the New York City police commissioner.[22] Although his tenure in the Boston Police Department was short, Bratton had had an important impact—he had started a process of change. He also had the wisdom to appoint Paul Evans, the man who would succeed him as commissioner, as his second in command. Not only was Evans a favorite of the police union, but he also had a strong commitment to working closely with the community. Reform in the department would proceed under the dual banners of professionalism and community relations.[23]

What Miracle?

Whereas Boston began the 1990s with the racial animosities of the past rekindled and its police department under broad attack, it ended the decade as a model for effective crime control based on a community-policing model (San Diego would be another American city to have a strong claim to this title). As already noted, homicides had declined by 80 percent during the 1990s. More remarkably, as time went on, a key component of the effort to deal with youth violence was a partnership between the police department and a group of black inner-city ministers known as the Ten Point Coalition. Not only did homicides drop precipitously, but complaints against police also dropped by over 60 percent during the 1990s.[24]

The Ten Point Coalition was formed after the May 1992 tragedy at the Morning Star Baptist Church in Mattapan, one of the three core Boston inner-city neighborhoods. During a funeral for a gang member, members of another gang entered the church and stabbed a gang member multiple times. The minister fell on the intended victim in order to protect him from further harm. Pandemonium broke out, and four hundred individuals attempted to flee the church.[25]

The Morning Star Baptist Church incident was a wake-up call to many African American clergy that they needed to get involved in the life of the streets.[26] And so the Ten Point Coalition was created. Although, since the coalition's inception, the number of its members has varied from forty-five to seventy-two, at its core for most of the 1990s have been three ministers — the Reverends Jeffery Brown, Raymond Hammond, and Eugene Rivers.[27] In the past, Rivers had a very hostile relationship with the police. He was quoted in the *Globe* series cited above making very derogatory comments about the police and was generally known as a "cop basher."[28] He reports that, for many years, the police were convinced that he was one of the major drug dealers in Boston's inner city. More generally, the early 1990s were a nadir in the relationship between the police department and Boston's black community.[29]

The Ten Point Coalition did not initially work directly with the police, which is hardly surprising given the difficult relationship that existed between the department and Rivers. What is surprising is that the partnership between the groups became one of the core components of the effort to deal with the problem of violence, particularly youth violence, in the 1990s. This partnership continues to this day. This was a second miracle that occurred in Boston in the 1990s. The story of how it occurred is complex and cannot be detailed here.[30] The short version is that, over time, both police and ministers came to realize that they had a common goal — "to keep the next kid from getting killed" — and that their efforts could complement each other. The relationship between the police and Ten Point became formalized when, toward the end of 1996, the ministers became regular participants a series of "gang forums" that the police had initiated earlier in the year as a part of a citywide strategic plan to deal with youth violence.[31] Gang members would be "invited" to the forums. The police, ministers, and other individuals from various criminal justice and social service agencies would then demand that these young people stop their gang banging, promise that, if they did, they would help them out in any of a variety of ways (school, jobs, family, etc.) but that, if they did not, they would work as hard as they could to see them put in jail since they were a danger both to themselves and to the community and the last thing that the ministers wanted to do was preside over their funeral. The police presence in these meetings was critical for letting these young people know that the ministers meant business. And, in fact, a number of gang members who continued gang banging were sent to jail."[32]

Whose Miracle?

As noted above, the media have given the Boston Police Department's policy and its partnership with the Ten Point Coalition the majority of the credit for the sharp decline in homicides that occurred during the 1990s. This claim is made nowhere more strongly than on an extensive website created by the Boston Police Department.[33] This multiple-page site provides the official version of the Boston story. A broad set of excerpts from statements by numerous individuals — patrolmen, ministers, street workers, and police brass — is offered, as is detailed information on the accomplishments of the police department and its work with the Ten Point ministers. The website appears to contain more than a hundred separate pages. It is essentially a book on the Web.

Whether the Boston police strategy is, in fact, responsible for the dramatic drops in homicide, particularly youth homicide, observed in the 1990s is difficult to determine. There are arguments on both sides. Arguing against the importance of policing policy is the fact that homicide rates fell significantly across the country in the 1990s and dramatically in other cities than Boston. Figure 2 shows the trends in the homicide rates for ten other cities.[34] As can be seen, dramatic drops in homicide rates occurred over the 1990s in Detroit, Dallas, Houston, Los Angeles, New York, San Antonio, and San Diego. In some cases — New York and San Diego in particular — dramatic drops occurred in cities that had adopted innovative policing policies, though policies distinctly different from those adopted in Boston. In the other cities, however, there were no explicit changes in policing policies that might account for the observed drops in homicide. Also note that, in some cities (Chicago, Phoenix), there was little or no drop. This is also the case in other cities not shown in the figure, such as Las Vegas, Baltimore, Washington, D.C., and San Jose.[35]

The fact that a number of cities experienced large drops in homicide rates, but that others didn't, suggests that there was a set of processes shared by some, but not all, cities. That is, the drop in Boston may simply be a function of processes common to other cities. Alternatively, it is certainly possible that rates would not have dropped, or at least dropped to the extent that they did, without the innovative policies adopted in Boston.

The strongest evidence that the Boston strategy caused the observed drop

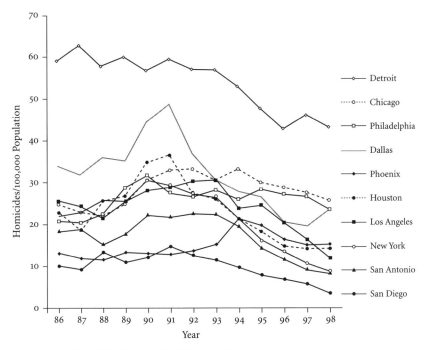

FIGURE 2 Homicide Trends for Various Cities, 1986–98
Note: Reprinted with the permission of Cambridge University Press.

in homicide comes from a paper by Anthony Braga and his colleagues at Harvard's Kennedy School that explicitly evaluates the impact of the Boston program. The key piece of analysis is reported in figure 3, which shows the monthly homicide rate for individuals age twenty-four and younger from June 1991 through May 1998. The major program implemented by the Boston Police Department was an effort named Operation Ceasefire, an inter-agency problem-oriented policing intervention that tightly focused criminal justice and social service attention on a small number of chronically offending gang-involved youths who were responsible for a majority of the city's youth violence problem. The forums described above were a key part of this program.

Operation Ceasefire was initiated in June 1996. As can be seen in figure 3, there is a 63 percent reduction in the monthly youth homicide rate precisely at this point. Braga et al. investigate the robustness of their finding by estimating multivariate models that allow them to control for other variables that

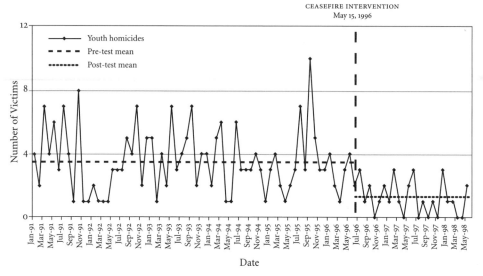

FIGURE 3 Monthly Counts of Youth Homicides in Boston
Note: Reprinted by permission of Sage Publications.

could potentially have affected the youth homicide rate. In addition, they examine data from other cities to see whether there is any evidence of a break in youth homicide similar to that observed for Boston in 1996. Neither analysis provides any evidence that the reduction in the Boston rate is due to factors other than Operation Ceasefire.[36]

What are we to conclude? There is little doubt that the Braga et al. analysis provides strong evidence that Operation Ceasefire reduced the youth homicide rate in Boston. Two concerns remain, however. First, how do we reconcile the drops in homicide in other cities with the claim that it was the Boston policy that specifically reduced that city's homicide rate? Second, how much of the overall credit for the 80 percent drop in homicide does the Boston policy deserve? In another paper from the Kennedy School group, Kennedy and Braga examine what they call the *epidemic* of youth homicide that occurred in Boston during the late 1980s and early 1990s. They conclude in part that "the epidemic was contained largely within Boston's young black male population," that "virtually all the increase in homicide victimization was firearm victimization," that the epidemic was "consistent with a picture of growing and increasingly disorderly drug markets involving young people," and that "youth associated with firearms . . [had] extensive criminal records."[37]

If Kennedy and Braga are correct that disorderly drug markets were the initial cause of the youth gun violence, this may allow us to reconcile the observed effects of the Boston policing strategy and the observed decreases seen in other cities that did not adopt similar policies. Just as drug markets and the streets more generally are likely to experience periods during which they become more disorderly and more violent, they are also likely to experience periods during which they become more orderly and less violent. Orderliness is likely as markets and other activities move off the street and/or implicit understandings are reached as to who controls which neighborhoods.[38] If this is correct, then we would expect gun violence to subside as the streets would no longer be sites of contestation. One hypothesis suggests that the Boston policing strategy may have reduced homicide rates by pushing gangs off the street and causing drug markets to move indoors earlier and to a greater extent than would have occurred otherwise. In other cities, gangs and drug markets may have moved indoors over time as well, but perhaps more slowly and not to nearly as significant a degree. This would be consistent with the fact that, in most other cities, youth homicide rates did not fall nearly as fast or to as great a degree as they did in Boston. The one notable exception is New York, which also adopted a set of policies that made it very difficult for gang and drug activity to continue on the streets.

But how much of the overall drop in youth homicide can be attributed to the Boston policy? Braga et al.'s analysis suggests that most of it can be, but that a sizable drop might have occurred after June 1996 even in the absence of Operation Ceasefire is also consistent with the Kennedy School group's findings. An analogy might be an expanding balloon that is popped with a pin. In a real sense, the pin caused the balloon to pop. Yet, left alone, the balloon might also have eventually deflated, achieving the same result. What remains unclear is what would have happened in the absence of Operation Ceasefire.

What the Boston Police and the Ten Point Coalition clearly deserve credit for is their decision to work together to deal with the problem of youth violence and the effects that this has had on police-community relations specifically and racial politics in Boston more generally. As detailed above, because they did decide to work together, Boston has been able to deal with a number of incidents and issues, both within and outside the criminal justice system, that could have been racially explosive. To understand what might have occurred had they not decided to work together, one need only look south to New York City. New York's homicide rate dropped nearly as much in the 1990s as Boston's. However, New York pursued a heavy-handed form of policing under the banners of fixing broken windows and of zero tolerance.[39] What this meant was that young minority males were frequently stopped and, from their perspective, harassed. Furthermore, when police mishaps such as the Diallo shooting or the Louima assault occurred, there has been enormous racial protest.[40]

Is the Miracle of the 1990s Over?

As noted earlier, homicides shot up in Boston from an all-time low of thirty-one in 1999, to thirty-nine in 2000, to sixty-eight in 2001. Although the figure of sixty-eight murders is still below the historic level of eighty to a hundred in the several decades prior to the mid-1990s, it does raise the question whether the miracle of the 1990s is over. More important, it raises the question whether the Boston approach is still effective.

In his farewell speech as mayor of New York, Rudy Giuliani, ever sensitive to criticism of his police department (and, perhaps, because of the historic competition between Boston and New York in terms of baseball and so many other areas of life), declared his city's methods "triumphant." Giuliani used as evidence the fact that, in 2001, the homicide rate had risen dramatically in Boston but fallen slightly in New York. Many in the Boston establishment bridled at his remarks and the implicit assumption that Boston's miracle was over or, even worse, had never occurred.[41]

The issue of the comparative effectiveness of New York's and Boston's policing policies, however, goes beyond civic pride. It speaks to the question of how our cities should best be policed. Interestingly, as noted earlier, William Bratton was police commissioner of both cities at different times during the 1990s and deserves some, if not much, of the credit for changes in the 1990s in both departments.[42] Under his leadership, both departments moved to a more proactive form of policing where the goal was, not simply to solve crimes after they occurred, but also to prevent crime from happening in the first place. In addition, both cities set up procedures for identifying crime hot spots where police would intervene immediately and aggressively.

Despite these similarities, there are also critical differences in the two cities' policing philosophies. Boston has worked very hard to develop a program that is community friendly, particularly with regard to its inner-city residents.[43] The cornerstone of this effort has been the Ten Point Coalition. (Both the Coalition and partnership will be considered further below.) New York, however, has seen the authority of police officers as residing in their professional status. As such, police and the policies they pursue are determined by the police hierarchy, and, significantly, community involvement in decisionmaking is eschewed. As a result, when mishaps and tragedies involving the police occur in New York, there has been enormous protest by the minority community over police practices.

In part, the question of which city has a better policing policy has implicitly become a debate about morality as much as a debate about effectiveness. The legitimacy of the Boston approach is based on its police department working with the community, strikingly with a group of black ministers. The legitimacy of the New York approach is founded, first, on the relationship between the police and the state and, second, on the approach's effectiveness. The fact that Giuliani, who had just been named *Time* magazine's man of the year, would comment on the ineffectiveness of Boston's policing practices in his farewell address to the public is remarkable. It indicates how much is at stake — both politically and morally — in the support for policing policies that involve very different postures with respect to a city's minority community.

The question whether the Boston model is flawed raises the question whether effective policing policy can be community oriented and friendly. Although one could certainly imagine other community-friendly approaches than Boston's, the failure of the Boston model is bound to have significant political consequences. Specifically, it is likely that that failure will be used by some to justify more heavy-handed approaches to dealing with violence in the inner city.

Providing a satisfactory answer to these questions is difficult given that we have observed a large increase in homicides for only a single year. As can be seen in figure 1 above, the homicide rate in Boston varies considerably over time, both on a year-to-year basis and over longer-term cycles. A one-year increase does not make a trend. Without knowing what will occur in the future, it is difficult to know whether 2001 is an aberration or the beginning of a long-term upward increase in Boston's murder rate.

Despite this caveat, a number of observations provide insight into the causes of the large increase in 2001. In contrast to the upsurge in the homicide rate that occurred in 2001, the number of crimes committed with firearms (homicide, robbery, and aggravated assault) increased only modestly from 1,096 to 1,212, a change of a little less than 11 percent. More generally, the perception among police, ministers, and street workers is that there has been not a substantial increase in day-to-day street violence. How do we reconcile these observations with the large increase in homicide rates?

Reports from police officers and street workers indicate that many more shootings are occurring indoors, that the shootings appear to be premeditated, and that specific individuals have been targeted. Furthermore, much of the increase has occurred in a single age group. In 1999, 2000, and 2001, the numbers of homicide victims were, respectively, five, seven, and ten among those aged fourteen to nineteen; nine, ten, and fourteen among those aged twenty to twenty-four; and eleven, ten, and nineteen for those aged thirty-three and older. In sharp contrast, during the same period, the numbers of homicide victims among those aged twenty-five to thirty-two increased from four in 1999, to ten in 2000, to twenty-two in 2001.[44] What is driving these large increases in homicides in this particular age group?

There had been in 2000 and 2001 a large increase in the number of felons returning to the community from prison—as many as 250 each month.[45] Many of these individuals were previously involved in the gang conflicts. The belief is that many recent killings involve retribution and/or attempts to re-take lost drug markets. Whereas the early 1990s might be characterized as a period of hot-blooded street shootings, 2001 has seen mostly targeted, cold-blooded murders.

If homicide rates fell in Boston during the 1990s because relationships between gangs, within gangs, and among drug dealers became more stable, the fact that they have increased more recently may well mean that those relationships are being destabilized now by the large increase in returning felons, the upsurge in the number of young people generally, and the flood of guns into the inner city. And, if those relationships are, in fact, being destabilized, that may explain why homicide rates have increased, not only in the twenty-five- to thirty-two-year-old age group, but in adjacent age groups as well. External shocks to the system may well be undermining the peace that was established in the 1990s, resulting in increased homicides in all age groups.

All this suggests that Boston is faced with a new type of problem. Whereas the problem individuals of the 1990s were often young, immature, and hot-blooded and had never been to prison, those of 2001 are prison-hardened criminals who are returning to the community after having acquired a jail-house education in how to employ violence effectively. A simple message from ministers and police to knock off the "noise" or go to prison is likely to have little effect, especially since these individuals no longer fear prison. Rather, what is needed is a focus on "impact players" — those seen "as having a negative effect in neighborhoods regarding gang activity, drug trafficking, and firearm violence"[46] — in order to identify them and, if they are committing crimes, ensure that they are incarcerated as quickly as possible.

The Response

As one might expect, Boston is working hard to deal with its new violence problem. The police department has launched what it calls Boston Strategy II, the key feature of which is "the collaboration and partnerships between the police, community, and clergy." This new effort has three components: enforcement; intervention; and prevention. Enforcement involves warrant apprehension efforts, efforts to disrupt firearm trafficking, and gang and drug investigations. Intervention involves prison reentry programs run jointly by police, clergy, and individuals from other agencies; the revitalization of an earlier police/probation program, Operation Nitelite; the revitalization of Operation Ceasefire; and the creation of Operation Homefront, which involves home visits to high-risk individuals by teams of police and clergy. Prevention involves a host of new and existing programs, including youth service officers, summer jobs, a junior police academy, and summer camps. In addition, forums at which police and clergy meet with gang members in an attempt to resolve their conflicts have been revived, and sweeps have been conducted targeting the members of a particular gang, who have been arrested — often on federal charges — on drug and gun charges.[47]

Looking toward the Future

Given the Boston Police Department's mission statement — "We dedicate ourselves to work to fight crime, reduce fear and improve the quality of life in our neighborhoods. Our Mission is Neighborhood policing"[48] — it would seem superfluous to ask whether its partnership with the clergy of the Ten Point Coalition will continue to be important. It is, however, meaningful to ask whether that partnership will be important beyond its PR value.

A number of events that occurred in the winter of 2002 while this essay was being drafted have provided an important test of whether Boston will rise to the occasion and respond aggressively and cooperatively to the new violence that it faces.

On January 24, three-year-old Malik Andrade-Percival was shot dead in his home. His father Ian Percival had ten years earlier been involved in the infamous Morning Star Baptist Church incident described above. The shooter was dressed in a police uniform. He had knocked on the door at approximately nine in the evening, saying that he had been called to investigate a disturbance. The shooter and Ian Percival scuffled, and, in the process, little Malik was shot and killed.[49] The public claim was that the shooter, knowing that the father was a major drug dealer, planned to rob him of drugs and money.[50] The word on the street, however, was that the shooter had coldly planned to execute the father in front of his family.[51] In ways analogous to the Morning Star Baptist Church incident, this killing has become a rallying cry for the clergy and Boston more generally to reengage in working to deal with the problem of inner-city violence.[52] Boston's newspapers ran stories on the incident for weeks, covering not only the shooting and the investigation but the boy's funeral as well. On February 3, a "peace march" was held demanding an end to the violence.[53]

On February 11, a sixteen-year-old brazenly shot at a city bus from an MBTA train station during the afternoon rush hour.[54] On February 13, at four in the morning, Willie Murray, a thirty-seven-year-old black man, was shot and killed while sitting in the driver's seat of his car by a black Boston police officer, Shawn West. While there is typically one killing of a civilian by a police office in Boston in a year, this was the sixth in fifteen months. As they are in many police shootings, the circumstances in this case were unclear. The only witness was an individual in the backseat of Murray's car. It is said that West has claimed that his life was threatened by Murray's actions and that the shooting was, therefore, justified.[55]

The *Boston Globe* immediately raised the question — one almost certainly on the minds of many community members, black and white — whether the

Murray killing indicated that the police were using excessive force in the inner city.[56] The police commissioner, Paul Evans, responded to these charges by attending a joint meeting—held the day after the shooting—of the Boston Ten Point Coalition and the Black Ministerial Alliance, Boston's more traditional organization of African American churches.[57] Speaking at the meeting, Evans explained what he knew about the circumstances of the shooting, indicated that the incident was being thoroughly examined by internal investigations, suggested that it might not have been justified, and recognized the concern of the clergy as well as the city generally about the recent high numbers of killings of civilians by police officers. The approximately thirty-five African American clergy attending the meeting had no questions for the commissioner.[58]

The police department did eventually send the case to a grand jury, essentially admitting that the shooting was not justified. Five days later, the *Boston Globe* published an op-ed piece by the Reverends Ray Hammond and Wesley Roberts, the respective heads of the Ten Point Coalition and the Black Ministerial Alliance, that called for the renewal of efforts against violence. Hammond and Roberts also claimed that the partnerships of the past were now fully active and necessary if Boston was to counter its new crime problem.[59]

Boston's new resolve, however, has been tested once more. On January 4, 2002, the district attorney for Suffolk County (the county in which Boston is located), Ralph Martin, an African American and the most important Republican in elected office in the state next to the governor, resigned his position to go into private practice. A group of ministers from the Ten Point Coalition and the Black Ministerial Alliance requested a meeting with the governor in order to discuss both the issue of who would replace Martin and their more general concerns about the rising crime rates in Boston's inner city. A meeting was set but then canceled, and the governor announced the appointment of Dan Conley, a white Irish city council member from the Hyde Park neighborhood, as the new district attorney without ever conferring with African American ministers. The black *Globe* columnist Adrian Walker wrote a piece lambasting the white establishment for its handling of the appointment—supposedly at the request of some of the ministers.[60]

Walker's column was, however, far from prescient. Immediately, the new district attorney was making the rounds, meeting with different groups of black ministers, including those in Ten Point Coalition and the Black Ministerial Alliance.[61] The ministers had a long list of demands, and the district attorney was acceding to their requests. He needed to get elected several years hence. The ministers suddenly realized that they now had more leverage over the new district attorney than they had ever had over Ralph Martin.[62] Perhaps most ironically, the governor announced that she would not run for election in the fall, and she did not. This was partly in recognition of the fact that, since becoming governor the previous year when the elected governor, Paul Celucci, became the U.S. ambassador to Canada, she had made a number of political blunders, including mishandling the appointment of the new district attorney.

The Boston Police Department has shown no such tendency to bumble things political. On March 1, 2002, above the fold on the front page of the city section, the *Boston Globe* ran a detailed story about how the police department intended to deal with a spate of shootings in Boston's Cape Verdean community. The story described how a vastly disproportionate share of Boston's homicides both recently and in the past had involved conflicts in the Cape Verdean community. It also discussed how various efforts had failed and how the department believed that it now had to crack down on some of the more violence-prone individuals in the community.[63] Clearly, the story could not have been written without the full cooperation of the police department. It represented both a new level of transparency and a new level of communication between the department and Boston's various communities.

Conclusion

The decade of the 1990s was certainly a remarkable one for Boston. During that time, homicide rates plummeted, and the police and a group of inner-city black ministers were able to collaborate in dealing with the problem of youth violence. Is the Boston Miracle now over?

If by *the Boston Miracle* one means the remarkably low homicide rates of the 1990s, then, yes, the miracle is over. It was probably unrealistic, however, to think that such low rates could be maintained. Cities are periodically hit by exogenous factors — new drugs, large numbers of individuals being released from prison — that are likely to cause homicide rates to increase. And homicide rates have, indeed, risen recently, though they are still well below the historic averages of the past.

. If, however, by *the Boston Miracle* one means the ability of a previously race-torn city to develop a highly effective working partnership between its police department and the black ministerial community, then the miracle is still very much alive. Whatever one wants to consider as constituting the Boston Miracle, the critical point is that an enduring legacy of the 1990s has been that Boston has been able to build a sustainable relationship between its police department and its inner-city community through that community's churches. In doing so, the city has continued to be able to deal with multiple issues surrounding policing and inner-city crime. This is an achievement of no small order.

Notes

This research was supported by grants from the Smith Richardson Foundation and the National Science Foundation. I am grateful to Anthony Braga, Jeffery Fagan, James Jordan, David Kennedy, and R. Drew Smith for comments on an early draft of this essay.

1 Statistics supplied by the Boston Police Department.

2 Jenny Berrien and Christopher Winship, "An 'Umbrella of Legitimacy': Boston's Police Department–Ten Point Coalition Collaboration," in *Securing Our Children's Future: New Approaches to Juvenile Justice and Youth Violence*, ed. Gary Katzmann (Washington, D.C.: Brookings Institution, 2002); Christopher Winship and Jenny Berrien, "Boston Cops and Black Churches," *Public Interest* 136 (1999): 52–68. See also Jenny Berrien, Omar McRoberts, and Christopher Winship, "Religion and the Boston Miracle: The Effect of Black Ministry on Youth Violence," in *Who Will Provide? The Changing Role of Religion in American Social Welfare*, ed. Mary Jo Bane, Brent Coffin, and Ronald Thiemann (Boulder: Westview, 2000); Jenny Berrien and Christopher Winship, "Lessons Learned from Boston's Police-Community Collaboration," *Federal Probation Review* 63, no. 2 (December 1999): 24–32.

3 John Leland, "Savior of the Streets," *Newsweek*, June 1, 1998, 20–25.

4 Statistics supplied by the Boston Police Department.

5 Daniel Cork, "Examining Space-Time Interaction in City-Level Homicide Data: Crack Markets and the Diffusion of Guns among Youth," *Journal of Quantitative Criminology* 15, no. 4 (1999): 379–406, and "The Juvenile Homicide Epidemic: Spatio-Temporal Dynamics of Homicide in American Cities" (Ph.D. diss., Carnegie Mellon University, 2000); Bruce Johnson, Andrew Golub, and Eloise Dunlap, "The Rise and Decline of Hard Drugs, Drug Markets, and Violence in Inner-City New York," in *The Crime Drop in America*, ed. Alfred Blumstein and Joel Waldman

(Cambridge: Cambridge University Press, 2000); Jeff Grogger and Michael Willis, "The Emergence of Crack Cocaine and the Rise of Urban Crime Rates," *Review of Economics and Statistics* 82, no. 4 (2000): 519–29.

6 Statistics supplied by the Boston Police Department.

7 The material in this paragraph is drawn from Berrien and Winship, "An 'Umbrella of Legitimacy.'"

8 A detailed account of the Carol Stuart murder can be found in Sean Flynn, *Boston DA: The Battle to Transform the American Justice System* (New York: TV Books, 2000).

9 Ronald P. Formisano, *Boston against Busing: Race, Class, and Ethnicity in the 1960's and 1970's* (Chapel Hill: University of North Carolina Press, 1991).

10 Informant interviews. See also "Minister Dies as Cops Raid Wrong Apartment," *Boston Herald*, March 26, 1994, 0001.

11 Informant interviews. See also "Alleged Beating of Undercover Cop Probed," *Boston Herald*, February 3, 1995, 016.

12 Informant interviews. See also "Prosecutor Slain; Assistant AG Shot in Apparent Execution," *Boston Herald*, September 26, 1995, 001.

13 Berrien and Winship, "An 'Umbrella of Legitimacy.'" See also "Police, Clergy Working to Avert Racial Tension," *Boston Globe*, September 29, 1995, 004.

14 Informant interview.

15 Informant interview. See also "Menino Ups Ante on School Vote; Seeks Link to Political Future," *Boston Globe*, November 4, 1996, B1.

16 Informant interviews.

17 William Bratton, *Turnaround: How America's Top Cop Reversed the Crime Epidemic* (New York: Random House, 1998). See also Flynn, *Boston DA*.

18 "Family of Youth Killed by Officer Files Suit against Police," *Boston Globe*, November 21, 1991, 72.

19 "Flynn Urges Police Panel to Focus on Questions," *Boston Globe*, August 2, 1991, 19.

20 James St. Clair, "Report of the Boston Police Department Management Review Committee" (Boston Police Department, January 14, 1992).

21 "State Law Restricts Mayor on Firing of City's Police Chief," *Boston Globe*, August 13, 1991, 16.

22 Informant interview.

23 Informant interview.

24 Statistics supplied by the Boston Police Department.

25 Informant interviews. See also Berrien and Winship, "An 'Umbrella of Legitimacy.'"

26 "Clergy's Anger Can Bring Hope," *Boston Globe*, May 3, 1992, A13.

27 Other ministers in the city, such as Bruce Wall and Michael Haynes, have been involved in intensive street ministry. But their work has not generated as much publicity as has that of the three key Ten Point ministers.

28 Berrien and Winship, "An 'Umbrella of Legitimacy.'"

29 Informant interview.

30 A detailed account can be found in Christopher Winship and Jenny Berrien, "How Can Bitter Enemies Become the Best of Allies: Boston's Police Department and the Ten Point Coalition of Black Ministers" (Harvard University, Department of Sociology, July 1999, typescript).

31 Anthony A. Braga, David M. Kennedy, Elin J. Waring, and Anne M. Piehl, "Problem-Oriented Policing, Deterrence, and Youth Violence: An Evaluation of Boston's Operation Ceasefire," *Journal of Research in Crime and Delinquency* 38, no. 3 (2001): 195–225; and Boston Police Department, "Strategic Plan for Neighborhood Policing: Citywide Strategic Plan" (Boston Police Department, July 1996).

32 Informant interviews; field notes.

33 See www.Bostonstrategy.com (copy on file with the author).

34 John Eck and Edward MaGuire, "Have Changes in Policing Reduced Violent Crime?" in Blumstein and Waldman, eds., *The Crime Drop in America*.

35 Berrien and Winship, "An 'Umbrella of Legitimacy.' "

36 Braga et al., "Problem-Oriented Policing."

37 David Kennedy and Anthony Braga, "The Youth Homicide Epidemic in Boston" (Harvard University, Kennedy School of Government, 1999, typescript), 40–42.

38 Johnson, Golub, and Dunlap, "The Rise and Decline of Hard Drugs."

39 Andrew Karmen, *New York Murder Mystery: The True Story behind the Crime Crash of the 1990's* (New York: New York University Press, 2000); George L. Kelling and Catherine M. Coles, *Fixing Broken Windows: Restoring Order and Reducing Crime in Our Communities* (New York: Touchstone, 1996); George L. Kelling and William H. Sousa Jr., "Do Police Matter? An Analysis of the Impact of New York City's Police Reforms," Manhattan Institute Civic Report no. 22 (New York: Manhattan Institute, 2001).

40 Orlando Patterson and Christopher Winship, "Boston's Police Solution," editorial, *New York Times*, March 3, 1999, sec. A1, p. 17; Berrien and Winship, "Boston Cops and Black Churches"; Andrea McArdle and Tanya Erzen, eds., *Zero Tolerance: Quality of Life and the New Police Brutality in New York City* (New York: New York University Press, 2001).

41 "Despite Giuliani's Gibes, Locals Laud Police Work," *Boston Globe*, December 29, 2001.

42 Bratton, *Turnaround*.

43 Boston Police Department, "Strategic Plan for Neighborhood Policing."

44 Boston Police Department, "Violent Crime in the City of Boston: Trends, Challenges, and Reduction Strategies: A Collaborative Effort" (Boston Police Department, January 2002, powerpoint presentation).

45 Ibid.

46 Ibid.

47 Ibid.

48 Ibid.

49 Informant interview. See also "Boy, 3, Slain—and Mother Asks 'Why?'" *Boston Globe*, January 26, 2002.

50 "Slayer Planned Robbery, Prosecutors Say, Arraignment Held in Death of 3-Year Old," *Boston Globe*, February 6, 2002, B1.

51 Informant interview.

52 "Pastor Hopes Child Death Will Be City's Wake-Up Call," *Boston Globe*, January 29, 2002, A4.

53 "Boy's Slaying Prompts Peace March," *Boston Globe*, February 3, 2002, B6.

54 "Gunman Fires into T Bus at Rush Hour," *Boston Globe*, February 12, 2002, B7.

55 Informant interview. See also "Driver Is Shot, Killed by Boston Police Officer," *Boston Globe*, February 13, 2002, A1.

56 "Police Questions," *Boston Globe*, February 14, 2002, A18; "Suspect Shootings," *Boston Globe*, February 21, 2002, A16.

57 During the 1990s there was some tension between the Ten Point Coalition and the Black Ministerial Alliance, especially as Ten Point's power and visibility increased. In recent years, however, the two groups have worked closely together, even sharing staff. Many churches are members of both organizations, and there is now even talk of a merger.

58 Field notes. See also "Evans Asks Patience in Shooting Case," *Boston Globe*, February 14, 2002, A18.

59 Ray Hammond and Wesley Roberts, "Renewing Efforts against Violence," *Boston Globe*, February 19, 2002, A11.

60 Informant interview. Adrian Walker, "The Miracle Is Now Dead," *Boston Globe*, February 21, 2002, B1.

61 Field notes. See also "Conley Seeks to Reach Out," *Boston Globe*, March 6, 2002, B1.

62 Field notes; informant interviews.

63 "Out of Answers," *Boston Globe*, March 1, 2002, B1.

9

AFRICAN AMERICAN CHURCHES AND THE

EVOLUTION OF ANTIAPARTHEID ACTIVISM

Columba Aham Nnorom

In 1983, a "coalition of conscience" emerged that included members of the civil rights groups of the 1960s (including churches and organized labor) and newer groups representing peace activists, environmentalists, the Hispanic movement, and the women's rights movement. In the summer of 1983, this coalition helped facilitate a march on Washington attended by 500,000 people, in commemoration of the 1963 March on Washington. The coalition identified fourteen pieces of legislation for passage in Congress. Among those were the "Martin Luther King Holiday" bill and a legislative amendment proposed by Congressman William Gray III (D-PA), which banned new investments by American corporations in South Africa. In 1984, leaders of this coalition, including Congressman Walter Fauntroy (D-DC), Randall Robinson, the executive director of TransAfrica, Dr. Mary Frances Berry, of the U.S. Civil Rights Commission, and Eleanor Holmes Norton, the chair of the Equal Employment Opportunity Commission, strategized a sit-in at the South African embassy in Washington, D.C. The sit-in was to take place on Thanksgiving Eve by two in the afternoon — four hours before prime time on "a slow press day in the nation's capital" — in order to maximize exposure to the issue of racial injustice in South Africa. On the appointed date, the antiapartheid activists staged the sit-in and were arrested, handcuffed, and taken to jail amid a blaze of attention from television and radio networks, wire services, and every important news publication in America. Behind the media representative jamming the sidewalks in front of the embassy were demonstrators chanting "Freedom Yes! Apartheid No!"[1]

Two days after the sit-in, Fauntroy, Robinson, Berry, and Norton announced the founding of the Free South Africa Movement, its "principal objective" being "the passage of comprehensive economic sanctions against South Africa."[2] The demonstrations that the organizers had planned to last only one week wound up lasting for more than a year and spread throughout the country. More than three thousand people were arrested at the South African embassy in Washington, D.C., and more than two thousand at South African consulates in Los Angeles, New York, Boston, Chicago, and other cities. Those arrested included clergy, elected officials, schoolchildren, university students, and professionals from various walks of life.

By early 1986, several different antiapartheid bills sponsored by congressmen such as William Gray III (D-PA), Ronald Dellums (D-CA), Stephen Solarz (D-NY), Julian Dixon (D-CA), and Charles Rangel (D-NY) were combined into one and passed in the House of Representatives. Within the Senate, antiapartheid initiatives by Edward Kennedy (D-MA), Richard Lugar (R-IN), Nancy Kassebaum (R-KA), and others were also combined and passed. The House and Senate bills were then consolidated and the combined bill sent to President Ronald Reagan, who vetoed it. The House overrode the president's veto by a vote of 313–83, and the Senate did the same by a vote of 78–21—thereby passing the Comprehensive Anti-Apartheid Act of 1986 (CAAA). This historic legislation banned, among other things, all U.S. import of South African iron, steel, coal, uranium, textiles, and agricultural products and the sale of krugerrands. It also banned new loans and investment in South Africa and forbade South Africa Airlines from landing in the United States.

That African Americans played a prominent role in events leading up to the passing of this important legislation, and in the broader range of antiapartheid activism, is not surprising. There has always existed within black communities an *anawin* (a remnant)—composed mostly of African American professionals (scholars, lawyers, doctors, pastors, and others) who vocally and organizationally kept the links with Africa alive in America.[3] Malcolm X acknowledged the power of the African connection when he said: "I've got ghosts of Africa swimming in my blood."[4] African American denominations such as the African Methodist Episcopal (AME) Church certainly have a long and rich history of involvement in South Africa and South African affairs, a history dating back to the 1800s. AME churches led the way in these early days in raising African American consciousness about Africa.

Antiapartheid activism among African Americans during the mid- to late twentieth century built directly on this AME legacy as well as on the civil rights movement and many of the clergy activists who emerged from it. According to the prominent antiapartheid activist Bishop John Hurst Adams, senior bishop of the AME Church, all African American churches were involved in the passage of the CAAA. However, despite the inclusiveness of Adams's statement, there was clearly a variation in denominational involvement. Adams certainly symbolized the activist core within the AME Church —he himself serving as the first chairman of TransAfrica (an Africa and Caribbean advocacy organization) and as a board member of Africaire (an Africa development organization) and the Joint Center for Political and Economic Studies (a black public policy think tank). Nonetheless, antiapartheid activism by Adams and other AME clergy was not always highly visible, perhaps, as Adams stated, because African American churches were able to avail themselves of the services and expertise of black institutions such as TransAfrica and there was "no point duplicating things."[5]

It was, instead, an activist core of clergy within the Progressive National Baptist Convention (PNBC)—many of whom were civil rights movement veterans—that provided some of the most visible African American church leadership within the antiapartheid movement. This activist core included clergymen such as Congressmen Walter Fauntroy and William Gray III, Leon Sullivan (founder of the Opportunities Industrialization Center and author of the Sullivan Principles on U.S. investment in South Africa), Wyatt Tee Walker (a chairman of the American Committee on Africa (ACOA) and the Southern Christian Leadership Conference chief of staff under Martin Luther King Jr.), Otis Moss Jr. (a chairman of the PNBC Civil Rights Commission and a confidant of "Daddy" King and Martin King Jr.), and other PNBC clergy as well.

This antiapartheid activism by African American church leaders was part of a broader context of antiapartheid activism in which American churches affiliated largely with the National Council of Churches (NCC) also played a significant role. The NCC, in fact, opened an office on corporate responsibility in the early 1970s that led the way in the call for corporations, universities, and city and state governments to divest financially from South Africa. The AME Church and the PNBC provided an additional "direct action" front that successfully facilitated the emergence and effectiveness of a cadre of activist clergy who helped mobilize the mass action component of American antiapartheid activism. This brand of church activism was well established among African American churches, dating back before the civil rights movement. The antiapartheid activism of the PNBC grew directly out of its civil rights activism, with many of the leading PNBC antiapartheid activists — Fauntroy, Gray, Sullivan, Walker, Moss, and others — having also been prominent civil rights activists. The antiapartheid activism of AME churches drew similarly on their civil rights movement involvements as well as on the AME Church's rich legacy of Africa involvement dating back to Turner, Dwane, and others.[6] Details of the AME Church's and the PNBC's relationship to South Africa and to the antiapartheid struggle will be outlined in this discussion.

Ecclesiastical Approaches to African American Church Involvement with Africa

Robert Bellah and Carl Brill have identified "two important moments" when American churches had significant influence on the United States. The first occurred during the "Evangelical Revival or Second Awakening" of the early nineteenth century, when America deliberately maintained a low global military and political profile while "Uncle Sam's" missionaries transmitted his values abroad. The second was the "moment of social responsibility," when the churches decided that the struggle against poverty and injustice in the United States must go hand in hand with efforts to bring justice and equality to the world.[7] With respect to the first moment, both black and white religious groups participated in the missionary explosion of the nineteenth century that exerted an early influence on politics in Southern Africa and on U.S. policy toward the region. Nevertheless, black and white reactions to the issues of racism and colonialism differed in many respects.

The period between 1834 and 1948 was a time when white American missionaries gave significant support to the U.S. government's pro-European colonial policy and to the pro-Boer racist domination of Africans; entered into an alliance with Cecil Rhodes, the architect of British imperialism in southern Africa, who often gave them land violently taken from the Africans to build churches; and even gave a copy of the U.S. Constitution on which the Boers "based their Volksroad (elected assembly)."[8] At the same time, U.S. missionary interests were buttressed by strong economic relations to American multinational companies in South Africa such as Mobil, General Electric, and, later, Honeywell and Allis-Chalmers. Indeed, as early as 1896, the year that an AME Church bishop, Henry McNeal Turner, made his maiden visit to the country, "half of South Africa's mines were run by American engineers, one of whom (John Hays Hammond) had become the dominant force in South African mining two years before. American engineers brought with them to South Africa American equipment and American capital, which combined to establish an American foothold in South Africa's nascent economy."[9]

African American missionaries, on the other hand, were less tolerant of European and Boer domination of southern Africa. In fact, they played a pivotal role in "proto-opposition" to white supremacy in the region. This opposition can be traced to the birth of Ethiopianism in South Africa in 1892 and the crucial connections that that movement established with African American churches in the United States. The Annual Conference of the Ethiopian Church, meeting in Pretoria on March 17, 1894, passed a resolution for the merger of the Ethiopian and AME Churches. The Reverends James Dwane and Jacobus Xaba, leaders of the Ethiopian Church, were sent to the United States to effect the union. Fully aware of the great opportunity that the moment presented, Bishop Henry McNeal Turner of the AME Church convened a special session of the AME North Georgia Conference in Atlanta on June 19, 1896, at which the union was consummated and Rev. Dwane appointed general superintendent for South Africa.[10] The merger of both churches set in motion a chain reaction of events and relationships in the United States and South Africa whose impact was felt in the antiapartheid movement in both countries.

In 1898, barely two years after Ethiopian forces defeated the Italians at the Battle of Adowa, Bishop Turner went on a five-week blitz through Cape Colony and the Transvaal and Orange Free State Republics to formally visit the AME churches in the region. His visit is symbolic of some of the immediate benefits of the Ethiopianist-AME connection as well as a more humane and symbiotic approach toward the racial problems in southern Africa. On the religious plane, he praised the Ethiopian spirit that inspired South Africans to "discover that churches of their own race would be of far more benefit in a pragmatic measure than worshipping among white, where they are compelled to occupy a subordinate status." Consequently, Turner promoted Rev. Dwane from superintendent to vicar bishop of the South African district of the church; he also ordained thirty-one elders and twenty deacons to the AME ministry. Turner broke South Africa's white supremacist laws, traveling, living, and eating "wherever he wished without incident," and visiting and shaking hands with Paul Krugger, the Afrikaner president of Transvaal, who conceded: "You are the first black man whose hand I have ever shaken." In his public speeches, Turner hid his political inclinations and seemed to blame the black South African victims rather than the colonial system that had oppressed them for so long. But, before private and all-black congregations, the AME bishop showed his true colors — as an "arch-critic of U.S. imperialism and racism and outspoken emigrationist," emphasizing the "need for the international solidarity of blacks, the efficacy of assertive and concerted action to redress their common grievances, and the necessity for defensive violence."[11] Thus, by promoting the unity of the Ethiopian and AME Churches, and by identifying the sufferings of black South Africans with those of black Americans. Turner played a leading role in the promotion of evangelical Pan-Africanism and proto-opposition by an African American church to European colonialism in Africa.[12]

Another fruit of the AME-Ethiopian connection was both educational and political and facilitated the freedom struggle in southern Africa. In the late nineteenth century and the early twentieth, "at least forty mission-educated Christians went on to higher education in the United States. . . . Many African leaders came to feel that they could learn much from the Black experience in the U.S.A." Soon, the AME Church was not only building churches but also establishing schools, including Bethel Institute in Cape Town and Wilberforce Institute. Indeed, the greatest attraction of the AME Church for Africans was neither theological nor doctrinal but, rather, educational, that is, the educational opportunities that it provided to a people whom the white establishment would have preferred to see wallowing in ignorance. The white community in South Africa was understandably worried by the African American connection. The South African graduates from U.S. black colleges, they complained, "returned indoctrinated with the dangerous poison of race hatred which they spread to their gullible and uneducated brethren." Black American "notions of democracy, liberty, equality, education and self government," they said, made Africans "difficult to control." Moreover, Turner's activities during his visit to South Africa — only two years after the Battle of Adowa — and the discovery of a letter by a Haitian domestic servant predicting that "ultimately Africans would 'whip' the British back to the Thames as the Haitians had repelled the French" only inflamed their fears. There were also rumors among whites that African Americans were buying large tracts of land in central South Africa to establish a nation governed by blacks.[13]

The real and imagined dangers of the AME Church–Africa links led to a white backlash. African Americans were blamed for everything "from the fractious behavior of chiefs to an apparent epidemic of 'native insolence' on the highveld farms." Calling AME ministers "American agitators" hiding under the "guise of religion," some state governments canceled their sacramental licenses. While a government inquiry found no evidence of seditious behavior on the part of the AME ministers, they were, nonetheless, made to feel unwelcome in the region. White South Africans were especially disturbed by the proprietary attitude of AME ministers toward Africa as they saw themselves as the "true sons of the soil." It was, therefore, not surprising that African American missionaries would soon be banned from the area and declared "persona non grata in southern Africa" even until 1926. For there was, indeed, a genuine fear among whites, especially the missionaries, that the AME ministers, whom they saw as "missionary raiders" with an unscrupulous habit of taking advantage of their color, would "steal" most of white missionaries' converts, who had hitherto looked to the white church for guidance and inspiration. Moreover, there was also trepidation that, unless this incipient relationship was "nipped in the bud," it could foment an African revolution against the colonial system.[14]

All the same, the actual impact of the Ethiopianist-AME connection should not be exaggerated. After all, many African American missionaries in Southern Africa were rather conservative in their challenge to white supremacy. In fact, some of them supported British imperialism in Africa and saw their role as primarily a "civilizing mission," an opportunity to bring millions of Africans out of "ignorance, degradation and barbarism." They opined that the "African had to prove himself worthy of being placed on a par with 'civilized' peoples by improving himself morally, intellectually, and financially." Indeed, some AME ministers displayed "an overt and covert sense of cultural chauvinism that went to an extreme." Dwane, who became an AME bishop, severed his connection with the church because most African American churches preferred light-skinned to dark-skinned ministers. Moreover, the colonial authorities treated black Americans differently from the Africans, giving them certain special privileges that racism had denied them in America. Such treatment was patently evident during Turner's visit. One AME bishop called the African American presence in South Africa outright imperialism.[15]

The AME Church's approach to antiapartheid activism was not burdened by these kinds of cultural tensions, but it did reflect some of the same hierarchical ecclesiastical style. AME Church opposition to colonialism and apartheid was based on the "legacy of Turner" and repeatedly buttressed by the "unanimous position of AME church Bishops that everything be done to end apartheid."[16] In various statements by the General Conference (the supreme body of the church) and the Council of Bishops and reports from the social action committees, the church made crystal clear its position on African liberation. At the forty-second session of its general conference, held in Kansas City, Missouri, July 7–15, 1984, it declared that its mission was based on the teachings of Jesus, who "admonishes us in no uncertain terms to feed the hungry, give drink to those who are thirsty, welcome the weary, clothe the naked, care for the sick, and visit prisoners." Also outlined were other challenges that it saw as a part of its mission, including combating racism in all forms and enabling liberation for the poor and oppressed, especially blacks; enhancing the desire for self-determination and self-development of African people and people of African descent through Christian concern and outreach; promoting voter education, registration, and participation as well as greater representation in public policymaking and decisionmaking at all levels; formulating programs that emphasize human development and economic development; and planning and implementing programs that strengthen and enhance the black family. On South Africa, the convention declared: "Our sisters and brothers in South Africa, unfortunately, may qualify for the dubious honor of being identified as the most oppressed people on the face of the earth. Once men find jobs, they are separated from their families for one year. Those who bring diamonds from the bowels of the earth, earn $12 per week. Black men must work for one white man for ten years before they are allowed to live in an urban area." The resolution recommended that "each Social Action Commission at the local level, the Annual Conference level, the Episcopal District level and at the Conventional level, petition our U.S. Congress persons to press the present and future administration to divest our holdings in South Africa until this abominable situation is redressed." Further, it encouraged "all black Americans to not purchase diamonds until equity and dignity are achieved in South Africa. Further, we call on all blacks and call for African Methodism to boycott *all* companies with holdings in South Africa. We now join in their struggle which is both difficult and dangerous."[17]

At the forty-third quadrennial session of its general conference, held in Fort Worth, Texas, July 6–14, 1988, the AME Church adopted by far its strongest resolutions against South Africa's apartheid regime. It noted with immense concern the continued existence of the most oppressive state of emergency in South Africa; the continued callousness and practiced brutality of the South Africa Police and the South Africa Defense Force as they perpetrated atrocities against the black people in South Africa; the continued shackling dominance that the evil of apartheid maintained over black people, depriving them of their human dignity and their own being; and the intensified struggle of their black brothers and sisters in South Africa. And it called for all to work for the absolute dismantling of the evil system. The general conference also unanimously passed a resolution calling on the church to support and reaffirm its position on mandatory and absolute sanctions as a peaceful means to a total dismantling of the system of apartheid; deplore in the strongest terms the practice of detention without trial, especially the detention of children, appeal for the unconditional release of all political prisoners, and call for the return of all South African refugees; support the efforts of the liberation movements such as the South West Africa People's Organization, the African National Congress (ANC), and the Pan Africanist Congress (PAC) in southern Africa to bring an end to the tragic situation now prevalent; support the Lusaka Declaration of May 1987; pray for an end to the unjust white-minority rule by observing June 16 (Soweto Day) and March 21 (Sharpeville Day) as conventional days of prayer; commit to continuing to work for an immediate end to the apartheid system of South Africa by lobbying and writing letters to the U.S. Congress and South African State President N. W. Botha; and press for a stay of execution of the Sharpeville Six, twenty-six other patriots whose execution was scheduled for July 19, 1988, and other political persons being tried in court cases across the country.[18]

At the forty-fourth session of the general conference, held in Orlando, Florida, July 8–15, 1992, the church resolved to condemn the deliberate attempt on the part of the white-minority regime in South Africa through atrocities committed by the South African security forces to retard and/or derail the peace process in that country; condemn the failure of the South African regime to bring to justice those members of the security forces responsible for those atrocities; strongly support the insistence of Nelson Mandela and other respectful leaders for UN mediation of problems encountered by the South African nation; pledge the continued support of the AME Church through prayers and other means for brothers and sisters in the Republic of South Africa, believing that God will, in due time, allow the South African nation to rid itself of the ills of apartheid and make it possible for a just, undivided, nonracial, and democratic dispensation to be established; charge the Women's Missionary Society, in its status as a nongovernment organization within the United Nations, with the responsibility and mission for monitoring the sentiments expressed in this resolution; and call for the immediate introduction of an interim government and constitutional assembly.[19]

It is important to note that AME resolutions against apartheid were often greatly influenced by the input and recommendations of "sister" churches in South Africa. It is doubtful that AME annual conferences would issue an anti-apartheid statement that had the potential of inflicting harm on its 180,000 members in South Africa. Another characteristic of AME churches is that they were more likely to engage in contacts with top U.S. politicians and government officials rather than participate in demonstrations, marches, sit-ins, etc. In fact, a striking characteristic of the church is its access to powerful members of the American political establishment and the evangelistic zeal with which it pursues this mission. One AME Church scholar, Louis Charles Harvey, has warned about the dangers posed by the subordination of spirituality to politics within the denomination. According to Harvey: "The present tendency to overemphasize the political life of the Church has led to two potential problems both of which threaten the worship life of the Church and the exterior life of the Church." The problems that he identified were the danger of absolutizing the AME institution to the point that it becomes so "enamored of itself" that all other aspects of its corporate ministry are gravely affected and the "potential for self-deification" arises and the danger of an overly politicized ministry that sees the achievement, concentration, and control of ecclesiastical power as an end in itself. "Institutional politics for the sole purpose of personal aggrandizement," he warns, "is sinful, and should be discouraged. This power of politics interferes with the inner life of worship and the outer life of liberating witness."[20]

Yet, it would be naive to expect the AME Church to be a politically apathetic church. Founded on political protest against racism and discrimination, the church has historically been blessed with strong activist bishops who saw personal relationships within the church and close contacts with the political establishment as a sine qua non for protecting and advancing personal and ecclesiastical interests.

The AME church may also have been a victim of the tension between the "logic of mission and maintenance"—operative in every organization. The logic of mission nudges a church, not only to "talk the talk of faith," but also to "walk the walk of faith." The logic of maintenance demands that a "church protect its international unity, protect its internal cohesion, . . . protect the authority of the ecclesiastical government, . . . protect its economic base, and . . . maintain their solidarity with the powerful and the affluent of society, again putting them at odds with the preferential option for the poor."[21]

Mass-Based Action Approaches and the Evolution of the Antiapartheid Movement

After World War II, the racial climate in South Africa deteriorated. The postwar period may be divided into two parts—1949–76 and 1976–86. With the introduction of apartheid as the official government policy in 1948, the white-minority regime used extra force to maintain the status quo. Black resistance also rose. The Group Areas Act (1950) was imposed on the country leading to an ANC-sponsored mass labor strike during which eighteen people were killed by the police and thirty wounded. The first period also saw the organization by the ANC of its first nationwide campaign of resistance, the Defiance of Unjust Laws Campaign (1952), in which Mandela played a key role. The police responded by killing forty people and arresting eight thousand demonstrators. The ANC launched the Freedom Charter and created Unkonto We Siwe-Zulu for the "Spear of the Nation" (1961), which carried out its first bomb attack in Johannesburg on December 16, the Day of the Covenant ("holy day") when Afrikaners celebrate their victory over the Zulu at "Blood River." The post–World War II era also saw the creation of Poqo (the military wing of the PAC) and the rise of the South African Students Organization and of the black consciousness movement.

In the United States, various African American groups and individuals sought to counter the violence in South Africa in a variety of ways. One of them, the Council on African Affairs, founded in 1937, less than two years after Italy's invasion of Ethiopia, was described by Henry Jackson as the "longest lived and most influential American organization of its kind." With members like Ralph Bunche, who became associate of the State Department's Division of Dependent Affairs and a UN deputy secretary general, Paul Robeson, the world class actor and singer, Mordecai W. Johnson, a Howard University president, Max Yergan, a YMCA official with seventeen years of experience in Africa, Adam Clayton Powell Jr., the Harlem congressman, W. E. B. Du Bois, a Harvard-trained sociologist, and an elite group of Ph.D.'s, the council was guaranteed a high degree of access to U.S. political institutions and policymakers. It advocated independence for African countries and, in 1950, made an unprecedented demand for South Africa's expulsion from the United Nations. A group, Americans for South African Resistance, was formed in 1952 to encourage nonviolent protest against apartheid. The American Negro Leadership Conference on Africa (ANLCA) was organized in 1962 to promote civil rights in America and independence in Africa.[22]

Other African American leaders like Martin Luther King Jr. also spoke out against apartheid in South Africa. From the very beginning of his public ministry, King recognized the connection between the civil rights and the antiapartheid movements, and, in the 1950s and 1960s, he acted by seeking to uplift the poor and oppressed in South Africa, first, by developing a friendship with Albert Luthuli and admiration and respect for antiapartheid activists like Nelson Mandela and Robert Sobukwe. In a letter to Luthuli, King wrote: "Our struggle for freedom in the U.S. is not fundamentally different from that going on in South Africa. We share a common destiny."[23] Luthuli's response shows the strong bonds between the blacks of Africa and those of America: "My Negro friends were eager to hear about South Africa, and their readiness to help resolved itself many times to the question: Can we come over there to assist you."[24] King also lent support to antiapartheid groups. In 1960, he condemned the Sharpeville massacre and asked the U.S. government to impose diplomatic and economic sanctions against South Africa.

Together with the ACOA, he called for the recall of the American ambassador in Pretoria, the mobilization of U.S. public opinion, a consumer boycott of South African goods, putting pressure on private American companies in South Africa and on U.S. policymakers to compel South Africa to abandon apartheid, and, finally, raising legal defense and welfare funds for victims of apartheid.[25] In 1964, King and the ANLCA appealed to the Johnson administration to "take a firm stand against South Africa, prohibit future American investments there, and endorse an unsponsored oil embargo against the apartheid state."[26]

Among African American Baptists, the PNBC played a leadership role in the antiapartheid movement. The denomination also had probably "the largest group of activist pastors" during both the civil rights and the antiapartheid struggles. One top PNBC official once jokingly said "All the bomb throwers are in our Convention."[27] Among leading members of the church who were active participants in the South African movement were Dr. Wyatt Walker, chief of staff to Martin Luther King Jr., Congressman Walter Fauntroy, another King associate and confidante, the Reverend J. Alfred J. Smith, Dr. Joseph Roberts, Congressman William Gray, one of the first sponsors of antiapartheid legislation in Congress, Dr. William A. Jones, Dr. Gardner C. Taylor, Dr. Fred Lofton, the late Dr. Thomas Kilgore, the Reverend Otis Moss Jr., Dr. Marshall Lorenzo Shepard Jr., and others.

The PNBC was formed in 1961, an outgrowth of the dissatisfaction of progressive members of the National Baptist Convention (NBC) over the unduly long tenure of the top leadership within the NBC and the need for term limits. The birth of the PNBC was also a result of differences of opinion about how to respond to the struggle for black civil rights.[28] Progressives such as Martin Luther King Jr. who were committed to such provocative tactics as mass-based nonviolent civil disobedience were some of the PNBC's original founders. The PNBC embraced King's nonviolent philosophy and his tactics, and, by frequently putting those tactics into action across the United States in the 1960s, its activists were able to hone the protest skills that they would carry forward into antiapartheid activism during the 1970s, 1980s, and 1990s.

The tradition of African American opposition to apartheid continued in the 1970s among black secular and religious organizations. At Howard University in May 1972, the Congressional Black Caucus (CBC) sponsored an ANLCA meeting that, among other things, "proposed the establishment of a national black strategy on Africa and a nationwide program of support for African liberation struggles." In 1976, the CBC "produced the Afro-American Manifesto on Southern Africa, a document that allied black Americans to the goals of African liberation in that region."[29]

The period 1976–86 was crucial in the efforts of antiapartheid groups to dismantle the apartheid system in South Africa. In South Africa, the turning point was the Soweto Massacre of June 16, 1976, when the South Africa Police shot into a group of fifteen thousand schoolchildren in Soweto peacefully protesting the government's ruling that half of all classes in secondary schools must be taught in Afrikaans, the national language of the Boers, the architects of apartheid. About a thousand students were killed and over five thousand injured.[30] The fallout from the Soweto massacre was felt both in the United States and in South Africa. The impact of the uprising in South Africa—the hardening of the belief of black students and adults that violence was necessary to end apartheid, the exodus from South Africa of about ten thousand students for guerilla training in Tanzania, Angola, and Mozambique or education in Europe or America, and the shift in the focus of resistance to a younger generation and a more dispersed leadership—was remarkable. The impact of the uprising in the United States—the application of more pressure on Pretoria by American antiapartheid activists, especially African American secular and religious organizations—was equally remarkable.

In 1977, the Reverend Leon Sullivan introduced the Sullivan Principles, a code that "asked U.S. companies in South Africa to desegregate facilities, pay equal wages to Blacks, improve job training and advancement and the quality of their workers' lives." But the Sullivan Principles were vehemently condemned by some African American church leaders. At a summit meeting of black church leaders in New York in 1979, the Reverend William Jones Jr., president of the PNBC, decried the Sullivan code as "well-intentioned but no longer sufficient," especially since "the very presence of United States corporations in South Africa serves to legitimize the apartheid system of white supremacy." In a paper entitled "A Theological Basis for Armed Struggle," Reverend Jones justified resort to violence in South Africa on the following grounds: "Genocide, on a massive scale, is being practiced in South Africa. To be non-violent in the contest of genocide is to affirm violence and is tantamount to alliance with the adversary. To resist, by whatever means necessary, is the only sane and spiritual response to anyone who calls himself Christian."

And, under the leadership of the Reverend Wyatt Tee Walker, King's chief of staff during the civil rights movement, the International Freedom Mobilization against Apartheid, a black religious leaders' lobby, "was organized to seal their unequivocal opposition to Sullivan." The church leaders, who represented thirty-eight states and fifty cities, went beyond moral protest and "took the additional political step of declaring support for the African National Congress, one of the primary antiapartheid organizations within South Africa."[31]

With the election of Ronald Reagan to the U.S. presidency in 1980, American foreign policy embraced a rabid anticommunism unknown since the days of McCarthyism. Reagan's approach to South Africa, termed *constructive engagement*, emphasized the importance of South Africa as "a focal point of the region, and as an actor whose ties should be strengthened with its neighbors." It saw the Cuban presence in Angola as "totally anathema to American interests" and viewed the rebel group Union Nacional por la Independencee Totale do Angola as "a major actor in Southern Africa and one . . . the U.S. has to take into account." Consequently, the Reagan administration saw South Africa as a friend and ally and was unprepared to abandon "a country that has stood by us in every war we've ever fought, a country that is strategically essential to the free world in its production of minerals we all must have and so forth."[32] Thus, in order to encourage evolutionary as opposed to revolutionary change, the Reagan administration proposed that the United States should "engage constructively" with moderate African leaders so as to remove or neutralize the military presence and influence of Eastern Bloc countries in Southern Africa. Thus was born the policy of constructive engagement, which like an earthquake shook the internal politics of America and South Africa.

The constructive engagement policy had an immediate effect in the increase of economic and military dealings between Pretoria and Washington: for the first time, the United States became the premier exporter to, and importer from, South Africa to the tune of about $4.2 billion, an increase of over 24 percent from the Carter administration. In November 1981, Reagan supported a $1.1 billion credit to South Africa despite CBC opposition. Thus, from January 1981 to June 1982, U.S. bank loans to South Africa increased by 246 percent, bailing the apartheid regime out of a great economic crisis. In 1982, the United States lifted the ban on the sale of nonmilitary equipment to the South African military and police and loosened restrictions on nuclear-related exports to Pretoria in violation of the Nuclear Non-Proliferation Treaty. CIA Director William Casey visited South Africa in September 1982 to bolster Pretoria's security needs.[33]

Meanwhile, in South Africa, the white-minority regime interpreted the policy of constructive engagement and Reagan's reelection as giving it carte blanche to engage in one of the most brutal and repressive crackdowns in its already bloody and murderous history. Pretoria's objectives were fourfold: to destroy the liberation movement in South Africa; to co-opt what leaders in South Africa it could; to repress those unwilling to cooperate; and to prepare for total war — economic and military. Pretoria was also waging undeclared war on Mozambique and Zambia. Its forces were seeking to destroy black South African freedom fighters undergoing military training in preparation for sabotage forays into the racist enclave, and, in the process, they bombed Mozambique into submission, forcing the country's leadership to sign the infamous Nkomati Accord on March 16, 1984. "When the South African army invaded Angola, the United States was the only nation to veto the resolution condemning the South African government for that action."[34]

In March 1984, black South African students held nonviolent demonstrations against the inferior school system that trained and prepared then to work only in mines and factories while reserving for the minority white students the superior educational institutions that trained them to manage the economy and run the government. The government's response was to gun down the protesters, killing 134, and arrest their leaders. In early November 1984, the black trade union movement called the biggest strike in South Africa's history: some three thousand workers, supported by four thousand students, closed down the Johannesburg area for two days. By 1985, civil strife had spread to the Eastern Cape and other parts of the country, leading to a potential total breakdown of law and order. The response of South African security forces was bloody and brutal: about a thousand blacks were slaughtered by the end of the year.

But, as in the 1990s the white-minority regime, emboldened by Reagan's policy of constructive engagement, inflicted more terror on its hapless black-majority population, the PNBC stepped up its denunciations of these policies. At its twenty-third annual convention, held in 1984, over one hundred delegates voted to condemn South African apartheid and the disenfranchisement of black South Africans. They also called for the immediate end of apartheid, the release of all political prisoners, the development of a nonracially based democratic government, and sanctions of and disinvestments in businesses and governments dealing with South Africa until the demands of justice and democracy were met. A resolution adopted by delegates to the twenty-fourth annual convention, held in 1985, was similar except that it also appealed to members to participate in nonviolent demonstrations at the South African embassy in Washington, D.C., and at South African consulates across the country. Again at the twenty-fifth annual convention, held in 1986, virtually the same appeals were made as in previous years.

That the evil nature of apartheid in South Africa loomed large in the minds and consciousness of PNBC leaders is evident from the importance it was given and the unanimity it inspired at the conventions. It was almost always the subject of discussion at the PNBC Executive Board sessions held on the first and last day of the convention. After the presentation of resolutions and recommendations, which were traditionally supportive of black-majority rule and opposed to white-minority rule in South Africa, pastors were given the chance to voice their opinions on the issue. It is to the credit of the denomination that "not one single pastor was ever opposed to a resolution against the apartheid regime."[35]

Unlike some timid and nonactivist churches, which saw little value in Christian participation in public agitation, the PNBC leadership facilitated the participation of the members in public demonstrations against apartheid South Africa. In fact, the chairman of the PNBC Civil Rights Commission had a lot of latitude in organizing demonstrations. All he had to do was check with the PNBC president; check with the executive secretary, and get pastors and ministers to sign up. Prior to the passage of the CAAA in 1986, the Reverend Otis Moss, chairman of the Civil Rights Commission as well as of the Martin Luther King Center for Non-Violent Change, was mandated by the church to organize a group of ministers to go to Washington, D.C., to protest against the white-minority regime in South Africa. On the night before the demonstration at the South African embassy, a mass meeting was held at the Metropolitan Baptist Church in Washington. It was mostly a planning and orientation meeting, and the proceedings were made easier by the

presence of a great many ministers who were veterans of the civil rights movement and had honed their skills in the tactics of active nonviolent agitation.
During the meeting, Rev. Moss reminded the ministers that the demonstration must be conducted within the context of nonviolence, that they were
demonstrating as representatives of the Gospel of Jesus Christ, and that the
demonstration should be in concert with the goals of the ANC. The ANC was
demanding that a new constitution be created for South Africa; that the ban
on the ANC be lifted; that all political prisoners, including Nelson Mandela,
be freed; that violence and brutality on the part of the South African security
forces cease; and that global economic sanctions be continued and expanded
until all these conditions were met.[36]

At the South African embassy, the twenty-five PNBC ministers and their
supporters staged a demonstration reminiscent of the civil rights protests of
the 1960s. Carrying Bibles and placards, and singing "We Shall Overcome,"
they crossed the police line and demanded to see the ambassador. When the
demonstrators refused to leave after being asked to do so twice, a diplomat
called the police, and the group was promptly arrested. The demonstrators
were handcuffed, put in a paddy wagon, and taken to jail, where they were
detained for several hours, after which they posted bond. As they were being
arrested, the ministers asked the police that they be handcuffed "with their
hands in front rather than behind so as to hold in their hands the bibles to
read in jail."[37] Arriving in court the next morning, they were given the option
of returning the following morning for a court hearing or forfeiting bond ($50
each). All chose to forfeit the bond money. The PNBC was the only Baptist
convention to lead a demonstration at the South African embassy.[38]

But Rev. Moss and his group of activist ministers wanted the PNBC to
go beyond lending its support to the ANC and other antiapartheid groups.
They recommended during the 1986 midwinter session that the church take
a stronger role in the antiapartheid movement, a recommendation that was
adopted by the convention. The result was increased grassroots mobilization
by local pastors. For example, in 1986, local churches organized a takeover
of the South African consulate in Cleveland. Among the groups of activists
involved in the protest was one that was led by the PNBC minister the Reverend Mylian Waite, who was arrested, tried, and acquitted in a bench trial
presided over by an African American judge.[39] The PNBC also manifested its

support for the freedom struggle in South Africa in other ways. For example, Dr. J. Alfred Smith, a former president of the PNBC, raised money for the antiapartheid movement. He and other PNBC leaders sponsored U.S. speaking tours for Desmond Tutu and Allan Boesak, which raised American consciousness to the evils of the apartheid system and led to increased support for black-majority rule in South Africa.

But PNBC activists paid another price beyond the dangers posed by protest for their involvement in the antiapartheid movement. Some were banned from entering South Africa until the collapse of white-minority rule. For example, Rev. Moss and others were refused entry into South Africa to attend Tutu's ordination as the first African archbishop of Johannesburg on February 8, 1985. And, when Jesse Jackson and Otis Moss went to the South African embassy to try to get the ban lifted, the ambassador told Jackson that he would be allowed into the country only under certain conditions: that the visit be limited to thirty-six hours and that there be no public statements, no media contacts, and no interviews. Jackson rejected Pretoria's preconditions.[40]

PNBC pastors also pursued antiapartheid activism through channels other than the strictly ecclesiastical. As stated earlier, Walter Fauntroy and William Gray III took legislative and other formal action, and Fauntroy took the lead in organizing a number of important antiapartheid protest activities. Moreover, Fauntroy's ability to mobilize his existing networks proved indispensable to the antiapartheid cause. For example, as a coordinator of the 1963 March on Washington, Fauntroy had the names and addresses of about 100,000 of the 250,000 people who had come to the Mall. These contacts were augmented by the thousands of new activist groups who came to Washington, D.C., in 1983 for the twentieth anniversary of the march. Also, as a former chairman of the CBC and the Black Leadership Roundtable, Fauntroy had access to the cream of the African American political elite as well as to the leadership of over 150 national black organizations that were part of what was known as the Black Leadership Family. Fauntroy rallied these organizations to achieve at least two objectives: present alternatives to objectionable Reagan administration domestic and foreign policies and mobilize African American voters in those congressional districts (roughly 115 in ten states, including Alabama, Georgia, Louisiana, North Carolina, Florida, and

Maryland) with a large enough proportion of African Americans (10 percent or more) to influence the outcome of an election.[41] African American voters in these districts were given "talking points," asked to call candidates and demand their support for the Martin Luther King holiday bill and sanctions against South Africa, and prompted to conclude: "If you can't vote for [this legislation], we can't vote for you in November."[42] The latter proved strategic as a means of garnering support for the CAAA among congressional representatives who may have been soft, or uninterested in, the issue.

It would have been difficult for Fauntroy to reach his national black constituency without the use of some of the perks that come with being a congressman. One of those perks is franking privileges, which allow congressmen and senators to mail free of charge thousands of letters to citizens. Fauntroy used these "franks" in the task of mobilizing African American churches in the push for enactment of the CAAA. According to Fauntroy, African American churches are extremely attractive to politicians because they are seen as the "conscience of America," because there are tens of thousands of them in the United States, representing millions of churchgoing African Americans, and because, when mobilized, these churches constitute a powerful voting bloc that can determine the outcome of an election.

Conclusion

In the 1980s, members of civil rights groups and newer groups formed a "coalition of conscience" that engaged in antiapartheid activism. In this struggle, African American churches, especially the AME Church and the PNBC, provided the ecclesiastical forums that successfully facilitated the emergence and effectiveness of a cadre of activist clergy whose influence was felt beyond denominational boundaries and their individual contributions. In their public statements and private activities, both the AME Church and the PNBC were unswerving in their total commitment to the antiapartheid movement. Where the AME churches used personal relationships within the church and the political establishment to aid the antiapartheid cause, the PNBC applied mass-based tactics. The significant role played by the AME Church in the antiapartheid cause is partly a product of its rich legacy of Africa involvement dating back to the close relationship between Turner and the Ethiopian Church of South Africa as well as its involvement in the abolitionist movement. PNBC antiapartheid activism grew directly out of PNBC civil rights activism. African American churches played a prominent role in the evolution of antiapartheid activism. Their persistence and perseverance was crucial in facilitating the collapse of white-minority rule and the installation of black-majority rule in South Africa.

Notes

This study is dedicated to the memory of Dr. Marshall Lorenzo Shepard Jr., president of the National Baptist Convention from 1984 to 1986, whom I interviewed just prior to his passing. May his generous, gentle, but fiery antiapartheid spirit rest in perfect peace.

1 Randall Robinson, *Defending the Spirit: A Black Life in America* (New York: Plume, 1999), 96–97.

2 Ibid., 97.

3 Roland Oliver and John Page, "Short History of Africa," in *Black Americans and the Missionary Movement in Africa*, ed. Sylvia Jacobs (Westport: Greenwood, 1982), 9.

4 Malcolm X quoted in Jan Carew, *Ghosts in Our Blood* (Chicago: Lawrence Hill, 1994), 57.

5 Bishop John Hurst Adams, interview with author, Washington, D.C., February 21, 2002.

6 Gayraud S. Wilmore, *Black Religion and Black Radicalism* (New York: Orbis, 2002), 153.

7 Robert N. Bellah and Carl H. Brill, "Religious Influence on United States Foreign Policy," in *American Character and Foreign Policy*, ed. Michael Hamilton (Grand Rapids: Eerdmans, 1986), 55.

8 Clarence Glendenen, Robert Collins, and Peter Duignan, *American in Africa, 1865–1900* (Stanford: Stanford University Press, 1964), 114.

9 Robinson, *Defending the Spirit*, 129.

10 Wilmore, *Black Religion*, 153.

11 Carol A. Page, "Colonial Reaction to AME Missionaries in Africa: 1898–1910," in Jacobs, ed., *Missionary Movement in Africa*, 9.

12 Tony Martin, "Some Reflections on Evangelical PanAfricanism," in Jacobs, *Black Americans*, 191.

13 Page, "Colonial Reaction," 183.

14 Columba A. Nnorom, *American Churches and Southern Africa, Rhetoric and Reality* (New York: University Press of America, 1997), 9.

15 Carol A. Page, "Colonial Reaction to A.M.E. Missionaries in South Africa," in *Black Americans and the Missionary Movement in Africa*, ed. Sylvia Jacobs (Westport:

Greenwood, 1982), 185–86. To some extent, the AME Church has still not overcome this entirely, given that the persons who have served as the bishop responsible for overseeing AME churches in South Africa have been African American rather than African for almost the entire history of the AME Church presence in South Africa.

16 Bishop John Hurst Adams, interview with author.

17 Resolution to the Forty-second General Conference, Kansas City, Mo., July 7–15, 1984.

18 Resolution to the Forty-third General Conference, Fort Worth, Tex., July 6–14, 1988.

19 Resolution to the Forty-fourth General Conference, Sarasota, Fla., July 8–15, 1992.

20 Louis-Charles Harvey, "The African Methodist Episcopal Church: The Tension between Its Interior Life and Exterior Life," AME Working Paper 11 (Washington, D.C.: AME Church Archives, n.d.), 1–25.

21 Gregory Baum, "The Catholic Church's Contradictory Stances," in *Changes in Struggle*, ed. William K. Tabb (New York: Monthly Review Press, 1986), 131.

22 Henry F. Jackson, *From Congo to Soweto* (New York: Quill, 1984), 121 (quotation), 143, 145.

23 King quoted in Lewis B. Baldwin, *Toward the Beloved Community: Martin Luther King and South Africa* (Cleveland: Pilgrim, 1995), 33.

24 Albert J. Luthuli, *Let My People Go* (New York: World, 1962), 83.

25 Baldwin, *Beloved Community*, 33.

26 Jackson, *From Congo to Soweto*, 146.

27 Dr. Marshall Lorenzo Shepard Jr., telephone interview with author, March 13, 2002.

28 "Progressive National Baptist Convention," in *Directory of African American Religious Bodies*, ed. Wardell Payne (Washington, D.C.: Howard University Press, 1991), 48.

29 Jackson, *From Congo to Soweto*, 148.

30 Lyle Tatum and the American Friends Services Committee, *South Africa: Challenge and Hope* (Toronto: Collins, 1987), 64.

31 Jackson, *From Congo to Soweto*, 134, 149.

32 "A Conversation with the President" (CBS special news report with Walter Cronkite, March 3, 1981, transcript), 3.

33 Robinson, *Defending the Spirit*, 137.

34 Dismantling Apartheid," *Sojourners* 14, no. 2 (February 1985): 15.

35 Reverend Otis Moss, telephone interview with author, March 18, 2002.

36 Ibid.

37 Ibid.

38 It is important to note, however, that black Baptist congregations and clergy may be affiliated with more than one of the Baptist conventions simultaneously.

39 Reverend Otis Moss, telephone interview with author.

40 Ibid.

41 "Campaign Worker's Assistant Program Sheet: National Roundtable Targeted US Senate Races, November 4, 1986" (National Democratic Party, 1986, copy on file with the author).

42 Reverend Walter Fauntroy, interview with author, Washington, D.C., March 14, 2002.

APPENDIX A

OVERVIEW OF NATIONAL SAMPLE FOR

THE 1999–2000 BLACK CHURCHES

AND POLITICS SURVEY

Sampling Methodology

A list of approximately eleven thousand black churches was drawn from nineteen cities, twenty-six predominantly black rural counties, and two predominantly black suburbs. Within each city and the two suburban counties, all churches located within census block tracts that were 90 percent or more black were identified as part of the sample. Keyword searches were done of yellow pages databases in the cities to identify other obviously black churches that were outside the 90 percent black census tracts. Keywords included *African*, *Greater*, and COGIC (Church of God in Christ). Yellow pages telephone books were then manually consulted to include other churches listed within categories of obviously black churches that were not discerned through prior steps. Categories included African Methodist Episcopal churches, African Methodist Episcopal Zion churches, Christian Methodist Episcopal churches, Church of God in Christ (COGIC) churches, and any Baptist churches listed according to one of the black Baptist conventions. Churches were similarly identified in largely black rural counties in six Deep South states (two counties per state). Census tracts that were 70 percent black (instead of the 90 percent black standard applied to urban census tracts) were selected. This slightly increased the chances that the churches selected might not be black churches. Nevertheless, the smallness of these rural counties necessitated casting a wider net to increase the overall number of churches. (Surveys completed by churches that were not predominantly black were not included in the final database.)

Surveys were mailed to all the churches on the list, and churches that did not respond to the first mailing of the survey received a second mailing. Those that did not respond to the second mailing received a third mailing. Churches that did not respond after the three mailings received telephone calls and were asked to complete the survey over the telephone. In addition, in order to supplement initially low numbers of Pentecostal respondents, surveys were administered at a national meeting of the COGIC. Surveys completed at that meeting were included in the database only if they were from congregations in the cities, suburbs, or rural counties designated by the project as research sites. This multiple-step process yielded 1,956 completed surveys over a twelve-month period. With the completion of the nation survey, a follow-up survey soliciting additional information on public policy matters probed in the initial survey was conducted among the survey respondents. A total of 324 of the 1,956 church leaders who responded to the initial survey provided answers to the follow-up survey.

Sample Characteristics

The following metropolitan areas were covered in the sample: Atlanta (also suburban DeKalb County); Birmingham; Boston; Charlotte; Chicago; Columbus, Ohio; Dallas; Denver; Detroit; Jackson, Miss.; Los Angeles; Memphis; New Orleans; New York; Newark, N.J.; Oakland; Philadelphia; Trenton, N.J.; and Washington, D.C. (also Prince George's County, Md.).

The following rural counties were covered in the sample: Bullock, Greene, Lowndes, and Macon (including Tuskegee town) Counties, Alabama; Hamilton, Jefferson, and Madison Counties, Florida; Hancock, Stewart, and Talbot Counties, Georgia; East Carroll, Madison, and West Feliciana Parishes, Louisiana; Claiborne, Holmes, and Jefferson Counties, Mississippi; Hertford and Northampton Counties, North Carolina; Allendale, Lee, and Williamsburg Counties, South Carolina; Haywood, Hardeman, and Lauderdale Counties, Tennessee; and Greensville and Sussex Counties, Virginia.

APPENDIX B

Project Design and Areas of Inquiry

A major premise of the Public Influences of African-American Churches (PIAAC) Project is that there has been a visibly different range and frequency of political involvements by African American churches since 1965 that have not been sufficiently researched, analyzed, or documented. The PIAAC Project has sought to respond to this gap by gathering quantitative and qualitative data from multiple sources and by facilitating original and updated scholarly analysis on this topic.

The components of the project have included a random, national survey of black congregations; interviews with a select number of prominent ecclesiastical leaders and public officials and the gathering of formal denominational reports and resolutions bearing on denominational political engagement; and the mobilization of approximately thirty scholars with expertise on aspects of the relation between African American churches and public life to write on designated topics that drew on their preexisting research and research interests.

PROJECT SURVEY

The survey was administered to a representative cross section of predominantly black churches drawn from nineteen cities, twenty-six predominantly black rural counties, and two predominantly black suburbs. The cities that were selected represented variations in population size, regional location, and percentage black population. For example, the sample included large to midsize, predominantly black cities, such as Atlanta, Washington, D.C., and Detroit, and large to midsize cities with relatively small black populations, such as Los Angeles and Boston. Smaller cities were included as well, such as Trenton, N.J., and Oakland, Calif. Approximately eleven thousand predominantly black churches were identified in these geographic locations. Surveys were mailed, more than once, to each church, and follow-up calls were made. The process yielded completed mail-in and telephone surveys from 1,956 respondents — with 324 of these respondents completing follow-up telephone surveys as well.

The survey instruments contained questions pertaining to the theological and cultural underpinnings of the congregation's ministry and mission; the nature and extent of the its civic, electoral, and public policy involvements; the channels of activism utilized by politically active congregations; the congregation's size, income, and denominational affiliation; and its pastor's educational background. These questions were designed to probe a number of dynamics, among them whether there are certain membership sizes and socioeconomic attributes that characterize activist congregations; whether activist congregations characteristically align with particular denominations (e.g., historically black denominations [such as American Methodist Episcopal churches] vs. predominantly white ones [such as Presbyterian churches] or denominations characterized by certain kinds of governance or authority structures [e.g., with or without bishops]); whether church-based civic involvements have been motivated by a particular theological or religious agenda (e.g., liberation theology, evangelicalism, or Afrocentrism); and whether specific political tactics and strategies have been emphasized more than others by activist churches in recent years. Insights from the data on some of these matters are discussed below.

DIALOGUES WITH PUBLIC OFFICIALS AND ECCLESIASTICAL LEADERS
Dialogues were solicited with a select number of ecclesiastical leaders and public officials, either one-on-one or in a group setting. The purpose was to obtain perspectives on some of the ways in which churches engaged in public affairs collectively (as opposed to singularly), including perspectives on points of intersection between the political concerns of local congregations and those of denominational offices and advocacy organizations. Ecclesiastical leaders were asked about, for example, whether and how their denominations had been engaged in public affairs in recent years; whether their denominations collaborated with other denominations, civic groups, or public-sector entities on political matters; whether pastors and member congregations within their denomination were routinely informed about po-

litical advocacy initiated through the denominational offices; whether and in what ways member congregations were responsive to these denominational initiatives; and, conversely, whether member congregations mobilized denominational offices around specific civic and political concerns. Public officials were asked for their perspectives as well about ways in which churches, either individually or collectively, collaborated with the public sector and with advocacy organizations on public policy matters and other civic concerns. Insights from these discussions have been highlighted at various points in the present collection and, more systematically, in previously published reports on project conference dialogues.[1]

INVITED ESSAYS

Approximately thirty scholars were asked to write essays on various aspects of the civic involvements of black churches since 1965. The topics chosen were connected to one of three broad themes: churches and American civic culture; public policies and church impact; and churches and public life in American cities. Scholars writing on churches and American civic culture explored structural dynamics within the institutional and social contexts of black church activism that have influenced black church civic responsiveness; theological and moral imperatives that have shaped black church approaches to civic life, including womanist and Afrocentric imperatives that have served as challenges to mainstream American and African American social agendas; and emerging collaborations between black churches and government in matters related to economic development and social service provision. Scholars writing on public policies and church impact explored black church responses to national public policy issues; the factors internal and external to churches that shape those responses; and the implications and outcomes of these black church policy responses. Some of the policy areas that were examined included affirmative action, welfare reform, health care, criminal justice, education, and U.S. Africa policies. Scholars writing on churches and public life in American cities looked at local patterns of civic and public policy engagement by black churches in cities such as Atlanta, Chicago, Columbus, Ohio, Detroit, and Miami.

Although project scholars worked individually on their respective research topics, they interacted with each other as part of an ongoing working group that met once each of the first two years of the project. As part of this process, project scholars were afforded opportunities to make presentations for peer feedback. Project scholars also presented their work at the project's national conference in April 2001. The resulting essays have been organized into edited volumes, including two scheduled for publication by Duke University Press: the current volume and *New Day Begun*.[2]

Project Outreach to Partners and Stakeholders

OUTREACH TO DENOMINATIONAL AND JUDICATORY LEADERS

Top leaders in all the historically black denominations, in many mainline Protestant denominations, and in the Roman Catholic Church were contacted early on in the course of the project for discussion about the project's goals and strategies. And many of these contacts resulted in endorsements of the project. For example, the project received endorsements from top leaders of each of the historically black denominations and of the National Council of Churches. The brochure circulated to thousands of churches as part of the project's initial outreach to congregations included a number of these endorsements, and the surveys mailed to the project's sample of congregations were in most instances accompanied by an endorsement from the appropriate denomination.

The project was very fortunate to receive this level of support, a level of support engendered, we believe, by the importance of the project. More important, however, was that, beyond offering their support, black ecclesiastical leaders engaged in systematic dialogue with the project about current prospects for, and steps that should be taken to strengthen, black church influence in the public sphere. For example, leaders from prominent black Evangelical, Charismatic, Pentecostal, and Holiness denominations and church organizations attended a PIAAC Project roundtable convened to generate feedback from these rapidly growing church groups about their public-sphere involvements. Some of these same leaders, along with black church leaders from across the denominational spectrum, participated in the project's national conference as well. In both conference settings, church leaders candidly articulated the challenges that black churches, and initiatives such as the PIAAC Project, will face in an effort to increase black church influence in public affairs. It is hoped that these dialogues will be only the first in a series of denominational, interdenominational, and local-level dialogues between church leaders, scholars, and community leaders on religion and public life.

OUTREACH TO LOCAL CONGREGATIONS

Communicating PIAAC Project objectives and information to local congregations has been an extremely important part of the project work. Consequently, direct contact has been made with thousands of local congregations via a series of mailings and via project staff participation in the annual national assemblies of several of the historically black denominations. The eleven thousand black churches on the project mailing list received a variety of materials, including the brochure announcing the launching of the PIAAC Project; the project survey and endorsement letter; two project newsletters; and two publicity mailings about the national conference. A few hundred churches also received a synopsis of the national conference and the denominational roundtable. PIAAC Project staff also attended and gave presentations at annual assemblies of the National Baptist Convention, USA, the Progressive National Baptist Convention, the National Baptist Convention of America, the African Methodist Episcopal Church, the African Methodist Episcopal Zion Church, the Christian Methodist Episcopal Church, and the Church of God in Christ. At some of these gatherings, the project also sponsored special meals or receptions as a way of sharing details about the project with targeted church leaders and local pastors. The contacts made with local pastors and, in some instances, the relationships that were established will be strategic to the future work of the PIAAC Project — including the local policy roundtables that are being considered.

OUTREACH TO ELECTED OFFICIALS

The PIAAC Project was also endorsed by two of the largest bodies of black elected officials: the National Black Caucus of State Legislators (NBCSL) and the National Conference of Black Mayors (NCBM). The project enjoyed a particularly close working relationship with the NBCSL. For example, NBCSL members were featured speakers at and participants in the PIAAC roundtable and national conference, and the PIAAC Project played an active part in NBCSL's newly initiated Faith Roundtable. The hundreds of NBCSL and NCBM members also received PIAAC Project mailings, including the project brochure and newsletters. Moreover, a number of NBCSL and NCBM members shared perspectives on important matters related to black churches and public life via the PIAAC Project's conferences and targeted interviews. The feedback from black elected officials provided intriguing contrasts to that of black clergy on the role and contribution of black churches to public life. These contrasting perspectives represent a potentially rich area for further research and systematic dialogue.

OUTREACH TO SCHOLARS

Although a fairly rich body of scholarship has been established on the public roles of black churches during the civil rights movement and earlier, significantly less scholarship exists on that topic for the period since the civil rights movement. Therefore, a primary objective of the PIAAC Project has been the facilitation of multidisciplinary academic research and dialogue on black religion and public life during the last three decades. The project set out to identify as many scholars as possible engaged in research on recent black church activism, and approximately thirty such scholars were commissioned to join the project. These scholars were asked to gather periodically as a working group and, ultimately, to produce individual essays that would be organized into several anthologies on aspects of the topic black churches and public life. Scholarly interactions within the working group contributed insights from a variety of disciplines, including religious studies and the social sciences. This multidisciplinary aspect was facilitated through the convening of seminars and conferences that placed project scholars into direct dialogue with one another. The hope has been that such teamwork would energize and inspire current and future scholarship on black churches and public life.

OUTREACH TO EMERGING LEADERS

Half of the African American population in the United States is, according to the latest census, under age thirty-five, and there are numerous indicators that this generation of black youths and young adults is noticeably less involved in the voting process and in civic and social organizations than are middle-aged and senior blacks. Although there are many reasons for this, one factor has certainly been the lack of shared civic institutional space between emerging and established social leaders and spokespersons. Facilitating intergenerational dialogue has been a priority of the PIAAC Project. Its denominational roundtable and national conference included delegates and speakers representing a variety of generational perspectives. At these conference events, student leaders and civil rights movement leaders, and "old school" and "new school" political and religious leaders, could engage each other on critical issues of the day. The project even provided sponsorship for dozens of undergraduates, graduate students, and seminarians—especially students from the Atlanta University Center Schools—in order to ensure the youth presence at the national conference. The national conference also facilitated a strategy workshop on youth leadership development—which was one of the most informative, energetic, and well-attended workshops of the conference. The dialogue and recommendations that were generated by the workshop made clear the need for black churches and civic organizations to work much harder at encouraging and inviting contributions from younger generation leaders.[3]

Toward Broader Engagement by African American Churches: Challenges and Recommendations

Traditions of political activism have been strong, though by no means universally embraced, among African American churches. Still, there is an increasingly widespread expectation that churches will somehow play an integral part in addressing social concerns within the African American community. This expectation is driven in part by the sheer urgency of the social situation of many African Americans, but it is also driven by the fact that churches continue to represent one of the most viable and elemental institutions in the African American community. Nevertheless, from the perspective of the PIAAC Project (and many of the black church leaders who shared their insights with the project),[4] there are critical steps that need to be taken in order for African American churches to achieve the potentially broad-based political influence of which they are capable. Some of those steps are outlined in the sections that follow.

EXPANSION OF THE ADVOCACY INFRASTRUCTURE WITHIN
HISTORICALLY BLACK DENOMINATIONS

Church-Based Advocacy Offices and Organizations At the very least, it is important that each of the historically black denominations have a person or an office designated to represent that denomination's public policy concerns on Capitol Hill and, preferably, at the state and local levels as well. The majority of the historically black denominations have yet to designate such a person or office. The same could be said about the newer communions of black independent and nondenominational churches. Ideally, many of these black denominations and communions could collaborate with each other to develop an advocacy office or organization that advances their many mutual public policy interests and concerns.

Training and Curriculum Components The training needs of black clergy tend to outpace relevant and accessible training opportunities — especially when the need is training for civic leadership. For example, given the fact that quite a few black denominations and communions do not have formal education requirements for their clergy, the numbers of clergy who take advantage of broad-based, liberal arts curricula offered by colleges and universities may be somewhat low compared to professionals in other sectors.[5] These types of curricula can provide insights into the culture and mechanics of civic and political life, insights that are seldom emphasized in many of the Bible schools and theological institutions from which many black clergy receive their training. On the other hand, a factor that sometimes discourages matriculation by black clergy in liberal arts institutions is that theological and ministerial imperatives do not receive sufficient attention there. What could prove helpful are more institutions where black clergy, as well as lay leaders, can reflect theologically, and from the standpoint of social science disciplines, on the church's role within society. Bible schools and theological seminaries are two important contexts where a stronger emphasis on public affairs issues and social science analysis could contribute to the civic leadership of church leaders. Helpful, as well, would be special programs and conference events facilitated by ecclesiastical and educational institutions that focus on the church's public mission and that are offered to as many black clergy as possible. Such activities would begin to address the general absence of opportunities for training in public policy analysis and engagement.

Policy Research and Analysis Church-related policy advocacy and civic leadership training will need to be supported by a strong research and analytic component if it is to be effective. Currently, theological and social science assessments of the public roles of black churches are in short supply and, in any case, require constant updating and contextualizing. Moreover, available research on these topics must more systematically inform the relation between black churches and the public sphere. The task of both research production and research dissemination would benefit greatly from the creation of at least one black church–related political think tank that focuses on national politics and additional think tanks that focus on regional or local concerns.

FACILITATION OF YOUTH LEADERSHIP DEVELOPMENT

Shared Civic Institutional Space Very few of the national African American advocacy organizations or ecclesiastical groups have welcomed youth and young adult voices onto their organizational center stage. Youths and young adults are often subjects of discussion and function within organizations in an auxiliary capacity, but rarely are they positioned so that their concerns inform the organization's central agenda. If national black advocacy and ecclesiastical structures are not places where genuine intergenerational dialogue and leadership can take place, younger generation blacks will continue to seek alternative venues where their issues and leadership will be taken seriously. All too often, however, younger blacks find no viable alternatives and become lost to the civic and community-building process altogether. Black civic and ecclesiastical organizations can take steps to ensure that younger blacks who are well prepared to make valuable contributions are given ample opportunity to do so. These organizations can also take steps to facilitate leadership preparation among many other youths and young adults through internship and mentorship programs. Given the existence of more than eight thousand black elected officials, dozens of black civic and lobby groups, and numerous offices and divisions within black ecclesiastical structures — there can be at least that many internships devoted to leadership development and civic exposure for black youths and young adults.

Emerging Leaders Programs and Dialogues There is also a need for younger church leaders to dialogue systematically with leaders from across the government, nongovernment, and business sectors about the church's theological and social mission. Very few opportunities for this kind of dialogue are built into existing university or seminary curricula or into the leadership-training or -teaching components within ecclesiastical organizations — and many of the younger leaders who would benefit most from this kind of dialogue may not have immediate access to these institutions to begin with. A way to respond to this would be through emerging leaders programs that convene two- to three-day dialogues between twenty or so younger faith-based leaders and a smaller number of leaders from other sectors. Not only should dialogue between younger church leaders and leaders from other sectors be encouraged, but so too should dialogue among younger church leaders themselves, dialogue that cuts across racial/ethnic lines. Coalitions and collaborations among racial/ethnic minorities will become increasingly important given the anticipated demographic shifts in the coming years, and emerging leaders within these various communities will need as many creative opportunities as possible to grapple with issues and to search for common ground.

Project Conference Activities

RATIONALE

A primary objective of the PIAAC Project has been to increase scholarly focus and systematic dialogue among church leaders, policy officials, and scholars on matters pertaining to the contemporary political involvements of African American churches. Since not nearly enough attention has been paid to this particular analysis and dialogue, the PIAAC Project invested considerable time and effort in identifying and mobilizing persons that bring strategic analysis and strategic institutional and social positioning to bear on these matters. The project intentionally sought out scholars and ecclesiastical and political leaders who have attempted to integrate theological with political concerns and theory with practice. It also tried to ensure that a good mix of both younger and well-established scholars and leaders was involved in the multifaceted dialogue that it facilitated. The project events that formally facilitated this dialogue are outlined below. Lists of conference and round-table presenters and resource persons, and of project scholars, are included in separate reports (as indicated below).

2001 NATIONAL CONFERENCE

The conference "Black Churches and Political Leadership in the New Millennium" was held April 19–21, 2001, in the Washington, D.C., area. It facilitated a rare cross-sector dialogue between scholars, students, church leaders, and political leaders on black faith-based activism. The discussions drew on the broad social leadership of the approximately 250 persons in attendance and on a significant body of PIAAC Project–sponsored research. The project research featured at the conference included studies by twenty-five scholars across the country on the civic, electoral, and public policy involvements of black churches and preliminary results from the PIAAC Project survey of 1,956 African American churches. The conference also centered around six strategy working groups designed to gain insights from conferees about ways in which to position black churches within American public life more effectively. Working groups discussed strategies for strengthening the public leadership of women and youths and strategies for strengthening the contributions of ecclesiastical structures, theological education, and scholarly research to black public advocacy. Conferees and conference presenters represented liberal and conservative perspectives and a range of denominations, advocacy groups, government branches, and academic institutions. Also, while a large number of the presenters and attendees were either individually or by institutional association identified with well-established activist traditions and orientations, the conference also drew on the perspectives of and participation from black Evangelical, Charismatic, Pentecostal, and Holiness churches. A synopsis of the conference dialogue, including strategic recommendations, was published in the summer of 2001 and distributed to all conferees and to many others interested in the work of the project.[6]

2001 DENOMINATIONAL ROUNDTABLE

In March 2001, the roundtable discussion "Social Witness, Prophetic Discernment, and Post Civil Rights Churches" was convened. This gathering assembled thirty religious leaders from families of churches not historically at the forefront of black political activism—although very much at the forefront of important ecclesiastical evolutions within American Protestantism—to assess the involvements of these churches within contemporary American public life. The denominations and church bodies represented at the roundtable included the Church of God in Christ, the Full Gospel Baptist Church Fellowship, the Church of Christ Holiness, the Mount Sinai Holy Church of America, the National Black Evangelical Association, Mission Mississippi, and the National Ten Point Leadership Foundation. There were also representatives from a number of academic institutions and from a number of foundations, including the Annie E. Casey Foundation, the Ford Foundation, and the Pew Charitable Trusts. The roundtable was convened to explore the significant, though largely untapped, advocacy potential of black Evangelical, Charismatic, Pentecostal, and Holiness churches. The advocacy potential of these churches stems both from numerical growth (within the Pentecostal and Charismatic churches in particular) and from evidence of new thinking among these churches on the importance of extending their influence into public affairs. A synopsis of the roundtable dialogue, including strategic recommendations, was published in the spring of 2001 and distributed to the roundtable participants and to many others interested in the work of the project.[7]

PROJECT SCHOLARS SEMINARS

Two weekend seminars — the first in 1999, the second in 2000 — were attended by the thirty scholars commissioned to provide researched essays on various aspects of the civic, electoral, and public policy involvements of black churches. The general purpose of these gatherings was to facilitate dialogue among project scholars about the themes and methodologies that would guide their research. The 2000 seminar also provided the researchers with an opportunity to receive feedback on their essays from other project scholars and from a small group of evaluators.

Notes

1 See "Black Churches and Political Leadership in the New Millennium" (Atlanta: Morehouse College, PIAAC Project, summer 2001); and "Social Witness, 'Prophetic' Discernment, and Post–Civil Rights Era Churches" (Atlanta: Morehouse College, PIAAC Project, spring 2001). Both are available at www.morehouse.edu/pubinfl. Copies are also available from the Leadership Center at Morehouse College.

2 *New Day Begun: African American Churches and Civic Culture in Post–Civil Rights America*, ed. R. Drew Smith (Durham: Duke University Press, 2003).

3 For a synopsis of the workshop discussion, see "Black Churches and Political Leadership in the New Millennium" (Atlanta: Morehouse College, PIAAC Project, 2001), 11–14, available at www.morehouse.edu/pubinfl and also from the Leadership Center at Morehouse College.

4 For additional context on many of the recommendations outlined here, see "Black Churches and Political Leadership in the New Millennium"; and "Social Witness, 'Prophetic' Discernment, and Post–Civil Rights Era Churches."

5   Data on this subject are available in, for example, Smith, ed., *New Day Begun*; and
    C. Eric Lincoln and Lawrence Mamiya, *The Black Church in the African-American
    Experience* (Durham: Duke University Press, 1990), 131.

6   The conference synopsis is available on request from the Leadership Center at More-
    house College and also on the project website: www.morehouse.edu/pubinfl.

7   The roundtable synopsis is available on request from the Leadership Center at More-
    house College and also on the project website: www.morehouse.edu/pubinfl.

CONTRIBUTORS

Cathy J. Cohen is Professor of Political Science and Director of the Center for the Study of Race, Politics, and Culture at the University of Chicago.

Megan E. McLaughlin is the former Executive Director and Chief Executive Officer of the Federation of Protestant Welfare Agencies, Inc., New York City.

Columba Aham Nnorum is a Catholic priest and an independent scholar with an extensive background as a political activist.

Michael Leo Owens is Assistant Professor of Political Science at Emory University.

Desiree Pedescleaux is Associate Professor of Political Science and Associate Dean of Undergraduate Studies at Spelman College.

Barbara Dianne Savage is Associate Professor of History at the University of Pennsylvania.

R. Drew Smith is Director of the Public Influences of African-American Churches Project and Scholar-in-Residence at the Leadership Center at Morehouse College.

Emilie M. Townes is Professor of Christian Ethics at Union Theological Seminary, New York.

Christopher Winship is Professor of Sociology at Harvard University.

INDEX

abortion, 129–130, 133–134, 140 n.2, 140 n.7, 140 n.8, 141 nn.24–25

Adams, Charles, 154

Adams, John Hurst, 78, 135, 195

affirmative action, 13; corporate opposition to, 30; Democrats and, 29–30; definition, 28, 45–46; and One Florida Plan, 28, 32–37; opposition to, 28–32; Republicans and, 30–31

Africa: advocacy organizations, 16; churches and anti-apartheid activism, 195, 200, 205–212; churches and public policy on, 16–17; missions to, 197–199

African American Ministers Leadership Council, 39

African Methodist Episcopal Church (AME), 22, 34, 39, 90, 135, 197–201

African Methodist Episcopal Zion Church (AMEZ), 133–135, 141 n.14

African National Congress, 201, 203

AIDS National Interfaith Network, 122

Aid to Families with Dependent Children (AFDC), 52, 54; description, 98 n.1; faith-based organizations and, 75, 77–78

American Committee on Africa, 16, 195

Annie E. Casey Foundation, 59

apartheid, 203; resistance in South Africa, 206, 208

Ashcroft, John, 53, 77, 79

Balm in Gilead, 120–123

Baltimore United in Leadership Development, 84, 159

Baptists: affirmative action and, 38–42; anti-apartheid activism and, 195, 205–212; and policy activism, 21; reproductive health

and, 137–138; splits, 205; welfare reform and, 78

Berry, Mary Frances, 193

Black Churches and Politics (BCAP) Survey, 11–15, 18–23, 83–84, 127, 217–218

Black Church Initiative, 137–138

black elected officials: tensions with clergy, 43; welfare reform and, 60, 63, 78

black spirituality, 3

Blake, Charles, 88

Blum, Barbara, 59, 68

Boesak, Allan, 211

Bratton, William, 176, 182

Bread for the World, 59

Broadnax, Reginald D., 134–135

Brown, Jeffrey, 177

Bunche, Ralph, 204

Bush, George W., 89; faith-based initiative and, 82; Jeb Bush and, 30, 32

Bush, Jeb, 89; affirmative action and, 28–37, 40–41, 44; and One Florida Plan, 28–29, 32–33

Butler, Charles, 155

Butts, Calvin, 57, 59, 84

Caldwell, Kirbyjohn, 88

Call to Renewal, 66

Caribbean: churches and public policy, 16–17

Catholics: activism and, 22–24, 58–59, 82, 86, 96, 157

Catholic Charities: welfare reform and, 59, 75, 78–79, 96

charitable choice: block grants, 67, 79; churches and, 78–79, 81–82, 85–96; description, 53, 77, 81; public opinion and, 82–85

vouchers, 30–31, 34, 39, 54, 88. *See also* education and schools

Walker, Wyatt, 94, 96, 195, 205, 207
Washington, Booker T., 111–116
Washington Office on Africa, 16
welfare reform: behavioral issues and, 76, 82; increases in poverty and, 55–56; public opinion and, 82–87, 89–90; reduction of welfare recipients and, 55–56; stigmatization and, 60, 63

White, R. L., 161
White House Office of Faith-Based and Community Initiatives, 82, 89
Wilson, Willie, 157
Women of Color Partnership, 137
women's rights: affirmative action and, 42; church activism in policies, 14–16, 127; and leadership development, 14–16; and ordination of women clergy, 14–16
World Council of Churches, 22

youth violence, 177–182, 186

Library of Congress Cataloging-in-Publication Data

Long march ahead : African American churches and public

policy in post–civil rights America / R. Drew Smith, editor.

p. cm.— (The public influences of

African American churches ; v. 2)

Includes bibliographical references and index.

ISBN 0-8223-3358-9 (alk. paper)

1. African American churches—History—20th century.

2. Christianity and politics—United States—History—

20th century. I. Smith, R. Drew II. Series.

BR563.N4L64 2004

261.8′089′96073—dc22   2004013408